THE SWINDLER

AND OTHER STORIES

ETHEL M. DELL

The Swindler and Other Stories

Ethel M. Dell

© 1st World Library, 2006
PO Box 2211
Fairfield, IA 52556
www.1stworldlibrary.com
First Edition

LCCN: 2006935216

Softcover ISBN: 1-4218-2469-8
Hardcover ISBN: 1-4218-2369-1
eBook ISBN: 1-4218-2569-4

Purchase "*The Swindler and Other Stories*"
as a traditional bound book at:
www.1stWorldLibrary.com/purchase.asp?ISBN=1-4218-2469-8

1st World Library is a literary, educational organization
dedicated to:

- Creating a free internet library of downloadable ebooks

- Hosting writing competitions and offering book
publishing scholarships.

Interested in more 1st World Library books?
contact: literacy@1stworldlibrary.com
Check us out at: www.1stworldlibrary.com

1st World Library Literary Society

Giving Back to the World

"If you want to work on the core problem, it's early school literacy."

- James Barksdale, former CEO of Netscape

"No skill is more crucial to the future of a child, or to a democratic and prosperous society, than literacy."

- Los Angeles Times

Literacy... means far more than learning how to read and write... The aim is to transmit... knowledge and promote social participation."

- UNESCO

"Literacy is not a luxury, it is a right and a responsibility. If our world is to meet the challenges of the twenty-first century we must harness the energy and creativity of all our citizens."

- President Bill Clinton

"Parents should be encouraged to read to their children, and teachers should be equipped with all available techniques for teaching literacy, so the varying needs and capacities of individual kids can be taken into account."

- Hugh Mackay

CONTENTS

THE SWINDLER

"When you come to reflect that there are only a few planks between you and the bottom of the Atlantic Ocean, it makes you feel sort of pensive."

"I beg your pardon?"

The stranger, smoking his cigarette in the lee of the deck-cabins, turned his head sharply in the direction of the voice. He encountered the wide, unembarrassed gaze of a girl's grey eyes. She had evidently just come up on deck.

"I beg yours," she rejoined composedly. "I thought at first you were some one else."

He shrugged his shoulders, and turned away. Quite obviously he was not disposed to be sociable upon so slender an introduction.

The girl, however, made no move to retreat. She stood thoughtfully tapping on the boards with the point of her shoe.

"Were you playing cards last night down in the saloon?" she asked presently.

"I was looking on."

He threw the words over his shoulder, not troubling to turn.

The girl shivered. The morning air was damp and chill.

"You do a good deal of that, Mr. - Mr. -" She paused suggestively.

But the man would not fill in the blank. He smoked on in silence.

The vessel was rolling somewhat heavily, and the splash of the drifting foam reached them occasionally where they stood. There were no other ladies in sight. Suddenly the clear, American voice broke through the man's barrier of silence.

"I know quite well what you are, you know. You may just as well tell me your name as leave me to find it out for myself."

He looked at her then for the first time, keenly, even critically. His clean-shaven mouth wore a very curious expression.

"My name is West," he said, after a moment.

She nodded briskly.

"Your professional name, I suppose. You are a professional, of course?"

His eyes continued to watch her narrowly. They were blue eyes, piercingly, icily blue.

"Why 'of course,' if one may ask?"

She laughed a light, sweet laugh, inexpressibly gay. Cynthia Mortimer could be charmingly inconsequent when she chose.

"I don't think you are a bit clever, you know," she said. "I knew what you were directly I saw you standing by the gangway watching the people coming on board. You looked really professional then, just as if you didn't care a red cent whether you caught your man or not. I knew you did care though, and I was ready to dance when I knew you hadn't got him. Think you'll track him down on our side?"

Ethel M. Dell

West turned his eyes once more upon the heaving, grey water, carelessly flicking the ash from his cigarette.

"I don't think," he said briefly. "I know."

"You - know?" The wide eyes opened wider, but they gathered no information from the unresponsive profile that smoked the cigarette. "You know where Mr. Nat Verney is?" she breathed, almost in a whisper. "You don't say! Then - then you weren't really watching out for him at the gangway?"

He jerked up his head with an enigmatical laugh.

"My methods are not so simple as that," he said.

Cynthia joined quite generously in his laugh, notwithstanding its hard note of ridicule. She had become keenly interested in this man, in spite of - possibly in consequence of - the rebuffs he so unsparingly administered. She was not accustomed to rebuffs, this girl with her delicate, flower-like beauty. They held for her something of the charm of novelty, and abashed her not at all.

"And you really think you'll catch him?" she questioned, a note of honest regret in her voice.

"Don't you want him to be caught?"

He pitched his cigarette overboard and turned to her with less of churlishness in his bearing.

She met his eyes quite frankly.

"I should just love him to get away," she declared, with kindling eyes. "Oh, I know he's a regular sharper, and he's swindled heaps of people - I'm one of them, so I know a little about it. He swindled me out of five hundred dollars, and I can tell you I was mad at first. But now that he is flying from justice, I'm game enough to want him to get away. I suppose my sympathies generally lie with the hare, Mr. West. I'm sorry if it annoys you, but I was created that way."

West was frowning, but he smiled with some cynicism over her last remarks.

"Besides," she continued, "I couldn't help admiring him. He has a regular genius for swindling - that man. You'll agree with me there?"

A sudden heavy roll of the vessel pitched her forward before he could reply. He caught her round the waist, saving her from a headlong fall, and she clung to him, laughing like a child at the mishap.

"I think I'll have to go below," she decided regretfully. "But you've been good to me, and I'm glad I spoke. I've always been somewhat prejudiced against detectives till to-day. My cousin Archie - you saw him in the cardroom last night - vowed you were nothing half so interesting. Why is it, I wonder, that detectives always look like journalists?" She looked at him with eyes of friendly criticism. "You didn't deceive me, you see. But then" - ingenuously - "I'm clever in some ways, much more clever than you'd think. Now you won't cut me next time we meet, will you? Because - perhaps - I'm going to ask you to do something for me."

"What do you want me to do?"

The man's voice was hard, his eyes cold as steel, but his question had in it a shade - just a shade - of something warmer than mere curiosity.

She took him into her confidence without an instant's hesitation.

"My cousin Archie - you may have noticed - you were looking on last night - he's a very careless player, and headstrong too. But he can't afford to lose any, and I don't want him to come

Ethel M. Dell

to grief. You see, I'm rather fond of him."

"Well?"

The man's brows were drawn down over his eyes. His expression was not encouraging.

"Well," she proceeded, undismayed, "I saw you looking on, and you looked as if you knew a few things. So I thought you'd be a safe person to ask. I can't look after him; and his mother - well, she's worse than useless. But a man - a real strong man like you - is different. If I were to introduce you, couldn't you look after him a bit - just till we get across?"

With much simplicity she made her request, but there was a tinge of anxiety in her eyes. Certainly West, staring steadily forth over the grey waste of tumbling waters, looked sufficiently forbidding.

After several seconds of silence he flung an abrupt question:

"Why don't you ask some one else?"

"There is no one else," she answered.

"No one else?" He made a gesture of impatient incredulity.

"No one that I can trust," she explained.

"And you trust me?"

"Of course I do."

"Why?" Again he looked at her with a piercing scrutiny. His eyes held a savage, almost a threatening expression.

But the girl only laughed, lightly and confidently.

"Why? Oh, just because you are trustworthy, I guess. I can't think of any other reason."

West's look relaxed, became abstracted, and finally fell away from her.

"You appear to be a lady of some discernment," he observed drily.

She proffered her hand impulsively, her eyes dancing.

"My, that's the first pretty thing you've said to me!" she declared flippantly. "I just like you, Mr. West!"

West was feeling for his cigarette case. He gave her his hand without looking at her, as if her approbation did not greatly gratify him. When she was gone he moved away along the wind-swept deck with his collar up to his ears and his head bent to the gale. His conversation with the American girl had not apparently made him feel any more sociably inclined towards his fellow-passengers.

*   *   *   *   *

Certainly, as Cynthia had declared, young Archibald Bathurst was an exceedingly reckless player. He lacked the judgment and the cool brain essential to a good cardplayer, with the result that he lost much more often than he won. But notwithstanding this fact he had a passion for cards which no amount of defeat could abate - a passion which he never failed to indulge whenever an opportunity presented itself.

At the very moment when his cousin was making her petition on his behalf to the surly Englishman on deck, he was seated in the saloon with three or four men older than himself, playing and losing, playing and losing, with almost unvarying monotony, yet with a feverish relish that had in it something tragic.

He was only three-and-twenty, and, as he was wont to remark, ill-luck dogged him persistently at every turn. He never blamed himself when rash speculations failed, and he never profited by bitter experience. Simply, he was by nature a spendthrift, high-spirited, impulsive, weak, with little thought for the future and none at all for the past. Wherever he went he was popular. His gaiety and spontaneity won him favour. But no one took him very seriously. No one ever dreamed that his ill-luck was a cause for anything but mirth.

A good deal of money had changed hands when the party separated to dine, but, though young Bathurst was as usual a loser, he displayed no depression. Only, as he sauntered away to his cabin, he flung a laughing challenge to those who remained:

"See if I don't turn the tables presently!"

They laughed with him, pursuing him with chaff till he was out of hearing. The boy was a game youngster, and he knew how to lose. Moreover, it was generally believed that he could afford to pay for his pleasures.

But a man who met him suddenly outside his cabin read something other than indifference upon his flushed face. He only saw him for an instant. The next, Archie had swung past and was gone, a clanging door shutting him from sight.

When the little knot of cardplayers reassembled after dinner their number was augmented. A short, broad-shouldered man, clean-shaven, with piercing blue eyes, had scraped acquaintance with one of them, and had accepted an invitation to join the play. Some surprise was felt among the rest, for this man had till then been disposed to hold aloof from his fellow-passengers, preferring a solitary cigarette to any amusements that might be going forward.

A New York man named Rudd muttered to his neighbour that the fellow might be all right, but he had the eyes of a sharper. The neighbour in response murmured the words "private detective" and Rudd was relieved.

Archie Bathurst was the last to arrive, and dropped into the place he had occupied all the afternoon. It was immediately facing the stranger, whom he favoured with a brief and somewhat disparaging stare before settling down to play.

The game was a pure gamble. They played swiftly, and in silence. West seemed to take but slight interest in the issue, but he won steadily and surely. Young Bathurst, playing feverishly, lost and lost, and lost again. The fortunes of the other four players varied. But always the newcomer won his ventures.

The evening was half over when Archie suddenly and loudly demanded higher stakes, to turn his luck, as he expressed it.

"Double them if you like," said West.

Rudd looked at him with a distrustful eye, and said nothing. The other players were disposed to accede to the boy's vehement request, and after a little discussion the matter was settled to his satisfaction. The game was resumed at higher points.

Some onlookers had drawn round the table scenting excitement. Archie, sitting with his back to the wall, was playing with headlong recklessness. For a while he continued to lose, and then suddenly and most unexpectedly he began to win. A most rash speculation resulted in his favour, and from that moment it seemed that his luck had turned. Once or twice he lost, but these occasions were far outbalanced by several brilliant *coups*. The tide had turned at last in his favour.

He played as a man possessed, swiftly and feverishly. It seemed that he and West were to divide the honours. For West's luck scarcely varied, and Rudd continued to look at him askance.

For the greater part of an hour young Bathurst won with scarcely a break, till the spectators began to chaff him upon his outrageous success.

"You'd better stop," one man warned him. "She's a fickle jade, you know, Bathurst. Take too much for granted, and she'll desert you."

But Bathurst did not even seem to hear. He played with lowered eyes and twitching mouth, and his hands shook perceptibly. The gambler's lust was upon him.

"He'll go on all night," murmured the onlookers.

But this prophecy was not to be fulfilled.

It was a very small thing that stemmed the racing current of the boy's success - no more than a slight click audible only to a few, and the tinkle of something falling - but in an instant, swift as a thunderbolt, the wings of tragedy swept down upon the little party gathered about the table.

Young Bathurst uttered a queer, half-choked exclamation, and dived downwards. But the man next to him, an Englishman named Norton, dived also, and it was he who, after a moment, righted himself with something shining in his hand which he proceeded grimly to display to the whole assembled company. It was a small, folding mirror - little more than a toy, it looked - with a pin attached to its leathern back.

Deliberately Norton turned it over, examining it in such a way that others might examine it too. Then, having concluded his investigation of this very simple contrivance, he slapped it down upon the table with a gesture of unutterable contempt.

"The secret of success," he observed.

Every one present looked at Archie, who had sunk back in his chair white to the lips. He seemed to be trying to say something, but nothing came of it.

And then, quite calmly, ending a silence more terrible than any tumult of words, another voice made itself heard.

"Even so, Mr. Norton." West bent forward and with the utmost composure possessed himself of the shining thing upon the table. "This is my property. I have been rooking you fellows all the evening."

The avowal was so astounding and made with such complete *sang-froid* that no one uttered a word. Only every one turned from Archie to stare at the man who thus serenely claimed his own.

He proceeded with unvarying coolness to explain himself.

"It was really done as an experiment," he said. "I am not a card-sharper by profession, as some of you already know. But in the course of certain investigations not connected with the matter I now have in hand, I picked this thing up, and, being something of a specialist in certain forms of cheating, I made up my mind to try my hand at this and prove for myself its extreme simplicity. You see how easy it is to swindle, gentlemen, and the danger to which you expose yourselves. There is no necessity for me to explain the trick further. The instrument speaks for itself. It is merely a matter of dexterity, and keeping it out of sight."

He held it up a second time before his amazed audience, twisted it this way and that, with the air of a conjurer displaying his smartest trick, attached it finally to the lapel of his coat, and rose.

"As a practical demonstration it seems to have acted very well," he remarked. "And no harm done. If you are all satisfied, so am I."

He collected the notes at his elbow with a single careless sweep of the hand, and tossed them into the middle of the table; then, with a brief, collective bow, he turned to go. But Rudd, the first to recover from his amazement, sprang impetuously to his feet. "One moment, sir!" he said.

West stopped at once, a cold glint of humour in his eyes. Without a sign of perturbation he faced round, meeting the American's hostile scrutiny calmly, judicially.

"I wish to say," said Rudd, "on behalf of myself, and - I think I may take it - on behalf of these other gentlemen also, that your action was a most dastardly piece of impertinence, to give it its tamest name. Naturally, we don't expect Court manners from one of your profession, but we do look for ordinary common honesty. But it seems that we look in vain. You have behaved like a mighty fine skunk, sir. And if you don't see that there's any crying need for a very humble apology, you've got about the thickest hide that ever frayed a horsewhip."

Every one was standing by the time this elaborate threat was uttered, and it was quite obvious that Rudd voiced the general opinion. The only one whose face expressed no indignation was Archie Bathurst. He was leaning against the wall, mopping his forehead with a shaking hand.

No one looked at him. All attention was centred upon West, who met it with a calm serenity suggestive of contempt. He showed himself in no hurry to respond to Rudd's indictment, and when he did it was not exclusively to Rudd that he spoke.

"I am sorry," he coolly said, "that you consider yourselves aggrieved by my experiment. I do not myself see in what way I have injured you. However, perhaps you are the best judges of that. If you consider an apology due to you, I am quite ready to apologise."

His glance rested for a second upon Archie, then slowly swept the entire assembly. There was scant humility about him, apologise though he might.

Rudd returned his look with open disgust. But it was Norton

who replied to West's calm defence of himself.

"It is Bathurst who is the greatest loser," he said, with a glance at that young man, who was beginning to recover from his agitation. "It was a tom-fool trick to play, but it's done. You won't get another opportunity for your experiments on board this boat. So - if Bathurst is satisfied - I should say the sooner you apologise and clear out the better."

"We will confiscate this, anyway," declared Rudd, plucking the mirror from West's coat.

He flung it down, and ground his heel upon it with venomous intention. West merely shrugged his shoulders.

"I apologise," he said briefly, "singly and collectively, to all concerned in my experiment, especially" - he made a slight pause - "to Mr. Bathurst, whose run of luck I deeply regret to have curtailed. If Mr. Bathurst is satisfied, I will now withdraw."

He paused again, as if to give Bathurst an opportunity to express an opinion. But Archie said nothing whatever. He was staring down upon the table, and did not so much as raise his eyes.

West shrugged his shoulders again, ever so slightly, and swung slowly upon his heel. In a dead silence he walked away down the saloon. No one spoke till he had gone.

*   *   *   *   *

A black, moaning night had succeeded the grey, gusty day. The darkness came down upon the sea like a pall, covering the long, heaving swell from sight - a darkness that wrapped close, such a darkness as could be felt - through which the spray drove blindly.

There was small attraction for passengers on deck, and West

Ethel M. Dell

grimaced to himself as he emerged from the heated cabins. Yet it was not altogether distasteful to him. He was a man to whom a calm atmosphere meant intolerable stagnation. He was essentially born to fight his way in the world.

For a while he paced alone, to and fro, along the deserted deck, his hands behind him, the inevitable cigarette between his lips. But presently he paused and stood still close to the companion by which he had ascended. It was sheltered here, and he leaned against the woodwork by which Cynthia Mortimer had supported herself that morning, and smoked serenely and meditatively.

Minutes passed. There came the sound of hurrying feet upon the stairs behind him, and he moved a little to one side, glancing downwards.

The light at the head of the companion revealed a man ascending, bareheaded, and in evening dress. His face, upturned, gleamed deathly white. It was the face of Archie Bathurst.

West suddenly squared his shoulders and blocked the opening.

"Go and get an overcoat, you young fool!" he said.

Archie gave a great start, stood a second, then, without a word, turned back and disappeared.

West left his sheltered corner and paced forward across the deck. He came to a stand by the rail, gazing outwards into the restless darkness. There seemed to be the hint of a smile in his intent eyes.

A few more minutes drifted away. Then there fell a step behind him; a hand touched his arm.

"Can I speak to you?" Archie asked.

Slowly West turned.

"If you have anything of importance to say," he said.

Archie faced him with a desperate resolution.

"I want to ask you - I want to know - what in thunder you did it for!"

"Eh?" said West. "Did what?"

He almost drawled the words, as if to give the boy time to control his agitation.

Archie stared at him incredulously.

"You must know what I mean."

"Haven't an idea."

There was just a tinge of contempt this time in the words. What an unconscionable bungler the fellow was!

"But you must!" persisted Archie, blundering wildly. "I suppose you knew what you were doing just now when - when -"

"I generally know what I am doing," observed West.

"Then why -"

Archie stumbled again, and fell silent, as if he had hurt himself.

"I don't always care to discuss my motives," said West very decidedly.

"But surely -" Archie suddenly pulled up, realising that by this spasmodic method he was making no headway. "Look here, sir," he said, more quietly, "you've done a big thing for me to-night - a dashed fine thing! Heaven only knows what you did it for, but - "

"I have done nothing whatever for you," said West shortly. "You make a mistake."

"But you'll admit -"

"I admit nothing."

He made as if he would turn on his heel, but Archie caught him by the arm.

"I know I'm a cur," he said. And his voice shook a little. "I don't wonder you won't speak to me. But there are some things that can't be left unsaid. I'm going down now, at once, to tell those fellows what actually happened."

"Then you are going to make a big fool of yourself to no purpose," said West.

He stood still, scanning the boy's face with pitiless eyes. Archie writhed impotently.

"I can't stand it!" he said, with vehemence. "I thought I was blackguard enough to let you do it. But - no doubt I'm a fool, as you say - I find I can't."

"You can't help yourself," said West. He planted himself squarely in front of Archie. "Listen to this!" he said. "You know what I am?"

"They say you are a detective," said Archie.

West nodded.

"Exactly. And, as such, I do whatever suits my purpose without explaining why to the rest of the world. If you are fortunate enough to glean a little advantage from what I do, take it, and be quiet about it. Don't hamper me with your acknowledgments. I assure you I have no more concern for your ultimate fate than those fellows below that you've been swindling all the evening. One thing I will say, though, for your express benefit. You will never make a good, even an indifferently good, gambler. And as to card-sharping, you've no talent whatever. Better give it up."

His blue eyes looked straight at Archie with a stare that was openly supercilious, and Archie stood abashed.

"You - you are awfully good," he stammered at length.

West's brief laugh lived in his memory for long after. It held an indescribable sting, almost as if the man resented something. Yet the next moment unexpectedly he held out his hand.

"A matter of opinion," he observed drily. "Good-night! Remember what I have said to you."

"I shall never forget it," Archie said earnestly.

He wrung the extended hand hard, waited an instant, then, as West turned from him with that slight characteristic lift of the shoulders, he moved away and went below.

*   *   *   *   *

"I'd just like a little talk with you, Mr. West, if I may." Lightly the audacious voice arrested him, and, as it were, against his will, West stood still.

She was standing behind him in the morning sunshine, her hair blown all about her face, her grey eyes wide and daring, full of an alert friendliness that could not be ignored. She moved forward with her light, free step and stood beside him. West was smoking as usual. His expression was decidedly surly. Cynthia glanced at him once or twice before she spoke.

"You mustn't mind what I'm going to ask you," she said at length gently. "Now, Mr. West, what was it - exactly - that happened in the saloon last night? Surely you'll tell me by myself if I promise - honest Injun - not to tell again."

"Why should I tell you?" said West, in his brief, unfriendly style.

Cynthia was undaunted. "Because you're a gentleman," she said boldly.

He shrugged his shoulders. "I don't know what reason I have given you to say so."

"No?" She looked at him with a funny little smile. "Well then, I just feel it in my bones; and nothing you do or leave undone will make me believe the contrary."

"Much obliged to you," said West. His blue eyes were staring straight out over the sea to the long, blue sky-line. He seemed too absorbed in what he saw to pay much attention to the girl beside him.

But she was not to be shaken off. "Mr. West," she began again, breaking in upon his silence, "do you know what they are saying about you to-day?"

"Haven't an idea."

"No," she said. "And I don't suppose you care either. But I care. It matters a lot to me."

"Don't see how," threw in West.

He turned in his abrupt, disconcerting way, and gave her a piercing look. She averted her face instantly, but he had caught her unawares.

"Good heavens!" he said. "What's the matter?"

"Nothing," she returned, with a sort of choked vehemence. "There's nothing the matter with me. Only I'm feeling badly about - about what I asked you to do yesterday. I'd sooner have lost every dollar I have in the world, if I had only known, than - than have you do - what you did."

"Good heavens!" West said again.

He waited a little then, looking down at her as she leaned upon the rail with downcast face. At length, as she did not raise her head, he addressed her for the first time on his own initiative:

"Miss Mortimer!"

She made a slight movement to indicate that she was listening, but she remained gazing down into the green and white of the racing water.

Unconsciously he moved a little nearer to her. "There is no occasion for you to feel badly," he said. "I had my own reasons for what I did. It doesn't much matter what they were. But let me tell you for your comfort that neither socially nor professionally has it done me any harm."

"They are all saying: 'Set a thief to catch a thief,'" she interposed, with something like a sob in her voice.

"They can say what they like."

West's tone expressed the most stoical indifference, but she would not be comforted.

"If only I hadn't - asked you to!" she murmured.

He made his peculiar, shrugging gesture. "What does it matter? Moreover, what you asked of me was something quite apart from this. It had nothing whatever to do with it."

She stood up sharply at that, and faced him with burning eyes. "Oh, don't tell me that lie!" she exclaimed passionately. "I'm not such a child as to be taken in by it. You don't deceive me at all, Mr. West. I know as well as you do - better - that the man who did the swindling last night was not you. And I'm sick - I'm downright sick - whenever I think of it!"

West's expression changed slightly as he looked at her. He seemed to regard her as a doctor regards the patient for whom he contemplates a change of treatment.

"See here," he abruptly said. "You are distressing yourself all to no purpose. If you will promise to keep it secret, I'll tell you the facts of the case."

Cynthia's face changed also. She caught eagerly at the suggestion. "Yes?" she said. "Yes? I promise, of course. And I'm quite trustworthy."

"I believe you are," he said, with a grim smile. "Well, the fact of the matter is this. The man we want is on board this ship, but being only a private detective, I don't possess a warrant for his arrest. Therefore all I can do is to keep him in sight. And I can only do that by throwing him as far as possible off the scent. If he takes me for a card-sharper, all the better. For he's as slippery as an eel, and I have to play him pretty carefully."

He ceased. Cynthia's eyes were growing wider and wider.

"Nat Verney on board this ship?" she gasped.

He nodded.

"Yes. You wanted him to get away, didn't you? But I don't think he will, this time. He will probably be arrested directly we reach New York. But, meantime, I must watch out."

"Oh!" breathed Cynthia. "Then" - with sudden hope dawning in her eyes - "it really was your doing, that trick at the card-table last night?"

West uttered his brief, hard laugh.

"What do you take me for?"

She heaved a great sigh of relief.

"And it wasn't Archie, after all? I'm thankful you told me. I thought - I thought - But it doesn't matter, does it? Tell me, do tell me, Mr. West," drawing very close to him, "which - which is Mr. Nat Verney?"

West seemed to hesitate.

"Oh, do tell me!" she begged. "I know I'm only a woman, but I always keep my word. And it's only two days more to New York."

He looked closely into her eyes and yielded.

"I'm trusting you with my reputation," he said. "It's the stout, red-faced man called Rudd."

"Mr. Rudd?" She started back. "You don't say? That man?" There followed a short pause while she digested the information. Then, as on the previous morning, she suddenly extended her hand. "Well, I hate that man, anyway. And I believe you're really clever. If you like, Mr. West, I'll help you to watch out."

"Thanks!" said West. He took the little hand into a tight grip, still looking straight into her eyes. There was a light in his own that shone like a blue flame. "Thanks!" he said again, as he released it. "You're very good, Miss Mortimer. But you mustn't be seen with me, you know. You've got to remember that I'm a swindler."

The girl laughed aloud. It pleased her to feel that this taciturn

Ethel M. Dell

man had taken her into his confidence at last. "I shall remember," she said lightly.

And she went away, not only comforted, but gay of heart.

*   *   *   *   *

During the remainder of the voyage, West was treated with extreme coolness by every one. It did not seem to abash him in the least. He came and went in the crowd with the utmost *sang-froid*, always preoccupied, always self-contained. Cynthia observed him from a distance with admiration. The man had taken her fancy. She was keenly interested in his methods, as well as in his decidedly unusual personality. She observed Rudd also, and noted the obvious suspicion with which he regarded West. On the night before their arrival she saw the latter alone for a moment, and whispered to him that Mr. Rudd seemed uneasy. At which information West merely laughed sardonically. He was holding a small parcel, to which, after a moment, he drew her attention.

"I was going to ask you to accept this," he said. "It is nothing very important, but I should like you to have it. Don't open it before to-morrow."

"What is it?" asked Cynthia, in surprise.

He frowned in his abrupt way.

"It doesn't matter; something connected with my profession. I shouldn't give it you, if I didn't know you were to be trusted."

"But - but" - she hesitated a little - "ought I to take it?"

He raised his shoulders.

"I shall give it to the captain for you, if you don't. But I would rather give it to you direct."

In face of this, Cynthia yielded, feeling as if he compelled her.

"But mayn't I open it?"

"No." West's eyes held hers for a second. "Not till to-morrow. And, in case we don't meet again, I'll say good-bye."

"But we shall meet in New York?" she urged, with a sudden sense of loss. "Or perhaps in Boston? My father would really like to meet you."

"Much obliged," said West, with his grim smile. "But I'm not much of a society man. And I don't think I shall find myself in Boston at present."

"Then - then - I sha'n't see you again - ever?" Cynthia's tone was unconsciously tragic. Till that moment she had scarcely realised how curiously strong an attraction this man held for her.

West's expression changed. His emotionless blue eyes became suddenly more blue, and intense with a vital fire. He leaned towards her as one on the verge of vehement speech.

Then abruptly his look went beyond her, and he checked himself.

"Who knows?" he said carelessly. "Good-bye for the present, anyway! It's been a pleasant voyage."

He straightened himself with the words, nodded, and turned aside without so much as touching her hand.

And Cynthia, glancing round with an instinctive feeling of discomfiture, saw Rudd with another man, standing watching them at the end of the passage.

*   *   *   *   *

Ethel M. Dell

In the dark of early morning they reached New York. Most of the passengers decided to remain on board for breakfast, which was served at an early hour in the midst of a hubbub and turmoil indescribable.

Cynthia, with her aunt and Archie, partook of a hurried meal in the thick of the ever-shifting crowd. She looked in vain for West, her grey eyes searching perpetually.

One friend after another came up to bid them good-bye, stood a little, talking, and presently drifted away. The whole ship from end to end hummed like a hive of bees.

She was glad when at length she was able to escape from the noisy saloon. She had not slept well, and her nerves were on edge. The memory of that interrupted conversation with West, of the confidence unspoken, went with her continually. She had an almost feverish longing to see him once more, even though it were in the heart of the crowd. He had been about to tell her something. Of that she was certain. She had an intense, an almost passionate desire to know what it was. Surely he would not - he could not - go ashore without seeing her again!

She had not intended to open the packet he had given her till she was ashore herself, but a palpitating curiosity tugged ever at her resolution till at length she could resist it no longer. West was nowhere to be seen, and she felt she must know more. It was intolerable to be thus left in the dark. Through the scurrying multitude of departing passengers, she began to make her way back to her cabin. Her progress was of necessity slow, and once in a crowded corner she was stopped altogether.

Two men were talking together close to her. Their backs were towards her, and in the general confusion they did not observe her futile impatience to pass.

"Oh, I knew the fellow was a wrong 'un, all along," were the first words that filtered to the girl's consciousness as she stood. "But I didn't think he was responsible for that card trick, I must say. Young Bathurst looked so abominably hangdog."

It was the Englishman, Norton, who spoke, and the man who stood with him was Rudd. Cynthia realised the near presence of the latter with a sensation of disgust. His drawling tones grated upon her intolerably.

"Waal," he said, "it was just that card trick that opened my eyes - I shouldn't have noticed him, otherwise. I knew that young Bathurst was square. He hasn't the brains to be anything else. And when this chap butted in with his thick-ribbed impudence, I guessed right then that we hadn't got a beginner to deal with. After that I watched for a bit, and there were several little things that made me begin to reflect. So the next evening I got a wireless message off to my partner in New York, and I reckon that did the trick. When we came up alongside this morning, the vultures were all ready for him. I took them to his cabin myself. There was no fuss at all. He saw it was all up, and gave in without a murmur. They were only just in time, though. In another thirty seconds, he would have been off. It was a clever piece of work, I flatter myself, to net Mr. Nat Verney so neatly."

The Englishman began to laugh, but suddenly broke off short as a girl's face, white and quivering, came between them.

"Who is this man?" the high, breathless voice demanded. "Which - which is Mr. Nat Verney?"

Rudd looked down at her through narrowed eyes. He was smiling - a small, bitter smile.

"Waal, Miss Mortimer," he began, "I reckon you have first right to know -"

She turned from him imperiously.

"You tell me," she commanded Norton.

Ethel M. Dell

Norton looked genuinely uncomfortable, and, probably in consequence, he answered her with a gruffness that sounded brutal.

"It was West. He has been arrested. His own fault entirely. No one would have suspected him if he hadn't been a fool, and given his own show away."

"He wasn't a fool!" Cynthia flashed back fiercely. "He was my friend!"

"I shouldn't be in too great a hurry to claim that distinction," remarked Rudd. "He's about the best-known rascal in the two hemispheres."

But Cynthia did not wait to hear him. She had slipped past, and was gone.

In her own cabin at last, she bolted the door and tore open that packet connected with his profession which he had given her the night before. It contained a roll of notes to the value of a hundred pounds, wrapped in a sheet of notepaper on which was scrawled a single line: "With apologies from the man who swindled you."

There was no signature of any sort. None was needed! When Cynthia finally left her cabin an hour later, her eyes were bright with that brightness which comes from the shedding of many tears.

THE SWINDLER'S HANDICAP

A SEQUEL TO "THE SWINDLER"

Which I Dedicate to the Friend Who Asked for it.

I

"Yes, but what's the good of it?" said Cynthia Mortimer gently. "I can never marry you."

"You might be engaged to me for a bit, anyhow," he urged, "and see how you like it."

She made a quaint gesture with her arms, as though she tried to lift some heavy weight.

"I am very sorry," she said, in the same gentle voice. "It's very nice of you to think of it, Lord Babbacombe. But - you see, I'm quite sure I shouldn't like it. So that ends it, doesn't it?"

He stood up to his full height, and regarded her with a faint, rueful smile.

"You're a very obstinate girl, Cynthia," he said.

She leaned back in her chair, looking up at him with clear, grey eyes that met his with absolute freedom.

Ethel M. Dell

"I'm not a girl at all, Jack," she said. "I gave up all my pretensions to youth many, many years ago."

He nodded, still faintly smiling.

"You were about nineteen, weren't you?"

"No. I was past twenty-one." A curious note crept into her voice; it sounded as if she were speaking of the dead. "It - was just twelve years ago," she said.

Babbacombe's eyebrows went up.

"What! Are you past thirty? I had no idea."

She laughed at him - a quick, gay laugh.

"Why, it's eight years since I first met you."

"Is it? Great heavens, how the time goes - wasted time, too, Cynthia! We might have been awfully happy together all this time. Well" - with a sharp sigh - "we can't get it back again. But anyhow, we needn't squander any more of it, if only you will be reasonable."

She shook her head; then, with one of those quick impulses that were a part of her charm, she sprang lightly up and gave him both her hands.

"No, Jack," she said. "No - no - no! I'm not reasonable. I'm just a drivelling, idiotic fool. But - but I love my foolishness too well ever to part with it. Ever, did I say? No, even I am not quite so foolish as that. But it's sublime enough to hold me till - till I know for certain whether - whether the thing I call love is real or - or - only - a sham."

There was passion in her voice, and her eyes were suddenly full of tears; but she kept them upturned to his as though she pleaded with him to understand.

He looked down at her very kindly, very steadily, holding her hands closely in his own. There was no hint of chagrin on his clean-shaven face - only the utmost kindness.

"Don't cry!" he said gently. "Tell me about this sublime foolishness of yours - about the thing you call - love. I might help you, perhaps - who knows? - to find out if it is the real thing or not."

Her lips were quivering.

"I've never told a soul," she said. "I - am half afraid."

"Nonsense, dear!" he protested.

"But I am," she persisted. "It's such an absurd romance - this of mine, so absurd that you'll laugh at it, just at first. And then - afterwards - you will - disapprove."

"My dear girl," he said, "you have never entertained the smallest regard for my opinion before. Why begin to-day?"

She laughed a little, turning from him to brush away her tears.

"Sit down," she said, "and - and smoke - those horrid strong cigarettes of yours. I love the smell. Perhaps I'll try and tell you. But - mind, Jack - you're not to look at me. And you're not to say a single word till I've done. Just - smoke, that's all."

She settled herself on the low fender-cushion with her face turned from him to the fire. Lord Babbacombe sat down as she desired, and took out and lighted a cigarette.

As the scent of it reached her she began to speak in the high, American voice he had come to love. There was nothing piercing about it; it was a clear, sweet treble.

"It happened when I was travelling under Aunt Bathurst's wing. You know, it was with her and my cousin Archie that I first did Europe. My! It was a long time ago! I've been round the world four times since then - twice with poor dear Daddy, once with Mrs. Archie, after he died, and the last time - alone. And I didn't like that last time a mite. I was like the man in *The Pilgrim's Progress* - I took my hump wherever I went. Still, I had to do something. You were big-game shooting. I'd have gone with you if you'd have had me unmarried. But I knew you wouldn't, so I just had to mess around by myself. Oh, but I was tired - I was tired! But I kept saying to myself it was the last journey before - Jack, if you don't smoke your cigarette will go out. Where was I? I'm afraid I'm boring you. You can go to sleep if you like. Well, it was on the voyage back. There was a man on board that every one said was a private detective. It was at the time of the great Nat Verney swindles. You remember, of course? And somehow we all jumped to the conclusion that he was tracking him. I remember seeing him when we first went on board at Liverpool. He was standing by the gangway watching the crowd with the bluest eyes on earth, and I took him for a detective right away. But - for all that - there was something about him - something I kind of liked, that made me feel I wanted to know him. He was avoiding everybody, but I made him talk to me. You know my way."

She paused for a moment, and leaning forward, gazed into the heart of the fire with wide, intent eyes.

The man in the chair behind her smoked on silently with a drawn face.

"He was very horrid to me," she went on, her voice soft and slow as though she were describing something seen in a vision, "the only man who ever was. But I - do you know, I liked him all the more for that? I didn't flirt with him. I didn't try. He wasn't the sort one could flirt with. He was hard - hard as iron, clean shaven, with an immensely powerful jaw, and eyes that looked clean through you. He was one of those short, broad Englishmen - you know the sort - out of proportion everywhere, but so splendidly strong. He just hated me for making friends with him. It was very funny."

An odd little note of laughter ran through the words - that laughter which is akin to tears.

"But I didn't care for that," she said. "It didn't hurt me in the least. He was too big to give offence to an impudent little minx like me. Besides, I wanted him to help me, and after a bit I told him so. Archie - my cousin, you know; he was only a boy then - was mad on card-playing at that time. And I was real worried about him. I knew he would get into a hole sooner or later, and I begged my surly Englishman to keep an eye on him. Oh, I was a fool! I was a brainless, chattering fool! And I'm not much better now, I often think."

Cynthia's hand went up to her eyes. The vision in the fire was all blurred and indistinct.

Babbacombe was leaning forward, listening intently. The firelight flickered on his face, showing it very grave and still. He did not attempt to speak.

Nevertheless, after a moment, Cynthia made a wavering movement with one hand in his direction.

"I'm not crying, Jack. Don't be silly! I'm sure your cigarette is out."

It was. He pitched it past her into the fire.

"Light another," she pleaded. "I love them so. They are the kind he always smoked. That's nearly the end of the story. You can almost guess the rest. That very night Archie did get into a hole, a bad one, and the only way my friend could lift him out was by getting down into it himself. He saved him, but it was at his own expense; for it made people begin to reflect. And in the end - in the end, when we came into harbour, they came on board, and - and arrested him early in the morning - before I knew. You see, he - he was Nat Verney."

Cynthia's dark head was suddenly bowed upon her hands. She

was rocking to and fro in the firelight.

"And it was my fault," she sobbed - "all my fault. If - if he hadn't done that thing for me, no one would have known - no one would have suspected!"

She had broken down completely at last, and the man who heard her wondered, with a deep compassion, how often she had wept, in secret and uncomforted, as she was weeping now.

He bore it till his humanity could endure no longer. And then, very gently, he reached out, touched her, drew her to him, pillowed her head on his shoulder.

"Don't cry, Cynthia," he whispered earnestly. "It's heart-breaking work, dear, and it doesn't help. There! Let me hold you till you feel better. You can't refuse comfort from an old friend like me."

She yielded to him mutely for a little, till her grief had somewhat spent itself. Then, with a little quivering smile, she lifted her head and looked him straight in the face.

"Thank you, Jack," she said. "You - you've done me good. But it's not good for you, is it? I've made you quite damp. You don't think you'll catch cold?" - dabbing at his shoulder with her handkerchief.

He took her hand and stayed it.

"There is nothing in this world," he said gravely "that I would so gladly do as help you, Cynthia. Will you believe this, and treat me from this stand-point only?"

She turned back to the fire, but she left her hand in his.

"My dear," she said, in an odd little choked voice, "it's just like you to say so, and I guess I sha'n't forget it. Well, well! There's my romance in a nutshell. He didn't care a fig for me till just the last. He cared then, but it was too late to come to anything. They shipped him back again you know, and he was sentenced to fifteen years' penal servitude. He's done nearly twelve, and he's coming out next month on ticket-of-leave."

"Oh, Cynthia!"

Babbacombe bent his head suddenly upon her hand, and sat tense and silent.

"I know," she said - "I know. It sounds simply monstrous, put into bald words. I sometimes wonder myself if it can possibly be true - if I, Cynthia Mortimer, can really be such a fool. But I can't possibly tell for certain till I see him again. I must see him again somehow. I've waited all these years - all these years."

Babbacombe groaned.

"And suppose, when you've seen him, you still care?"

She shook her head.

"What then, Jack? I don't know; I don't know."

He pulled himself together, and sat up.

"Do you know where he is?"

"Yes. He is at Barren Hill. He has been there for five years now. My solicitor knows that I take an interest in him. He calls it philanthropy." Cynthia smiled faintly into the fire. "I was one of the people he swindled," she said. "But he paid me back."

She rose and went across the room to a bureau in a corner. She unlocked a drawer, and took something from it. Returning, she laid a packet of notes in Babbacombe's hands.

Ethel M. Dell

"I could never part with them," she said. "He gave them to me in a sealed parcel the last time I saw him. It's only a hundred pounds. Yes, that was the message he wrote. Can you read it? 'With apologies from the man who swindled you.' As if I cared for the wretched money!"

Babbacombe frowned over the writing in silence.

"Why don't you say what you think, Jack?" she said. "Why don't you call him a thieving scoundrel and me a poor, romantic fool!"

"I am trying to think how I can help you," he answered quietly. "Have you any plans?"

"No, nothing definite," she said. "It is difficult to know what to do. He knows one thing - that he has a friend who will help him when he comes out. He will be horribly poor, you know, and I'm so rich. But, of course, I would do it anonymously. And he thinks his friend is a man."

Babbacombe pondered with drawn brows.

"Cynthia," he said slowly, at length, "suppose I take this matter into my own hands, suppose I make it possible for you to see this man once more, will you be guided entirely by me? Will you promise me solemnly to take no rash step of any description; in short, to do nothing without consulting me? Will you promise me, Cynthia?"

He spoke very earnestly. The firelight showed her the resolution on his face.

"Of course I will promise you, Jack," she said instantly. "I would trust myself body and soul in your keeping. But what can you do?"

"I might do this," he said. "I might pose as his unknown friend - another philanthropist, Cynthia." He smiled rather grimly. "I might get hold of him when he comes out, give him something to do to keep his head above water. If he has any manhood in him, he won't mind what he takes. And I might - later, if I thought it practicable - I only say 'if,' Cynthia, for after many years of prison life a man isn't always fit company for a lady - I might arrange that you should see him in some absolutely casual fashion. If you consent to this arrangement you must leave that entirely to me."

"But you will hate to do it!" she exclaimed.

He rose. "I will do it for your sake," he said. "I shall not hate it if it makes you see things - as they are."

"Oh, but you are good," she said tremulously - "you are good!"

"I love a good woman," he answered gravely.

And with that he turned and left her alone in the firelight with her romance.

II

It was early on a dark November day that the prison gate at Barren Hill opened to allow a convict who had just completed twelve years' penal servitude to pass out a free man.

A motor car was drawn up at the side of the kerb as he emerged, and a man in a long overcoat, with another slung on his arm, was pacing up and down.

He wheeled at the closing of the gate, and they stood face to face.

There was a moment's difficult silence; then the man with the motor spoke.

"Mr. West, I think?"

The other looked him up and down in a single comprehensive glance that was like the flash of a sword blade.

"Certainly," he said curtly, "if you prefer it."

He was a short, thick-set man of past forty, with a face so grimly lined as to mask all expression. His eyes alone were vividly alert. They were the bluest eyes that Babbacombe had ever seen.

He accepted the curt acknowledgment with grave courtesy, and made a motion toward the car.

"Will you get in? My name is Babbacombe. I am here to meet you, as no doubt you have been told. You had better wear this" - opening out the coat he carried.

But West remained motionless, facing him on the grey, deserted road. "Before I come with you," he said, in his brief, clipped style, "there is one thing I want to know. Are you patronising me for the sake of philanthropy, or for - some other reason?"

As he uttered the question, he fixed Babbacombe with a stare that was not without insolence.

Babbacombe did not hesitate in his reply. He was not a man to be lightly disconcerted.

"You can put it down to anything you like," he said, "except philanthropy."

West considered a moment.

"Very well, sir," he said finally, his aggressive tone slightly modified. "In that case I will come with you."

He turned about, and thrust his arms into the coat Babbacombe held for him, turned up the collar, and without a backward glance, stepped into the waiting motor.

Babbacombe started the engine, and followed him. In another moment they had glided away into the dripping mist, and the prison was left behind.

Through mile after mile they sped in silence. West sat with his chin buried in his coat, his keen eyes staring straight ahead. Babbacombe, at the wheel, never glanced at him once.

Through villages, through towns, through long stretches of open country they glided, sometimes slackening, but never stopping. The sun broke through at length, revealing a country of hills and woods and silvery running streams. They had been travelling for hours. It was nearly noon.

For the first time since their start Babbacombe spoke.

"I hope I haven't kept you going too long. We are just getting in."

"Don't mind me," said West.

Babbacombe was slackening speed.

"It's a fine hunting country," he observed.

"Whose is it?" asked West.

"Mine, most of it." They were running smoothly down a long avenue of beech trees, with a glimpse of an open gateway at the end.

"It must take some managing," remarked West.

"It does," Babbacombe answered. "It needs a capable man."

They reached the gateway, passing under an arch of stone. Beyond it lay wide stretches of park land. Rabbits scuttled in the sunshine, and under the trees here and there they had glimpses of deer.

"Ever ridden to hounds?" asked Babbacombe.

The man beside him turned with a movement half savage.

"Set me on a good horse," he said, "and I will show you what I can do."

Babbacombe nodded, conscious for the first time of a warmth of sympathy for the man. Whatever his sins, he must have suffered infernally during the past twelve years.

Twelve years! Ye gods! It was half a life-time! It represented the whole of his manhood to Babbacombe. Twelve years ago he had been an undergraduate at Cambridge.

He drove on through the undulating stretches of Farringdean Park, his favourite heritage, trying to realise what effect twelve years in a convict prison would have had upon himself, what his outlook would ultimately have become, and what in actual fact was the outlook and general attitude of the man who had come through this long purgatory.

Sweeping round a rise in the ground, they came into sudden sight of the castle. Ancient and splendid it rose before them, its battlements shining in the sun - a heritage of which any man might be proud.

Babbacombe waited for some word of admiration from his companion. But he waited in vain. West was mute.

"What do you think of it?" he asked at last, determined to wring some meed of appreciation from him, even though he stooped to ask for it.

"What - the house?" said West. "It's uncommonly like a primeval sort of prison, to my idea. I've no doubt it boasts some very superior dungeons."

The sting in the words reached Babbacombe, but without offence. Again, more strongly, he was conscious of that glow of sympathy within him, kindling to a flame of fellowship.

"It boasts better things than that," he said quietly, "as I hope you will allow me to show you."

He was conscious of the piercing gaze of West's eyes, and, after a moment, he deliberately turned his own to meet it.

"And if you find - as you probably soon will - that I make but a poor sort of host," he said, "just remember, will you, that I like my guests to please themselves, and secure your own comfort?"

For a second, West's grim mouth seemed to hesitate on the edge of a smile - a smile that never developed.

"I wonder how soon you will tell me to go to the devil?" he

said cynically.

"Oh, I am a better host than that," said Babbacombe, with quiet humour. "If you ever prefer the devil's hospitality to mine, it won't be my fault."

West turned from him with a slight shrug of the shoulders, as if he deemed himself to be dealing with a harmless lunatic, and dropped back into silence.

III

Silence had become habitual to him, as Babbacombe soon discovered. He could remain silent for hours. Probably he had never been of a very expansive nature, and prison discipline had strengthened an inborn reticence to a reserve of iron. He was not a disconcerting companion, because he was absolutely unobtrusive, but with all the good-will in the world Babbacombe found it well-nigh impossible to treat him with that ease of manner which came to him so spontaneously in his dealings with other men.

Grim, taciturn, cynical, West baffled his every effort to reach the inner man. His silence clothed him like armour, and he never really emerged from it save when a fiendish sense of humour tempted him. This, and this alone, so it seemed to Babbacombe, had any power to draw him out. And the instant he had flung his gibe at the object thereof, he would retreat again into that impenetrable shell of silence. He never once spoke of his past life, never once referred to the future.

He merely accepted Babbacombe's hospitality in absolute silence, without question, without gratitude, smoked his cigarettes eternally, drank his wines without appreciation, rode his horses without comment.

The only point in his favour that Babbacombe, the kindliest of critics, could discover after a fort-night's patient study, was that the animals loved him. He conducted himself like a gentleman, but somehow Babbacombe had expected this much from the moment of their meeting. He sometimes told himself with a wry face that if the fellow had behaved like a beast he would have found him easier to cultivate. At least, he would have had something to work upon, a creature of flesh and blood, instead of this inscrutable statue wrought in iron.

With a sinking heart he recalled Cynthia's description of the man. To a certain extent it still fitted him, but he imagined

Ethel M. Dell

that those twelve years had had a hardening effect upon him, making rigid that which had always been stubborn, driving the iron deeper and ever deeper into his soul, till only iron remained. Many were the nights he spent pondering over the romance of the woman he loved. What subtle attraction in this hardened sinner had lured her heart away? Was it possible that the fellow had ever cared for her? Had he ever possessed even the rudiments of a heart?

The message he had read in the firelight - the brief line which this man had written - was the only answer he could find to these doubts. It seemed to point to something - some pulsing warmth - which could not have been kindled from nothing. And again the memory of a woman's tears would come upon him, spurring him to fresh effort. Surely the man for whom she was breaking her heart could not be wholly evil, nor yet wholly callous! Somewhere behind those steely blue eyes, there must dwell some answer to the riddle. It might be that Cynthia would find it, though he failed. But he shrank, with an aversion inexpressible, from letting her try, so deeply rooted had his conviction become that her cherished girlish fancy was no more than the misty gold of dreams.

Yet for her sake he persevered - for the sake of those precious tears that had so wrung his heart he would do that which he had set out to do, notwithstanding the utmost discourage ment. An insoluble enigma the man might be to him, but he would not for that turn back from the task that he had undertaken. West should have his chance in spite of it.

They were riding together over the crisp turf of the park one frosty morning in November, when Babbacombe turned quietly to his companion, pointing to the chimneys of a house half-hidden by trees, ahead of them.

"I want to go over that place," he said. "It is standing empty, and probably needs repairs."

West received the announcement with a brief nod. He never

betrayed interest in anything.

"Shall I hold your animal?" he suggested, as they reached the gate that led into the little garden.

"No. Come in with me, won't you? We can hitch the bridles to the post."

They went in together through a rustling litter of dead leaves. The house was low, and thatched - a picturesque dwelling of no great size.

Babbacombe led the way within, and they went from room to room, he with note-book in hand, jotting down the various details necessary to make the place into a comfortable habitation.

"I daresay you can help me with this if you will," he said presently. "I shall turn some workmen on to it next week. Perhaps you will keep an eye on them for me, decide on the decorations, and so forth. It is my agent's house, you know."

"Where is your agent?" asked West abruptly.

Babbacombe smiled a little. "At the present moment - I have no agent. That is what keeps me so busy. I hope to have one before long."

West strolled to a window and opened it, leaning his arms upon the sill.

He seemed about to relapse into one of his interminable silences when Babbacombe, standing behind him, said quietly, "I am going to offer the post to you."

"To me?" West wheeled suddenly, even with vehemence. "What for?" he demanded sharply.

Babbacombe met his look, still faintly smiling. "For our

mutual benefit," he said. "I am convinced that you have ample ability for this sort of work, and if you will accept the post I shall be very pleased."

He stopped at that, determined for once to make the man speak on his own initiative. West was looking straight at him, and there was a curious glitter in his eyes like the sparkle of ice in the sun.

When he spoke at length his speech, though curt, was not so rigorously emotionless as usual.

"Don't you think," he said, "that you have carried this tomfoolery of yours far enough?"

Babbacombe raised one eyebrow. "Meaning?" he questioned.

West enlightened him with most unusual vigour.

"Meaning that tomfoolery of this sort never pays. I know. I've done it myself in my time. If I were you, I should pull up and try some less expensive hobby than that of mending broken men. The pieces are always chipped and never stick, and the chances are that you'll cut your fingers trying to make 'em. No, sir, I won't be your agent! Find a man you can trust, and let me go to the devil!"

The outburst was so unexpected and so forcible that at first Babbacombe stared at the man in amazement. Then, with that spontaneous kindness of heart that made him what he was, he grabbed and held his opportunity.

"My dear fellow," he said, not pausing for a choice of words, "you are talking infernal rot, and I won't listen to you. Do you seriously suppose I should be such a tenfold ass as to offer the management of my estate to a man I couldn't trust?"

"What reason have you for trusting me?" West thrust back. "Unless you think that a dozen years in prison have deprived me of my ancient skill. Would you choose a man who has been a drunkard for your butler? No! Then don't choose a swindler and an ex-convict for your bailiff."

He swung around with the words and shut the window with a bang.

But again Babbacombe took his cue from that inner prompting to which he had trusted all his life. For the first time he liked the man; for the first time, so it seemed to him, he caught a glimpse of the soul into which the iron had been so deeply driven.

"Look here, West," he said, "I am not going to take that sort of refusal from you. We have been together some time now, and it isn't my fault if we don't know each other pretty well. I don't care a hang what you have been. I am only concerned with what you are, and whatever that may be, you are not a weak-kneed fool. You have the power to keep straight if you choose, and you are to choose. Understand? I make you this offer with a perfectly open mind, and you are to consider it in the same way. Would you have said because you had once had a nasty tumble that you would never ride again? Of course you wouldn't. You are not such a fool. Then don't refuse my offer on those grounds, for it's nothing less than contemptible."

"Think so?" said West. He had listened quite impassively to the oration, but as Babbacombe ended, his grim mouth relaxed sardonically. "You seem mighty anxious to spend your money on damaged goods, Lord Babbacombe. It's a tom-fool investment, you know. How many of the honest folk in your service will stick to you when they begin to find out what you've given them?"

"Why should they find out?" asked Babbacombe.

West shrugged his shoulders. "It's a dead certainty that they will."

"If I can take the risk, so can you," said Babbacombe.

"Oh, of course, I used to be rather good at that game. It is called 'sand-throwing' in the profession."

Babbacombe made an impatient movement, and West's hard smile became more pronounced.

"But you are not at all good at it," he continued. "You are almost obtrusively obvious. It is a charm that has its very material drawbacks."

Babbacombe wholly lost patience at that. The man's grim irony was not to be borne.

"Take it or leave it!" he exclaimed. "But if you leave it, in heaven's name let it be for some sounder reason than a faked-up excuse of moral weakness!"

West uttered an abrupt laugh. "You seem to have a somewhat exalted opinion of my morals," he observed. "Well, since you are determined to brave the risk of being let down, I needn't quibble at it any further. I accept."

Babbacombe's attitude changed in an instant. He held out his hand.

"You won't let me down, West," he said, with confidence.

West hesitated for a single instant, then took the proffered hand into a grip of iron. His blue eyes looked hard and straight into Babbacombe's face.

"If I let you down," he said grimly, "I shall be underneath."

IV

It was not till the middle of December that the new bailiff moved into his own quarters, but he had assumed his duties some weeks before that time, and Babbacombe was well satisfied with him. The man's business instincts were unusually keen. He had, moreover, a wonderful eye for details, and very little escaped him. It soon came home to Babbacombe that the management of his estate was in capable hands, and he congratulated himself upon having struck ore where he had least expected to find it. He supervised the whole of West's work for a time, but he soon suffered this vigilance to relax, for the man's shrewdness far surpassed his own. He settled to the work with a certain grim relish, and it was a perpetual marvel to Babbacombe that he mastered it from the outset with such facility.

Keepers and labourers eyed him askance for awhile, but West's imperturbability took effect before very long. They accepted him without enthusiasm, but also without rancour, as a man who could hold his own.

As soon as he was installed in the bailiff's house, Babbacombe left him to his own devices, and departed upon a round of visits. He proposed to entertain a house-party himself towards the end of January. He informed West of this before departing, and was slightly puzzled by a certain humourous gleam that shone in the steely eyes at the news. The matter went speedily from his mind. It was not till long after that he recalled it.

West wrote to him regularly during his absence, curt, businesslike epistles, which always terminated on a grim note of irony: "Your faithful steward, N. V. West." He never varied this joke, and Babbacombe usually noted it with a faint frown. The fellow was not a bad sort, he was convinced, but he would always be more or less of an enigma to him.

He returned to Farringdean in the middle of January with one

Ethel M. Dell

of his married sisters, whom he had secured to act as hostess to his party. He invited West to dine with them informally on the night of his return.

His sister, Lady Cottesbrook, a gay and garrulous lady some years his senior, received the new agent with considerable condescension. She bestowed scant attention upon him during dinner, and West presented his most impenetrable demeanour in consequence, refusing steadily to avail himself of Babbacombe's courteous efforts to draw him into the conversation.

He would have excused himself later from accompanying his host into the drawing-room, but Babbacombe insisted upon this so stubbornly that finally, with his characteristic lift of the shoulders, he yielded.

As they entered, Lady Cottesbrook raised her glasses, and favoured him with a close scrutiny.

"It's very curious," she said, "but I can't help feeling as if I have seen you somewhere before. You have the look of some one I knew years ago - some one I didn't like - but I can't remember who."

"Just as well, perhaps," said Babbacombe, with a careless laugh, though a faint flush of annoyance rose in his face. "Come over here, West. You can smoke. My sister likes it."

He seated himself at the piano, indicated a chair near him to his guest, and began to play.

West, with his back to the light, sat motionless, listening. Lady Cottesbrook took up a book, and ignored him. There was something unfathomable about her brother's bailiff to which she strongly objected.

An hour later, when he had gone, she spoke of it.

"That man has the eyes of a criminal, Jack. I am sure he isn'ttrustworthy. He is too brazen. Where in the world did you pick him up?"

To which Babbacombe made composed reply:

"I know all about him, and he is absolutely trustworthy. He was recommended to me by a friend. I am sorry you thought it necessary to be rude to him. There is nothing offensive about him that I can see."

"My dear boy, you see nothing offensive in a great many people whom I positively detest. However, he isn't worth an argument. Only, if you must ask the man to dine, for goodness' sake another time have some one else for me to talk to. I frankly admit that I have no talent for entertaining people of that class. Now tell me the latest about Cynthia Mortimer. Of course, she is one of the chosen guests?"

"She has promised to spend a week here," Babbacombe answered somewhat reluctantly. "I haven't seen her lately. She has been in Paris."

"What has she been doing there? Buying her trousseau?"

"I really don't know." There was a faint inflection of irritation in his voice.

"Doesn't her consenting to come here mean that she will accept you?" questioned Lady Cottesbrook. She never hesitated to ask in plainest terms for anything she wanted.

"No," Babbacombe said heavily. "It does not."

Lady Cottesbrook was silenced. After a little she turned her attention to other matters, to her brother's evident relief.

V

It was on a still, frosty evening of many stars that Cynthia came to Farringdean Castle. A young moon was low in the sky, and she paused to curtsey to it upon descending from the motor that had borne her thither.

She turned to find Babbacombe beside her.

"I hope it will bring you luck, Cynthia," he said.

She flashed a swift look at him, and gave him both her hands.

"Thank you, old friend," she said softly.

Her eyes were shining like the stars above them. She laughed a little tremulously.

"I couldn't get to the station to meet you," he said. "I wanted to. Come inside. There is no one here whom you don't know."

"Thank you again," she said.

In another moment they were entering the great hall. Before an immense open fireplace a group of people were gathered at tea. There was a general buzz of greeting as Cynthia entered. She was always popular, wherever she went.

She scattered her own greetings broadcast, passing from one to another, greeting each in her high, sweet drawl - a gracious, impulsive woman whom to know was to love.

Babbacombe watched her with a dumb longing. How often he had pictured her as hostess where now she moved as guest! Well, that dream of his was shattered, but the glowing fragments yet burned in his secret heart. All his life long he would remember her as he saw her that night on his own hearth. Her loveliness was like a flower wide open to the sun.

He thought her lovelier that night than she had ever been before. When she flitted away at length, he felt as if she took the warmth and brightness of the fireside with her.

There was no agreement between them, but he knew that she would be down early, and hastened his own dressing in consequence. He found her waiting alone in the drawing-room before a regal fire. She wore a splendid star of diamonds in her dark hair. It sparkled in a thousand colours as she turned. Her dress was black, unrelieved by any ornament.

"Cynthia," he said, "you are exquisite!"

The words burst from him almost involuntarily. She put out her hand to him with a gesture half of acknowledgment, half of protest.

"I may be good to look at," she said, with a little whimsical smile. "But - I tell you, Jack - I feel a perfect reptile. It's heads I win, tails you lose; and - I just can't bear it."

There was a catch in the high voice that was almost a sob. Babbacombe took her hand and held it.

"My dear," he said, "it's nothing of the sort. You have done me the very great honour of giving me your full confidence, and I won't have you abusing yourself for it."

She shook her head. "I hate myself - there! And - and I'm frightened too. Jack, if you want me to marry you - you had better ask me now. I won't refuse you."

He looked her closely in the eyes. "No, Cynthia," he said very gravely.

"I am not laughing," she protested.

He smiled a little. "It would be easier for me if you were," he said. "No, we will go through with this since we have begun.

Ethel M. Dell

And you needn't be scared. He is hardly a ladies' man, according to my judgment, but he is not a bounder. I haven't asked him to meet you to-night. I thought it better not. In fact, I -"

He broke off at the sound of a step behind him. With a start Cynthia turned.

A short, thick-set man in riding-dress was walking up the room.

"I beg your pardon," he said formally, halting a few paces from Babbacombe. "I have been waiting for you in the library for the last hour. I sent you a message, but I conclude it was not delivered. Can I speak to you for a few seconds on a matter of business?"

He spoke with his eyes fixed steadily upon Babbacombe's face, ignoring the woman's presence as if he had not even seen her.

Babbacombe was momentarily disconcerted. He glanced at Cynthia before replying; and instantly, in her quick, gracious way, she came forward with extended hand.

"Why, Mr. West," she said, "don't you know me? I'm Cynthia Mortimer - a very old friend of yours. And I'm very glad to meet you again."

There was a quiver as of laughter in her words. The confidence of her action compelled some species of response. West took the outstretched hand for a single instant; but his eyes, meeting hers, held no recognition.

"I am afraid," he said stonily, "that your memory is better than mine."

It was a check that would have disheartened many women; not so Cynthia Mortimer.

She opened her eyes wide for a second, the next quite openly she laughed at him.

"You are not a bit cleverer than you used to be," she said. "But I rather like you for it all the same. Come, Mr. West, I'm sure you will make an effort when I tell you that I want to be remembered. You once did a big thing for me which I have never forgotten - which I never shall forget."

West was frowning. "You have made a mistake," he said briefly.

She laughed again, softly, audaciously. There was a delicate flush on her face, and her eyes were very bright.

"No, Mr. Nat Verney West," she said, sinking her voice. "I'm a lot cleverer than you think, and I don't make mistakes of that sort."

He shrugged his shoulders, and was silent. She was laughing still.

"Why can't we begin where we left off?" she asked ingenuously. "Back numbers are so dull, and we were long past this stage anyway. Lord Babbacombe," appealing suddenly to her host, "can't you persuade Mr. West to come to the third act? I always prefer to skip the second. And we finished the first long ago."

Babbacombe came to her assistance with his courteous smile. "Miss Mortimer considers herself in your debt, Mr. West," he said. "I think you will hurt her feelings if you try to repudiate her obligation."

"Yes, of course," laughed Cynthia. "It was a mighty big debt, and I have been wondering ever since how to get even with you. Oh, you needn't scowl. That doesn't hurt me at all. Do you know you haven't altered a mite, you funny English bulldog? Come, you know me now?"

"Yes, I know you," West said. "But I think it is a pity that you have renewed your acquaintance with me, and the sooner you drop me again the better." He spoke briefly and very decidedly, and having thus expressed himself he turned to Babbacombe. "I am going to the library. Perhaps you will join me there at your convenience."

With an abrupt bow to Cynthia, he turned to go. But instantly the high voice arrested him.

"Mr. West!"

He paused.

"Mr. West!" she said again, her voice half-imperious, half-pleading.

Reluctantly he faced round. She was waiting for him with a little smile quivering about her mouth. Her grey eyes met his with perfect composure.

"I want to know," she said, in her softest drawl, "if it is for my sake or your own that you regret this renewal of acquaintance."

"For yours, Miss Mortimer," he answered grimly.

"That's very kind of you," she rejoined. "And why?"

Again he gave that slight lift of the shoulders that she remembered so well.

"You know the proverb about touching pitch?"

"Some people like pitch," said Cynthia.

"Not clean people," threw back West.

"No?" she said. "Well, perhaps not. Anyway, it doesn't apply in this case. So I sha'n't drop you, Mr. West, thank you all the same! Good-night!"

She offered him her hand with a gesture that was nothing short of regal. And he - because he could do no less - took it, gripped it, and went his way.

"Isn't he rude?" murmured Cynthia; and she said it as if rudeness were the highest virtue a man could display.

Ethel M. Dell

VI

The early winter dusk was falling upon a world veiled in cold, drifting rain. Away in the distance where the castle stood, many lights had begun to glimmer. It was the cosy hour when sportsmen collect about the fireside with noisy talk of the day's achievements.

The man who strode down the long, dark avenue towards the bailiff's house smiled bitterly to himself as he marked the growing illumination. It was four days since Cynthia Mortimer had extended to him the hand of friendship, and he had not seen her since. He was, in fact, studiously avoiding her, more studiously than he had ever avoided any one in his life before. His daily visits to the castle he now paid early in the morning, before Babbacombe himself was dressed, long before any of the guests were stirring. And his refusal either to dine at the castle or to join the sportsmen during the day was so prompt and so emphatic that Babbacombe had refrained from pressing his invitation.

Not a word had passed between them upon the subject of Cynthia's recognition. West adhered strictly to business during his brief interviews with his chief. The smallest digression on Babbacombe's part he invariably ignored as unworthy of his attention, till even Babbacombe, with all his courtly consideration for others, began to regard him as a mere automaton, and almost to treat him as such.

Had he realised in the faintest degree what West was enduring at that time, his heart must have warmed to the man, despite his repellent exterior. But he had no means of realising.

The rust of twelve bitter years had corroded the bolts of that closed door behind which the swindler hid his lonely soul, and it was not in the power of any man to move them.

So grimly he went his silent way, cynical, as only those can be to whom the best thing in life has been offered too late; proud, also, after his curious, iron-clad fashion, refusing sternly to bear a lance again in that field which had witnessed his dishonour.

He knew very well what those twinkling lights denoted. He could almost hear the clatter round the tea-table, the witless jests of the youngsters, the careless laughter of the women, the trivial, merry nonsense that was weaving another hour of happiness into the golden skein of happy hours. Contemptible, of course! Vanity of vanities! But how infinitely precious is even such vanity as this to those who stand outside!

The rain was beginning to patter through the trees. It would be a wet night. With his collar turned up to his ears, he trudged forward. He cared little for the rain. For twelve long years he had lived an outdoor life.

There were no lights visible in his own abode. The old woman who kept his house was doubtless gossiping with some crony up at the castle.

With his hand on the garden gate, he looked back at its distant, shining front. Then, with a shrug, as if impatient with himself for lingering, he turned to walk up the short, flagged pathway that led to his own door.

At the same instant a cry of pain - a woman's cry - came sharply through the dripping stillness of the trees. He turned back swiftly, banging the gate behind him.

A long slope rose, tree-covered, from the other side of the road. He judged the sound to have come from that direction, and he hurried towards it with swinging strides. Reaching the deep shadow, he paused, peering upwards.

At once a voice he knew called to him, but in such accents of agony that he hardly recognised it.

"Oh, come and help me! I'm here - caught in a trap! I can't move!"

In a moment he was crashing through the undergrowth with the furious recklessness of a wild animal.

"I am coming! Keep still!" he shouted as he went.

He found her crouched in a tiny hollow close to a narrow footpath that ran through the wood. She was on her knees, but she turned a deathly face up to him as he reached her. She was sobbing like a child.

"They are great iron teeth," she gasped, "fastened in my hand. Can you open them?"

"Don't move!" he ordered, as he dropped down beside her.

It was a poacher's trap, fortunately of a species with which he was acquainted. Her hand was fairly gripped between the iron jaws. He wondered with a set face if those cruel teeth had met in her delicate flesh.

She screamed as he forced it open, and fell back shuddering, half-fainting, while he lifted her torn hand and examined it in the failing light.

It was bleeding freely, but not violently, and he saw with relief that the larger veins had escaped. He wrapped his handkerchief round it, and spoke:

"Come!" he said. "My house is close by. It had better be bathed at once."

"Yes," she assented shakily.

"Don't cry!" he said, with blunt kindliness.

"I can't help it," whispered Cynthia.

He helped her to her feet, but she trembled so much that he put his arm about her.

"It's only a stone's throw away," he said.

She went with him without question. She seemed dazed with pain.

Silently he led her down to his dark abode.

"I'm giving you a lot of trouble," she murmured, as they entered.

To which he made gruff reply:

"It's worse for you than for me!"

He put her into an easy chair, lighted a lamp, and departed for a basin of water.

When he returned, she had so far mastered herself as to be able to smile at him through her tears.

"I know I'm a drivelling idiot to cry!" she said, her voice high and tremulous. "But I never felt so sick before!"

"Don't apologise," said West briefly. "I know."

He bathed the injury with the utmost tenderness, while she sat and watched his stern face.

"My!" she said suddenly, with a little, shaky laugh. "You are being very good to me, but why do you frown like that?"

He glanced at her with those piercing eyes of his.

"How did you do it?"

The colour came into her white face.

"I - was trying to spring the trap," she said, eyeing him doubtfully. "I didn't like to think of one of those cute little rabbits getting caught."

"Yes, but how did you manage to get your hand in the way?" said West.

She considered this problem for a little.

"I guess I can't explain that mystery to you," she said, at length. "You see, I'm only a woman, and women often do things that are very foolish."

West's silence seemed to express tacit agreement with this assertion.

"Anyway," she resumed, making a wry face, "it's done. You are not vexed because I made such a fuss?"

There was an odd wistfulness in her tone. West, busy bandaging, did not raise his eyes.

"I don't blame you for that," he said. "It must have hurt you infernally! If you take my advice, you will show it to a doctor."

She screwed her face up a second time.

"To please you, Mr. West?"

"No," he responded curtly. "As a sensible precaution."

"And if I don't happen to be remarkable for sense?" she suggested.

He shrugged his shoulders.

"Yes, I know," said Cynthia. "You say that to everything. It's getting rather monotonous. And I'm sure I'm very patient. You'll g rant me that, at least?"

He turned his ice-blue eyes upon her.

"I am not good at paying compliments, Miss Mortimer," he said cynically. "Twelve years in prison have rusted all my little accomplishments."

She met his look with a smile, though her lips were quivering still.

"My! What a pity!" she said. "Has your heart got rusty, too?"

"Very," said West shortly.

"Can't you rub it off?" she questioned.

He uttered his ironic laugh.

"There wouldn't be anything left if I did."

"No?" she said whimsically. "Well, give it to me, and let me see what I can do!"

His eyes fell away from her, and the grim line of his jaw hardened perceptibly.

"That would be too hard a job even for you!" he said.

She rose and put out her free hand to him. Her eyes were very soft and womanly. A quaint little smile yet hovered about her lips.

"I guess I'll have a try," she said gently.

He did not touch her hand, nor would he again meet her eyes.

"A hopeless task, I am afraid," he said. "And utterly unprofitable to all concerned. I am not a deserving object for your charity."

She laughed a trifle breathlessly.

"Say, Mr. West, couldn't you put that into words of one syllable? You try, and perhaps then I'll listen to you, and give you my views as well."

But West remained rigorously unresponsive. It was as if he were thinking of other things.

Cynthia uttered a little sigh and turned to go.

"Good-bye, Mr. West!" she said.

He went with her to the door.

"Shall I walk back with you?" he asked formally.

She shook her head.

"No. I'm better now, and it's quite light still beyond the trees. Good-bye, and - thank you!"

"Good-bye!" he said.

He followed her to the gate, opened it for her, and stood there watching till he saw her emerge from the shadow cast by the overarching trees. Then - for he knew that the rest of the journey was no more than a few minutes' easy walk - he turned back into the house, and shut himself in.

Entering the room he had just quitted, he locked the door, and there he remained for a long, long time.

VII

It was not till she descended to dinner that Cynthia's injured hand was noticed.

She resolutely made light of it to all sympathisers but it was plain to Babbacombe, at least, that it gave her considerable pain.

"Let me send for a doctor," he whispered, as she finally passed his chair.

But she shook her head with a smile.

"No, no. It will be all right in the morning."

But when he saw her in the morning, he knew at once that this prophecy had not been fulfilled. She met his anxious scrutiny with a smile indeed, but her heavy eyes belied it. He knew that she had spent a sleepless night.

"It wasn't my hand that kept me awake," she protested, when he charged her with this.

But Babbacombe was dissatisfied.

"Do see a doctor. I am sure it ought to be properly dressed," he urged. "I'll take you myself in the motor, if you will."

She yielded at length to his persuasion, though plainly against her will, and an hour later they drove off together, leaving the rest of the party to follow the hounds.

At the park gate they overtook West, walking swiftly. He raised his hat as they went by, but did not so much as look at Cynthia.

A sudden silence fell upon her, and it was not till some

minutes had passed that she broke it.

"Shall I tell you what kept me awake last night, Jack?" she said then. "I think you have a right to know."

He glanced at her, encountering one of those smiles, half-sad, half-humorous, that he knew so well. "You will do exactly as you please," he said.

"You're generous," she responded. "Well, I'll tell you. I was busy burying my poor foolish little romance."

A deep glow showed suddenly upon Babbacombe's face. He was driving slowly, but he kept his eyes fixed steadily upon the stretch of muddy road ahead.

"Is it dead, then?" he asked, his voice very low.

She made a quaint gesture as of putting something from her.

"Yes, quite; and buried decently without any fuss. The blinds are up again, and I don't want any condolences. I'm going out into the sun, Jack. I'm going to live."

"And what about me?" said Babbacombe.

She turned in her quick way, and laid her hand upon his knee.

"Yes, I've been thinking about you. I am going back to London to-morrow, and the first thing I shall do will be to find you a really good wife."

"Thank you," he said, smiling a little. "But you needn't go to London for that."

"Oh, shucks!" said Cynthia, colouring deeply. "There's more than one woman in the world, Jack."

"Not for me," he said quietly.

She was silent for a space. Then:

"And if that one woman is such a sublime fool, such an ungrateful little beast, as not to be able to - to love you as you deserve to be loved?" she suggested, a slight break in her voice.

He turned his head at that, and looked for an instant straight into her eyes.

"She is still the one woman, dear," he said, very tenderly. "Always remember that."

She shook her head in protest. Her lips were quivering too much for speech.

Babbacombe drove slowly on in silence.

At last the hand upon his knee pressed slightly.

"You can have her if you like, Jack," Cynthia murmured. "She's going mighty cheap."

He freed his hand for a moment to grasp hers.

"I shall follow her to London," he said, "and woo her there."

She smiled at him gratefully and began to speak of other things.

The doctor was out, to her evident relief. Babbacombe wanted to go in search of another, but she would not be persuaded.

"I'm sure it will be all right to-morrow. If not, I shall be in town, and I can go to a doctor there. Please don't make a fuss about it. It's too absurd."

Reluctantly he abandoned the argument, and they followed the hounds in the motor instead.

VIII

Babbacombe's guests departed upon the following day. Cynthia was among the first to leave. With a flushed face and sparkling eyes she made her farewells, and even Babbacombe, closely as he observed her, detected no hint of strain in her demeanour.

Returning from the station in the afternoon after speeding some of his guests, he dropped into the local bank to change a cheque. The manager, with whom he was intimate, chanced to be present, and led him off to his own room.

"By the way," he said, "we were just going to send you notice of an overdraft. That last big cheque of yours has left you a deficit."

Babbacombe stared at him. He had barely a fortnight before deposited a large sum of money at the bank, and he had not written any large cheque since.

"I don't understand," he said. "What cheque?"

The manager looked at him sharply.

"Why, the cheque for two hundred and fifty pounds, which your agent presented yesterday," he said. "It bore your signature and was dated the previous day. You wrote it, I suppose?"

Babbacombe was still staring blankly, but at the sudden question he pulled himself together.

"Oh, that! Yes, to be sure. Careless of me. I gave him a blank cheque for the Millsand estate expenses some weeks ago. It must have been that."

But though he spoke with a smiling face, his heart had gone

suddenly cold with doubt. He knew full well that the expenses of which he spoke had been paid by West long before.

He refused to linger, and went out again after a few commonplaces, feeling as if he had been struck a stunning blow between the eyes.

Driving swiftly back through the park, he recovered somewhat from the shock. There must be - surely there would be! - some explanation.

Reaching West's abode he stopped the motor and descended. West was not in and he decided to wait for him, chafing at the delay.

Standing at the window, he presently saw the man coming up the path. He moved slowly, with a certain heaviness, as though weary.

As he opened the outer door, Babbacombe opened the inner and met him in the hall.

"I dropped in to have a word with you," he said.

West paused momentarily before shutting the door. His face was in shadow.

"I thought so," he said. "I saw the motor."

Babbacombe turned back into the room. He was grappling with the hardest task he had ever had to tackle. West followed him in absolute silence.

With an immense effort, Babbacombe spoke:

"I was at the bank just now. I went to get some cash. I was told that my account was overdrawn. I can't understand it. There seems to have been some mistake."

He paused, but West said nothing whatever. The light was beginning to fail, but his expressionless face was clearly visible. It held neither curiosity nor dismay.

"I was told," Babbacombe said again, "that you cashed a cheque of mine yesterday for two hundred and fifty pounds. Is that so?"

"It is," said West curtly.

"And yet," Babbacombe proceeded, "I understood from you that the Millsand estate business was settled long ago."

"It was," said West.

"Then this cheque - this cheque for two hundred and fifty pounds - where did it come from, West?" There was a note of entreaty in Babbacombe's voice.

West jerked up his head at the sound. It was a gesture openly contemptuous. "Can't you guess?" he said.

Babbacombe stiffened at the callous question. "You refuse to answer me?" he asked.

"That is my answer," said West.

"I am to understand then that you have robbed me - that you have forged my signature to do so - that you - great heavens, man" - Babbacombe's amazement burst forth irresistibly - "it's incredible! Are you mad, I wonder? You can't have done it in your sober senses. You would never have been so outrageously clumsy."

West shrugged his shoulders.

"I am quite sane - only a little out of practice."

His words were like a shower of icy water. Babbacombe

contracted instantly.

"You wish me to believe that you did this thing in cold blood - that you deliberately meant to do it?"

"Certainly I meant to do it," said West.

"Why?" said Babbacombe.

Again he gave the non-committal shrug, no more. There was almost a fiendish look in his eyes, as if somewhere in his soul a demon leaped and jeered.

"Tell me why," Babbacombe persisted.

"Why should I tell you?" said West.

Babbacombe hesitated for an instant; then gravely, kindly, he made reply:

"For the sake of the friendship that has been between us. I had not the faintest idea that you were in need of money. Why couldn't you tell me?"

West made a restless movement. For the first time his hard stare shifted from Babbacombe's face.

"Why go into these details?" he questioned harshly. "I warned you at the outset what to expect. I am a swindler to the backbone. The sooner you bundle me back to where I came from, the better. I sha'n't run away this time."

"I shall not prosecute," Babbacombe said.

"You will not!" West blazed into sudden ferocity. He had the look of a wild animal at bay. "You are to prosecute!" he exclaimed violently. "Do you hear? I won't have any more of your damned charity! I'll go down into my own limbo and stay there, without let or hindrance from you or any other man. If you are fool enough to offer me another chance, as you call it, I am not fool enough to take it. The only thing I'll take from you is justice. Understand?"

"You wish me to prosecute?" Babbacombe said.

"I do!"

The words came with passionate force. West stood in almost a threatening attitude. His eyes shone in the gathering dusk like the eyes of a crouching beast - a beast that has been sorely wounded, but that will fight to the last.

The man's whole demeanour puzzled Babbacombe - his total lack of shame or penitence, his savagery of resentment. There was something behind it all - something he could not fathom, that baffled him, however he sought to approach it. In days gone by he had wondered if the fellow had a heart. That wonder was still in his mind. He himself had utterly failed to reach it if it existed. And Cynthia - even Cynthia - had failed. Yet, somehow, vaguely, he had a feeling that neither he nor Cynthia had understood.

"I don't know what to say to you, West," he said at length.

"Why say anything?" said West.

"Because," Babbacombe said slowly, "I don't believe - I can't believe - that simply for the sake of a paltry sum like that you would have risked so much. You could have swindled me in a thousand ways before now, and done it easily, too, with small chance of being found out. But this - this was bound to be discovered sooner or later. You must have known that. Then why, why in heaven's name did you do it? Apart from every other consideration, it was so infernally foolish. It wasn't like you to do a thing like that." He paused, then suddenly clapped an urgent hand upon the swindler's shoulder. "West," he said, "I'll swear that you never played this game with me for your own advantage. Tell the truth, man! Be honest with me in heaven's name! Give me the chance of judging you fairly! It isn't much to ask."

West drew back sharply.

"Why should I be honest with you?" he demanded. "You have never been honest with me from the very outset. I owe you nothing in that line, at all events."

He spoke passionately still, yet not wholly without restraint. He was as a man fighting desperate odds, and guarding some precious possession while he fought. But these words of his were something of a revelation to Babbacombe. He changed his ground to pursue it.

"What do you mean by that?"

"You know very well!" West flung the words from between set teeth, and with them he abruptly turned his back upon Babbacombe, lodging his arms upon the mantelpiece. "I am not going into details on that point or any other. But the fact is there, and you know it. You have never been absolutely straight in your dealings with me. I knew you weren't. I always knew it. But how crooked you were I did not know till lately. If you had been any other man, I believe I should have given you a broken head for your pains. But you are so damnably courteous, as well as such an unutterable fool!" He broke off with a hard laugh and a savage kick at the coals in front of him. "I couldn't see myself doing it," he said, "humbug as you are."

"And so you took this method of making me suffer?" Babbacombe suggested, his voice very quiet and even.

"You may say so if it satisfies you," said West, without turning.

"It does not satisfy me!" There was a note of sternness in the steady rejoinder. "It satisfies me so little that I insist upon an explanation. Turn round and tell me what you mean."

But West stood motionless and silent, as though hewn in granite.

Babbacombe waited with that in his face which very few had ever seen there. At last, as West remained stubborn, he spoke again:

"I suppose you have found out my original reason for giving you a fresh start in life, and you resent my having kept it a secret."

"I resent the reason." West tossed the words over his shoulder as though he uttered them against his will.

"Are you sure even now that you know what that reason was?" Babbacombe asked.

"I am sure of one thing!" West spoke quickly, vehemently, as a man shaken by some inner storm. "Had I been in your place - had the woman I wanted to marry asked me to bring back into her life some worthless scamp to whom she had taken a sentimental fancy when she was scarcely out of the schoolroom, I'd have seen him damned first, and myself too - had I been in your place. I would have refused pointblank, even if it had meant the end of everything."

"I believe you would," Babbacombe said. The sternness had gone out of his voice, and a certain weariness had taken its place. "But you haven't quite hit the truth of the matter. Since you have guessed so much you had better know the whole. I did not do this thing by request. I undertook it voluntarily. If I had not done so, some other means - possibly some less discreet means - would have been employed to gain the same end."

"I see!" West's head was bent. He seemed to be closely examining the marble on which his arms rested. "Well," he said abruptly, "you've told me the truth. I will do the same to you. This business has got to end. I have done my part towards bringing that about. And now you must do yours. You will have to prosecute, whether you like it or not. It is the only way."

"What?" Babbacombe said sharply.

West turned at last. The glare had gone out of his eyes - they were cold and still as an Arctic sky.

"I think we understand one another," he said. "I see you don't like your job. But you'll stick to it, for all that. There must be an end - a painless end if possible, without regrets. She has got to realise that I'm a swindler to the marrow of my bones, that I couldn't turn to and lead a decent, honourable life - even for love of her."

The words fell grimly, but there was no mockery in the steely eyes, no feeling of any sort. They looked full at Babbacombe with unflickering steadiness, that was all.

Babbacombe listened in the silence of a great amazement. Vaguely he had groped after the truth, but he had never even dimly imagined this. It struck him dumb - this sudden glimpse of a man's heart which till that moment had been so strenuously hidden from him.

"My dear fellow," he said at last; "but this is insanity!"

"Perhaps," West returned, unmoved. "They say every man has his mania. This is mine, and it is a very harmless one. It won't hurt you to humour it."

"But - good heavens! - have you thought of her?" Babbacombe exclaimed.

"I am thinking of her only," West answered quietly. "And I am asking you to do the same, both now and after you have married her."

"And send you to perdition to secure her peace of mind? A thousand times - no!" Babbacombe turned, and began to pace the room as though his feelings were too much for him. But very soon he stopped in front of West, and spoke with grave resolution. "Look here," he said, "I think you know that her happiness is more to me than anything else in the world, except my honour. To you it seems to be even more than that. And now listen, for as man to man I tell you the truth. You hold her happiness in the hollow of your hand!"

West's face remained as a mask; his eyes never varied.

"You can change all that," he said.

Babbacombe shook his head.

"I am not even sure that I shall try."

"What then?" said West. "Are you suggesting that the woman you love should marry an ex-convict - a notorious swindler, a blackguard?"

"I think," Babbacombe answered firmly, "that she ought to be allowed to decide that point."

"Allowed to ruin herself without interference," substituted West, sneering faintly. "Well, I don't agree with you, and I shall never give her the opportunity. You won't move me from that if you argue till Doomsday. So, in heaven's name, take what the gods offer, and leave me alone. Marry her. Give her all a good woman ever wants - a happy home, a husband who worships her, and children for her to worship, and you will soon find that I have dropped below the horizon."

He swung round again to the fire, and drove the poker hard into the coals.

"And find another agent as soon as possible," he said; "a respectable one this time, one who won't let you down when you are not looking, who won't call you a fool when you make mistakes - in short, a gentleman. There are plenty of them about. But they are not to be found in the world's rubbish heap. There's nothing but filth and broken crockery there."

He ended with his brief, cynical laugh, and Babbacombe knew that further discussion would be vain. For good or ill the swindler had made his decision, and he realised that no effort of his would alter it. To attempt to do so would be to beat against a stone wall - a struggle in which he might possibly hurt himself, but which would make no difference whatever to the wall.

Reluctantly he abandoned the argument, and prepared to take his departure.

But later, as he drove home, the man's words recurred to him and dwelt long in his memory. Their bitterness seemed to cloak something upon which no eye had ever looked - a regret unspeakable, a passionate repentance that found no place.

IX

"I have just discovered of whom it is that your very unpleasant agent reminds me," observed Lady Cottesbrook at the breakfast-table on the following morning. "It flashed upon me suddenly. He is the very image of that nasty person, Nat Verney, who swindled such a crowd of people a few years ago. I was present at part of his trial, and a more callous, thoroughly insolent creature I never saw. I suppose he is still in prison. I forget exactly what the sentence was, but I know it was a long one. I should think this man must be his twin-brother, Jack. I never saw a more remarkable likeness."

Babbacombe barely glanced up from his letter. "You are always finding that the people you don't like resemble criminals, Ursula," he said, with something less than his usual courtesy. "Did you say you were leaving by the eleven-fifty? I think I shall come with you."

"My dear Jack, how you change! I thought you were going to stay down here for another week."

"I was," he answered. "But I have had a line from Cynthia to tell me that her hand is poisoned from that infernal trap. It may be very serious. It probably is, or she would not have written."

That note of Cynthia's had in fact roused his deepest anxiety. He had fancied all along that she had deliberately made light of the injury. Soon after three o'clock he was in town, and he hastened forthwith to Cynthia's flat in Mayfair.

He found her on a couch in her dainty boudoir, lying alone before the fire. Her eyes shone like stars in her white face as she greeted him.

"It was just dear of you to come so soon," she said. "I kind of thought you would. I'm having a really bad time for once, and

I thought you'd like to know."

"Tell me about it," he said, sitting down beside her.

Her left hand lay in his for a few moments, but after a little she softly drew it away. Her right was in a sling.

"There's hardly anything to tell," she said. "Only my arm is bad right up to the shoulder, and the doctor is putting things on the wound so that it sha'n't leave off hurting night or day. I dreamt I was Dante last night. But no, I won't tell you about that. It was too horrible. I've never been really sick before, Jack. It frightens me some. I sent for you because I felt I wanted - a friend to talk to. It was outrageously selfish of me."

"It was the kindest thing you could do," Babbacombe said.

"Ah, but you mustn't misunderstand." A note of wistfulness sounded in the high voice. "You won't misunderstand, will you, Jack? I only want - a friend."

"You needn't be afraid, Cynthia," he said. "I shall never attempt to be anything else to you without your free consent."

"Thank you," she murmured. "I know I'm very mean. But I had such a bad night. I thought that all the devils in hell were jeering at me because I had told you my romance was dead. Oh, Jack! it was a great big lie, and it's come home to roost. I can't get rid of it. It won't die."

He heard the quiver of tears in her confession, and set his teeth.

"My dear," he said, "don't fret about that. I knew it at the bottom of my heart."

She reached out her hand to him again. "I hate myself for treating you like this," she whispered. "But I - I'm lonely, and I can't help it. You - you shouldn't be so kind."

Ethel M. Dell

"Ah, child, don't grudge me your friendship," he said. "It is the dearest thing I have."

"It's so hard," wailed Cynthia, "that I can give you so little, when I would so gladly give all if I could."

"You are not to blame yourself for that," he answered steadily. "You loved each other before I ever met you."

"Loved each other!" she said. "Do you really mean that, Jack?"

He hesitated. He had not intended to say so much.

"Jack," she urged piteously, "then you think he really cares?"

"Don't you know it, Cynthia?" he asked, in a low voice.

"My heart knows it," she said brokenly. "But my mind isn't sure. Do you know, Jack, I almost proposed to him because I felt so sure he cared. And he - he just looked beyond me, as if - as if he didn't even hear."

"He thinks he isn't good enough for you," Babbacombe said, with an effort. "I don't think he will ever be persuaded to act otherwise. He seems to consider himself hopelessly handicapped."

"What makes you say that?" whispered Cynthia.

He had not meant to tell her. It was against his will that he did so; but he felt impelled to do it. For her peace of mind it seemed imperative that she should understand.

And so, in a few words, he told her of West's abortive attempt to plunge a second time into the black depths from which he had so recently escaped, of the man's absolutely selfless devotion, of his rigid refusal to suffer even her love for him to move him from this attitude.

Cynthia listened with her bright eyes fixed unswervingly upon Babbacombe's face. She made no comment of any sort when he ended. She only pressed his hand.

He remained with her for some time, and when he got up to go at length, it was with manifest reluctance. He lingered beside her after he had spoken his farewell, as though he still had something to say.

"You will come again soon," said Cynthia.

"To-morrow," he answered. "And - Cynthia, there is just one thing I want to say."

She looked up at him questioningly.

"Only this," he said. "You sent for me because you wanted a friend. I want you from now onward to treat me and to think of me in that light only. As I now see things, I do not think I shall ever be anything more to you than just that. Remember it, won't you, and make use of me in any way that you wish. I will gladly do anything."

The words went straight from his heart to hers. Cynthia's eyes filled with sudden tears. She reached out and clasped his hand very closely.

"Dear Jack," she said softly; "you're just the best friend I have in the world, and I sha'n't forget it - ever."

He called early on the following day, and received the information that she was keeping her bed by the doctor's orders. Later in the day he went again, and found that the doctor was with her. He decided to wait, and paced up and down the drawing-room for nearly an hour. Eventually the doctor came.

Babbacombe knew him slightly, and was not surprised when, at sight of him in the doorway, the doctor turned aside at

Ethel M. Dell

once, and entered the room.

"Miss Mortimer told me I should probably see you," he said, "and if I did so, she desired me to tell you everything. I am sorry to say that I think very seriously of the injury. I have just been persuading her to go into a private nursing-home. This is no place to be ill in, and I shall have to perform a slight operation to-morrow which will necessitate the use of an anaesthetic."

"An operation!" Babbacombe exclaimed, aghast.

"It is absolutely imperative," the doctor said, "to get at the seat of the poison. I am making every effort to prevent the mischief spreading any further. Should the operation fail, no power on earth will save her hand. It may mean the arm as well."

Babbacombe listened to further explanations, sick at heart.

"When do you propose to move her?" he asked presently.

"At once. I am going now to make arrangements."

"May I go in and see her if she will admit me?"

"I don't advise it to-night. She is excited and overstrung. To-morrow, perhaps, if all goes well. Come round to my house at two o'clock, and I will let you know."

But Babbacombe did not see her the next day, for it was found advisable to keep her absolutely quiet. The doctor was very reticent, but he gathered from his manner that he entertained very grave doubts as to the success of his treatment.

On the day following he telephoned to Babbacombe to meet him at the home in the afternoon.

Babbacombe arrived before the time appointed, and spent half an hour in sick suspense, awaiting the doctor's coming.

The latter entered at last, and greeted him with a serious face.

"I am going to let you see Miss Mortimer," he said. "What I feared from the outset has taken place. The mischief was neglected too long at the beginning. There is nothing for it but amputation of the hand. And it must be performed without delay."

Babbacombe said something inarticulate that resolved itself with an effort into:

"Have you told her?"

"Yes, I have." The doctor's voice was stern. "And she absolutely refuses to consent to it. I have given her till to-morrow morning to make up her mind. After that -" He paused a moment, and looked Babbacombe straight in the face. "After that," he said, with emphasis, "it will be too late."

When Babbacombe entered Cynthia's presence a few minutes later, he walked as a man dazed. He found her lying among pillows, with the sunlight streaming over her, transforming her brown hair into a mass of sparkling gold. The old quick, gracious smile welcomed him as he bent over her. There were deep shadows about her eyes, but they were wonderfully bright. The hand she gave him was as cold as ice, despite the flush upon her cheeks.

"You have been told?" she questioned. "Yes, I see you have. Now, don't preach to me, Jack - dear Jack. It's too shocking to talk about. Can you believe it? I can't. I've always been so clever with my hands. Have you a pencil? I want you to take down a wire for me."

In her bright, imperious way, she dominated him. It was well-nigh impossible to realise that she was dangerously ill.

He sat down beside her with pencil and paper.

Ethel M. Dell

"Address it to Mr. West," said Cynthia, her eyes following his fingers. "Yes. And now put just this: 'I am sick, and wanting you. Will you come? - Cynthia.' And write the address. Do you think he'll come, Jack?"

"Let me add 'Urgent,'" he said.

"No, Jack. You are not to. Add nothing. If he doesn't come for that, he will never come at all. And I sha'n't wait for him," she added under her breath.

She seemed impatient for him to depart and despatch the message, but when he took his leave her eyes followed him with a wistful gratitude that sent a thrill to his heart. She had taken him at his word, and had made him her friend in need.

X

"If he doesn't come for that, he will never come at all."

Over and over Cynthia whispered the words to herself as she lay, with her wide, shining eyes upon the door, waiting. She was a gambler who had staked all on the final throw, and she was watching, weak and ill as she was after long suffering, watching restlessly, persistently, for the result of that last great venture. Surely he would come - surely - surely!

Once she spoke imperiously to the nurse.

"If a gentleman named West calls, I must see him at once, whatever the hour."

The nurse raised no obstacle. Perhaps she realised that it would do more harm than good to thwart her patient's caprice.

And so hour after hour Cynthia lay waiting for the answer to her message, and hour followed hour in slow, uneventful procession, bringing her neither comfort nor repose.

At length the doctor came and offered her morphia, but she refused it, with feverish emphasis.

"No, no, no! I don't want to sleep. I am expecting a friend."

"Won't it do in the morning?" he said persuasively.

Her grey eyes flashed eager inquiry up at him.

"He is here?"

The doctor nodded.

"He has been here some time, but I hoped you would settle down. I want you to sleep."

Ethel M. Dell

Sleep! Cynthia almost laughed. How inexplicably foolish were even the cleverest of men!

"I will see him now," she said. "And, please, alone," as the doctor made a sign to the nurse.

He moved away reluctantly, and again she almost laughed at his imbecility.

But a minute later she had forgotten everything in the world save that upon which her eyes rested - a short, broad-shouldered man, clean-shaven, with piercing blue eyes that looked straight at her with something - something in their expression that made the heart within her leap and quiver like the strings of an instrument under a master hand.

He came quietly to the bedside, and stood looking down upon her, not uttering a word.

She stretched up her trembling hand.

"I'm very glad to see you," she said weakly. "You got my message? It - it - I hope it didn't annoy you."

"It didn't," said West.

His voice was curt and strained. His fingers had closed very tightly upon her hand.

"Sit down," murmured Cynthia. "No, don't let go. It helps me some to have you hold my hand. Mr. West, I've got to tell you something - something that will make you really angry. I'm rather frightened, too. It's because I'm sick. You - you must just make allowances."

A light kindled in West's eyes that shone like a blue flame, but still he held himself rigid, inflexible as a figure hewn in granite.

"Pray don't distress yourself, Miss Mortimer," he said stiffly.

"Wouldn't it be wiser to wait till you are better before you go any further?"

"I never shall be better," Cynthia rejoined, a tremor of passion in her voice, "I never shall go any further, unless you hear me out to-night."

West frowned a little, but still that strange light shone in his steady eyes.

"I am quite at your service," he said, "either now or at any future time. But if this interview should make you worse -"

"Oh, shucks!" said Cynthia, with a ghostly little smile. "Don't talk through your hat, Mr. West!"

West became silent. He was still holding her hand in a warm, close grasp that never varied.

"Let's get to business," said Cynthia, with an effort to be brisk. "It begins with a confession. You know better than any one how I managed to hurt my hand so badly. But even you don't know everything. Even you never suspected that - that it wasn't an accident at all; that, in fact, I did it on purpose."

She broke off for a moment, avoiding his eyes, but clinging tightly to his hand.

"I did it," she went on breathlessly - "I did it because I heard you in the drive below, and I wanted to attract your attention. I couldn't see you, but I knew it was you. I was just going to spring the trap with my foot, and then - and then I heard you, and I stooped down - it came to me to do it, and I never stopped to think - I stooped down and put my hand in the way. I never thought - I never thought it would hurt so frightfully, or that it could come to this."

She was crying as she ended, crying piteously; while West sat like a stone image, gazing at her.

"Oh, do speak to me!" she sobbed. "Do say something! Do you know what they want to do? But I won't let them - I won't let them! It - it's too dreadful a thing to happen to a woman. I can't bear it. I won't bear it. It will be much easier to die. But you shall know the truth first."

"Cynthia, stop!" It was West's voice at last, but not as she had ever heard it. It came from him hoarse and desperate, as though wrung by the extreme of torture. He had sunk to his knees by the bed. His face was nearer to hers than it had ever been before. "Don't cry!" he begged her huskily. "Don't cry! Why do you tell me this if it hurts you to tell me?"

"Because I want you to know!" gasped Cynthia. "Wait! Let me finish! I wanted - to see - if - if you really cared for me. I thought - if you did - you wouldn't be able to go on pretending. But - but - you managed to - somehow - after all."

She ended, battling with her tears; and West, the strong, the cold, the cynical, bowed his head upon her hand and groaned.

"It was for - your own sake," he muttered brokenly, without looking up.

"I know," whispered back Cynthia. "That was just what made it so impossible to bear. Because, you see, I cared, too."

He was silent, breathing heavily.

Cynthia watched his bent head wistfully, but she did not speak again till she had mastered her own weakness.

"Mr. West," she said softly at length.

He stirred, pressing her hand more tightly to his eyes.

"I am going to tell you now," proceeded Cynthia, "just why I asked you to come to me. I suppose you know all about this trouble of mine - that I shall either die very soon, or else have to carry my arm in a sling for the rest of my life. Now that's where you come in. Would you - would you feel very badly if I died, I wonder?"

He raised his head at that, and she saw his face as she had seen it once long ago - alert, vital, full of the passionate intensity of his love for her.

"You sha'n't die!" he declared fiercely. "Who says you are going to die?"

Cynthia's eyes fell before the sudden fire that blazed at her from his. "Unless I consent to be a cripple all my days," she said, with a curious timidity wholly unlike her usual dainty confidence.

"Of course you will consent," West said, sweeping down her half-offered resistance with sheer, overmastering strength. "You'll face this thing like the brave woman you are. Good heavens! As if there were any choice!"

"There is," Cynthia whispered, looking at him shyly, through lowered lids. "There is a choice. But it rests with you. Mr. West, if you want me to do this thing - if you really want me to, and it's a big thing to do, even for you - I'll do it. There! I'll do it! I'll go on living like a chopped worm for your sake. But - but - you'll have to do something for me in return. Now I wonder if you can guess what I'm hinting at?"

West's face changed. The eagerness went out of it. Something of his habitual grimness of expression returned.

Yet his voice was full of tenderness when he spoke.

"Cynthia," he said very earnestly, "there is nothing on this earth that I will not do for you. But don't ask me to be the means of ruining you socially, of depriving you of all your friends, of degrading you to a position that would break your heart."

Ethel M. Dell

A glimmer of amusement flashed across Cynthia's drawn face.

"Oh!" she said, a little quiver in her voice. "You are funny, you men, dull as moles and blind as bats. My dear, there's only one person in this little universe who has the power to break my heart, and it isn't any fault of his that he didn't do it long ago. No, don't speak. There's nothing left for you to say. The petition is dismissed, but not the petitioner; so listen to me instead. I've a sentimental fancy to be able to have 'Mrs. Nat V. West' written on my tombstone in the event of my demise to-morrow. I want you to make arrangements for the same."

"Cynthia!"

The word was almost a cry, but she checked it, her fingers on his lips.

"You great big silly!" she murmured, laughing weakly. "Where's your sense of humour? Can't you see I'm not going to die? But I'm going to be Mrs. Nat V. West all the same. Now, is that quite understood, I wonder? Because I don't want to cry any more - I'm tired."

"You wish to marry me in the morning - before the operation?" West said, speaking almost under his breath.

His face was close to hers. She looked him suddenly straight in the eyes.

"Yes, just that," she told him softly. "I want - dear - I want to go to sleep, holding my husband's hand."

XI

"It's a clear case of desertion," declared Cynthia imperturbably, two months later. "But never mind that now, Jack. How do you like my sling? Isn't it just the cutest thing in creation?"

"You look splendid," Babbacombe said with warmth, but he surveyed her with slightly raised brows notwithstanding.

She nodded brightly in response.

"No, I'm not worrying any, I assure you. You don't believe me, I see. So here's something for you to read that will set your mind at rest."

Babbacombe read, with a slowly clearing face. The note he held was in his agent's handwriting.

> "I am leaving you to-day, for I feel, now you are well again, that you will find it easier in my absence to consider very carefully your position. Your marriage to me was simply an act of impulse. I gave way in the matter because you were in no state to be thwarted. But if, after consideration, you find that that act was a mistake, dictated by weakness, and heaven knows what besides of generosity and pity, something may yet be done to remedy it. It has never been published, and, if you are content to lead a single life, no one who matters need ever know that it took place. I am returning to my work at Farringdean for the present. I am aware that you may find some difficulty in putting your feelings in this matter into words. If so, I shall understand your silence.
>
> Yours,
>
> "N. V. WEST."

"Isn't he quaint?" said Cynthia, with a little gay grimace.

Ethel M. Dell

"Now do you know what I'm going to do, Jack? I'm going to get a certain good friend of mine to drive me all the way to Farringdean in his motor. It's Sunday, you know, and all the fates conspire to make the trains impossible."

"How soon do you wish to start?" asked Babbacombe.

"Right away!" laughed Cynthia. "And if we don't get run in for exceeding the speed limit, we ought to be there by seven."

It was as a matter of fact barely half-past six when Babbacombe turned the motor in at the great gates of Farringdean Park. A sound of church-bells came through the evening twilight. The trees of the avenue were still bare, but there was a misty suggestion of swelling buds in the saplings. The wind that softly rustled through them seemed to whisper a special secret to each.

"I like those bells," murmured Cynthia. "They make one feel almost holy. Jack, you're not fretting over me?"

"No, dear," said Babbacombe steadily.

She squeezed his arm.

"I'm so glad, for - honest Injun - I'm not worth it. Good-bye, then, dear Jack! Just drive straight away directly you've put me down. I shall find my own way in."

He took her at her word as he always did, and, having deposited her at the gate under the trees that led to his bailiff's abode, he shot swiftly away into the gathering dusk without a single glance behind.

West, entering his home a full hour later, heavy-footed, the inevitable cigarette between his lips, was surprised to discover, on hanging up his cap, a morsel of white pasteboard stuck jauntily into the glass of the hatstand. It seemed to fling him an airy challenge. He stooped to look. A lady's visiting-card!

Mrs. Nat V. West!

A deep flush rose suddenly in his weather-beaten face. He seized the card, and crushed it against his lips.

But a few moments later, when he opened his dining-room door, there was no hint of emotion in his bearing. He bore himself with the rigidity of a man who knows he has a battle before him.

The room was aglow with flickering firelight, and out of the glow a high voice came - a cheery, inconsequent voice.

"Oh, here you are at last! Come right in and light the lamp. Did you see my card? Ah, I knew you would be sure to look at yourself directly you came in. There's nobody at home but me. I suppose your old woman's gone to church. I've been waiting for you such a while - twelve years and a bit. Just think of it."

She was standing on the hearth waiting for him, but since he moved but slowly she stepped forward to meet him, her hand impetuously outstretched.

He took it, held it closely, let it go.

"We must talk things over," he said.

"Splendid!" said Cynthia. "Where shall we begin? Never mind the lamp. Let's sit by the fire and be cosy."

He moved forward with her - it was impossible to do otherwise - but there was no yielding in his action. He held himself as straight and stiff as a soldier on parade. He had bitten through his cigarette, and he tossed it into the fire.

"Now sit down!" said Cynthia hospitably. "That chair is for you, and I am going to curl up on the floor at your feet as becomes a dutiful wife."

Ethel M. Dell

"Don't, Cynthia!" he said under his breath. But she had her way, nevertheless. There were times when she seemed able to attain this with scarcely an effort.

She seated herself on the hearthrug with her face to the fire.

"Go on," she said, in a tone of gentle encouragement; "I'm listening."

West's eyes stared beyond her into the flames.

"I haven't much to say," he said quietly at length. "Only this. You are acting without counting the cost. There is a price to pay for everything, but the price you will have to pay for this is heavier than you realise. There should be - there can be - no such thing as equality between a woman in your position - a good woman - and a blackguard in mine."

Cynthia made a little gesture of impatience without turning her head.

"Oh, you needn't treat me as if I were on a different plane," she said. "I'm a sinner, too, in my own humble way. It's unreasonable of you to go on like that, unkind as well. I may be only a sprat in your estimation, but even a sprat has its little feelings, its little heartaches, too, I daresay." She broke off with a sigh and a laugh; then, drawing impulsively nearer to him, but still without turning: "Do you remember once, ages and ages ago, you were on the verge of saying something to me, of - telling me something? And we were interrupted. Mr. West, I've been waiting all these years to hear what that something was."

West did not stir an eyelid. His face was stern and hard.

"I forget," he said.

She turned upon him then, raising a finger and pointing straight at him.

"That," she said, with conviction, "is just one of your lies!"

West became silent, still staring fixedly into the fire.

Cynthia drew nearer still. She touched his breast with her outstretched finger.

"Mr. West," she said gravely, "I suppose you'll have to leave off being a blackguard, and take to being an honest man. That's the only solution of the difficulty that I can think of now that you have got a crippled wife to look after."

He gripped her wrist, but still he would not look at her.

"This is madness," he said, grinding out the words through clenched teeth. "You are making a fatal mistake. I am not fit to be your husband. It is not in my power to give you happiness."

She did not shrink from his hold, though it was almost violent. Her eyes were shining like stars.

"That," she said, with quaint assurance, "is just another of your lies."

His hand relaxed slowly till her wrist was free.

"Do you know," he said, still with that iron self-suppression, "that only a few weeks ago I committed forgery?"

"Yes," said Cynthia. "And I know why you did it, too. It wasn't exactly clever, but it was just dear of you all the same."

The swindler's face quivered suddenly, uncontrollably. He tried to laugh - the old harsh laugh - but the sound he uttered was akin to something very different. He leaned forward sharply, and covered his face with his hands.

And in that moment Cynthia knew that the walls of the citadel had fallen at last, so that it lay open for her to enter in.

She knelt up quickly. Her arm slipped round his neck. She drew his head with soft insistence to her breast.

"My own boy, it's over; forget it all. It wasn't meant to handicap you always. We'll have another deal now, please God, and start afresh as partners."

There followed a pause - a silence that had in it something sacred. Then West raised himself, and took her face between his hands. For a moment he looked deep into her eyes, his own alight with a vital fire.

Then, "As lovers, Cynthia," he said, and kissed her on the lips.

THE NONENTITY

I

"It is well known that those fight hardest who fight in vain," remarked Lord Ronald Prior complacently. "But I should have thought a woman of your intellect would have known better. It's such a rank waste of energy to struggle against Fate."

He spoke in the easy drawl habitual to him. His grey eyes held the pleasant smile that was seldom absent from them. Not in any fashion a striking personality, this; his kindest friend could not have called him imposing, nor could the most uncharitable have described him as anything worse than dull. Enemies he had none. His invariable good temper was his safeguard in this particular. The most offensive remark would not have provoked more than momentarily raised eyebrows.

He was positively characterless, so Beryl Denvers told herself a dozen times a day. How could she possibly marry any one so neutral? And yet in his amiable, exasperatingly placid fashion he had for some time been laying siege to her affections. He had shaved off his beard because he had heard her say that she objected to hairy men, and he seemed to think that this sacrifice on his part entitled him to a larger share of her favour than the rest of the world, certainly much more than she was disposed to bestow.

He had, in fact, assumed almost an air of proprietorship over

Ethel M. Dell

her of late - a state of affairs which she strongly resented, but was powerless to alter. He had a little money, but no prospects to mention, and had never done anything worth doing in all his five-and-thirty years. And yet he seemed to think himself an eligible *parti* for one of the most popular women in the district. His social position gave him a certain precedence among her other admirers, but Beryl herself refused to recognise this. She thought him presumptuous, and snubbed him accordingly.

But Lord Ronald's courtship seemed to thrive upon snubs. He was never in the least disconcerted thereby. He hadn't the brains to take offence, she told herself impatiently, and yet somewhere at the back of her mind there lurked a vagrant suspicion that he was not always as obtuse as he seemed.

She had been rude to him on the present occasion and he had retaliated with his smiling speech regarding her intellect which had made her feel vaguely uncomfortable. It might have been - it probably was - an effort at bluff on his part, but, uttered by any other man, it would have had almost a hectoring sound.

"I haven't the smallest notion what you mean," she said, after a decided pause.

"Charmed to explain," he murmured.

"Pray don't trouble!" she rejoined severely. "It doesn't signify in the least. Explanations always bore me."

Lord Ronald smiled his imperturbable smile and flicked a gnat from his sleeve.

"Especially when they are futile, eh, Mrs. Denvers? I'm not fond of 'em myself. Haven't much ability for that sort of thing."

"Have you any ability for anything, I wonder?" she said.

He turned his smooth, good-humoured countenance towards her. It wore a speculative look, as though he were wondering if by any chance she could have meant to be nasty.

"Oh, rather!" he said. "I can do quite a lot of things - and decently, too - from boiling potatoes to taming snakes. Never heard me play the cornet, have you?"

Beryl remarked somewhat unnecessarily that she detested the cornet. She seemed to be thoroughly exasperated with him for some reason, and evidently wished that he would take his leave. But this fact had not apparently yet penetrated to Lord Ronald's understanding, for he was the most obliging of men at all times, and surely would never have dreamed of intruding his presence where it was unwelcome.

He sat on his favourite perch, the music-stool, and swung himself gently to and fro while he mildly upheld the virtues of the instrument she had slighted.

"I was asked to perform at a smoker the other night at the barracks," he said. "The men seemed to enjoy it immensely."

"Soldiers like anything noisy," said Beryl Denvers scathingly.

And then - because he had no retort ready - her heart smote her.

"But it was kind of you to go," she said. "I am sure you wouldn't enjoy it."

"Oh, but I did," he said, "on the whole. I should have liked it better if Fletcher hadn't been in the chair, and so, I think, would they. But it passed off very fairly well."

"Why do you object to Major Fletcher?" Beryl's tone was slightly aggressive.

Lord Ronald hesitated a little.

"He isn't much liked," he told her vaguely.

She frowned.

"But that is no answer. Are you afraid to answer me?"

He laughed at that, laughed easily and naturally, in the tolerant fashion that most exasperated her.

"Oh, no; I'm not afraid. But I don't like hurting people's feelings - especially yours."

"I do not see how that is possible," she rejoined, with dignity, "where my feelings are not concerned."

"Ah, but that's where it is," he responded. "You like Fletcher well enough to be extremely indignant if anyone were to tell you that he is not a nice person for you to know."

"I object to unpleasant insinuations regarding any one," she said, with slightly heightened colour. "They always appear to me cowardly."

"Yes; but you asked, you know," Lord Ronald reminded her gently.

Her colour deepened. It was not often that he got the better of her; not often, indeed, that he exerted himself to do so. She began to wish ardently that he would go. Really, he was quite insufferable to-day.

Had he been a man of any perception whatever she would almost have thought that he fathomed her desire, for at this point he rose in a leisurely fashion as though upon the point of departure.

She rose also from behind the tea-table with a little inward pricking of conscience for wishing him gone. She wondered if he deemed her inhospitable, but if he did he disguised it very carefully, for his eyes held nothing but friendliness as they met her own.

"Has it never occurred to you," he said, "that you lead a very unprotected existence here?"

Something in his expression checked her first impulse to resent the question. Her lip quivered unexpectedly.

"Now and then," she said.

"Are you a man-hater?" he asked deliberately.

She laughed a little.

"Why do you ask such an absurd question?"

He seemed to hesitate momentarily.

"Because - forgive me - wouldn't you be a good deal happier if you were to marry again?"

Again her colour rose hotly. What did the man mean by assuming this attitude? Was he about to plead his own cause, or that of another?

"I think it exceedingly doubtful," she replied stiffly, meeting his steady eyes with a hint of defiance.

"You have never thought of such a thing perhaps?" he suggested.

She smiled a woman's pitying smile.

"Of course I have thought of it."

"Then you have not yet met the man to whom you would care to entrust yourself?" he asked.

She took fire at this. It was an act of presumption not to be borne.

"Even if I had," she said, with burning cheeks, "I do not think I should make Lord Ronald Prior my confidant."

"No?" he said. "Yet you might do worse."

Her eyes shot scorn.

"Can a man be worse than inept?" she asked.

"Yes," he answered. "Since you ask me, I think he can - a good deal worse."

"I detest colourless people!" she broke in vehemently.

He smiled.

"In fact, you prefer black sheep to grey sheep. A good many women do. But it doesn't follow that the preference is a wise one."

The colour faded suddenly from her face. Did he know how ghastly a failure her first marriage had been? Most people knew. Could it be to this that he was referring? The bare suspicion made her wince.

"That," she said icily, "is no one's affair but my own. I am not wholly ignorant of the ways of the world. And I know whom I can trust."

"You trust me, for instance?" said Lord Ronald.

She looked him up and down witheringly.

"I should say you are quite the most harmless man I know."

"And you don't like me in consequence," he drawled, meeting the look with eyes so intent that, half-startled, she lowered her own.

She turned away from him with an impatient gesture. He had never managed to embarrass her before.

"I should like you better if you weren't so officious," she said.

"But you have no one else to look after you," objected Lord Ronald.

"Well, in any case, it isn't your business," she threw back, almost inclined to laugh at his audacity.

"It would be if you married me," he pointed out, as patiently as if he were dealing with a fractious child.

"If I -"

She wheeled abruptly, amazed out of her disdain. It was the most prosaic proposal she had ever had.

"If you married me," he repeated, keeping his eyes upon her. "You admit that I am harmless, so you would have nothing to fear from me. And as a watch-dog, I think you would find me useful - and quite easy to manage," he added, with his serene smile.

Beryl was staring at him in wide astonishment. Was the man mad to approach her thus?

"No," he said. "I am quite sane; eccentric perhaps, but - as you are kind enough to observe - quite harmless. I never proposed to any woman before in my life, or so much as wanted to, so that must be my excuse for doing it badly. Really, you know, Mrs. Denvers, you might do worse than marry me. You might indeed."

But at that her indignation broke bounds. If he were not mad,

Ethel M. Dell

it made him the more intolerable. Did he fancy himself so desirable, then, that he had merely to fling her the handkerchief - to find her at his feet? His impertinence transcended belief. But she would pay him back in his own coin. He should never again imagine himself irresistible.

"Really, Lord Ronald," she said, "if I actually needed a protector - which I do not - you are the very last person to whom I should turn. And as to a husband -"

She paused a moment, searching for words sufficiently barbed to penetrate even his complacency.

"Yes?" he said gently, as if desirous to help her out.

"As to a husband," she said, "if I ever marry again, it will be a man I can respect - a man who can hold his own in the world; a man who is really a man, and not - not a nonentity!"

Impetuously she flung the words. For all his placidity, he seemed to possess the power to infuriate her. She longed intensely to move him to anger. She felt insulted by his composure, hating him because he remained so courteously attentive.

He made no attempt to parry her thrust, nor did he seem to be disconcerted thereby. He merely listened imperturbably till she ceased to speak. Then:

"Ah, well," he said good-humouredly, "you mustn't take me too seriously. It was only a suggestion, you know." He picked up his hat with the words. "A pity you can't see your way to fall in with it, but you know best. Good-bye for the present."

Reluctantly, in response to his evident expectation, she gave him her hand.

"I wish you to understand, Lord Ronald," she said stiffly as she did so, "that my reply is final."

He lifted his eyebrows for a second, and she fancied - could it have been mere fancy? - that the grey eyes shone with a certain steely determination that was assuredly foreign to his whole nature as he made deliberate reply:

"That is quite understood, Mrs. Denvers. It was awfully kind of you to be so explicit. As you know, I am not good at taking hints."

And with that he was gone, unruffled to the last, perfectly courteous, almost dignified, while she stood and watched his exit with a vague and disquieting suspicion that he had somehow managed to get the best of it after all.

II

When Beryl Denvers first came to Kundaghat to be near her friend Mrs. Ellis, the Commissioner's wife, society in general openly opined that she had come to the populous Hill station to seek a husband. She was young, she was handsome, and she was free. It seemed the only reasonable conclusion to draw. But since that date society had had ample occasion to change its mind. Beryl Denvers plainly valued her freedom above every other consideration, and those who wooed her wooed in vain. She discouraged the attentions of all mankind with a rigour that never varied, till society began to think that her brief matrimonial experience had turned her into a man-hater. And yet this was hard to believe, for, though quick-tempered, she was not bitter. She was quite willing to be friendly with all men, up to a certain point. But beyond this subtle boundary few dared to venture and none remained. There was a wonderful fascination about her, a magnetism that few could resist; but notwithstanding this she held herself aloof, never wholly forgetting her caution even with those who considered themselves her intimates.

Having dismissed Lord Ronald Prior, with whom she was almost unreasonably angry, she ordered her rickshaw and went out to cool her hot cheeks. The recent interview had disquieted her to the depths. She tried to regard his presumption as ludicrous, yet failed to do so. For what he had said was to a large extent true. She was unprotected, and she was also lonely, though this she never owned. She stifled a sigh as she set forth. Hitherto she had always liked Lord Ronald. Why had he couched his proposal in such impossible terms?

She went to the polo-ground to watch the practice, and here found several friends in whose society she tried to forget her discomfiture. But it remained with her notwithstanding, and was still present when she returned to prepare for dinner. She was dining with the Ellises that night, and she hoped ardently that Lord Ronald would not make one of the party.

But she was evidently destined for mortification that day, for the first thing she saw upon entering the drawing-room was his trim figure standing by her hostess. And, "Lord Ronald will take you in, dear," said Nina Ellis, as she greeted her.

Beryl glanced at him, and he bowed in his courtly way. "I hope you don't mind," he murmured.

She did mind exceedingly, but it was impossible to say so. She could only yield to the inevitable and rest the tips of her fingers upon his sleeve.

It was with a decided sense of relief that she found Major Fletcher seated on her other side. A handsome, well-mannered cavalier was Major Fletcher, by every line of his figure a soldier, by every word of his conversation a gentleman. Exceedingly self-possessed at all times, it was seldom, if ever, that he laid himself open to a snub. It was probably for this very reason that Beryl liked him better than most of the men in Kundaghat, was less distant with him, and usually granted the very little that he asked of her.

She turned to him at once with a random remark about the polo-players, wondering if they would be able to hold their own against a native team with whom a match had been arranged for the following week.

"Oh, I think so," he said. "The Farabad men are strong, but our fellows are hard to beat. It won't be a walkover for either side."

"Where will the match be played?" she asked, nervously afraid of letting the subject drop lest Lord Ronald should claim her attention.

"Here," said Major Fletcher. "It was originally to have been at Farabad, but there was some difficulty about the ground. I was over there arranging matters only this evening. The whole place is being turned upside down for a native fair which is to

Ethel M. Dell

be held in a few days, when the moon is full. You ought to see it. It is an interesting sight - one which I believe you would enjoy."

"No doubt I should," she agreed. "But it is rather a long way, isn't it?"

"Not more than twelve miles." Fletcher's dark face kindled with a sudden idea. "I could drive you down some morning early if you cared for it."

Beryl hesitated. It was not her custom to accept invitations of this sort, but for once she felt tempted. She longed to demonstrate her independence to Lord Ronald, whose suggestions regarding her inability to take care of herself had so sorely hurt her pride. Might she not permit herself this one small fling for his benefit? It would be so good for him to realise that she was no incompetent girl, but a woman of the world and thoroughly well versed in its ways. And at least he would be forced to recognise that his proposal had been little short of an absurdity. She wanted him to see that, as she wanted nothing else on earth.

"You think it would bore you?" asked Fletcher.

"No," she said, flushing slightly; "I think I should like it."

"Well done!" he said, with quiet approval. "You are such a hermit, Mrs. Denvers, that it will be quite a novelty for us both."

She met his eyes for an instant, assailed by a sudden memory of Lord Ronald's vague remarks concerning him. But they were very level, and revealed nothing whatever. She told herself indignantly that there was nothing to reveal. The man had simply made her a friendly offer, and she determined to accept it in a like spirit.

"It was kind of you to think of it," she said. "I will come with much pleasure."

On her other side she heard Lord Ronald's leisurely tones conversing with his neighbour, and wondered if aught of the project had reached him. She hoped it had, though the serenity of his demeanour made her doubtful. But in any case he would surely know sooner or later.

III

Major Fletcher was well versed in the ways of natives, and as they drove in his high dog-cart to Farabad a few days later, he imparted to his companion a good deal of information regarding them of which, till then, she had been quite ignorant.

He succeeded in arousing her interest, and the long drive down the hillside in the early morning gave her the keenest enjoyment. She had been feeling weary and depressed of late, a state of affairs which could not fairly be put down to the score of ill-health. She had tried hard to ignore it, but it had obtruded itself upon her notwithstanding, and she was glad of the diversion which this glimpse of native life afforded her. Of Lord Ronald Prior she had seen nothing for over a week. He had left Kundaghat on the day following the dinner-party, dropping unobtrusively, without farewell, out of her life. She had told herself a dozen times, and vehemently, that she was glad of it, but the humiliating fact remained that she missed him - missed him at every turn; when she rode, when she danced, when she went out in her rickshaw, and most of all in her drawing-room.

She had grown so accustomed to the sight of the thick-set, unromantic figure swinging lazily to and fro on her sorely tried music-stool, watching her with serene grey eyes that generally held a smile. She wished she had not been quite so severe. She had not meant to send him quite away. As a friend, his attitude of kindly admiration was all that could be desired. And he was so safe, too, so satisfactorily solid. She had always felt that she could say what she liked to him without being misunderstood. Well, he had gone, and as they finally alighted, and went forward on foot through the fair, she resolutely dismissed him from her mind.

She made one or two purchases under Fletcher's guidance, which meant that she told him what she wanted and stood by while he bargained for her in Hindustani, an amusing business from her point of view.

Undoubtedly she was beginning to enjoy herself, when he surprised her by turning from one of these unintelligible colloquies, and offering for her acceptance a beautifully wrought gold filigree bracelet.

She looked at him blankly, not without a vague feeling of dismay.

"Won't you have it?" he said. "Won't you permit me this small favour?"

She felt the colour go out of her face. It was so unexpected, this from him - in a fashion, almost staggering. For some reason she had never regarded this man as a possible admirer. She felt as if the solid ground had suddenly quaked beneath her.

"I would rather not," she said at last, avoiding his eyes instinctively. "Please don't think me ungracious. I know you mean to be kind."

"If you really believe that," said Fletcher, smiling faintly, "I don't see your objection."

The blood rushed back in a burning wave to her face. She, who prided herself upon being a woman of the world, blushed hotly, overwhelmingly, like any self-conscious girl.

"I would rather not," she repeated, with her eyes upon the ground.

But Fletcher was not to be turned lightly from his purpose.

"I wouldn't distress you for the world, Mrs. Denvers," he said, "but don't you think you are a trifle unreasonable? No one expects a woman in your position to be a slave to convention. I would never have bought the thing had I dreamed that it could be an offence."

There was a tinge of reproach in his voice, no more, but she felt inexplicably ashamed as she heard it. She looked up sharply, and the conviction that she was making herself ridiculous swept quickly upon her. She held out her hand to him, and mutely suffered him to slip the bangle on to her wrist.

IV

A curious rattling sound made them turn sharply the next moment, and even though it proved to be the warning signal of an old snake-charmer, Beryl welcomed the diversion. She looked at the man with a good deal of interest, notwithstanding her repulsion. He was wrapped in a long, very dirty, white *chuddah*, from which his face peered weirdly forth, wrinkled and old, almost supernaturally old, she thought to herself. It was very strangely adorned with red paint, which imparted to the eyes a ghastly pale appearance in the midst of the swarthy skin. A wiry grey beard covered the lower part of the face, and into this he was crooning a tuneless and wholly unintelligible song, while he squatted on the ground in front of a large, covered basket.

"He has got a cobra there," Fletcher said, and took Beryl's arm quietly.

She moved slightly, with a latent wish that he would take his hand away. But natives were beginning to crowd and press about them to see the show, and she realised that his action was dictated by necessity.

"Shall I take you away before we get hemmed in?" he asked her once.

But she shook her head. A nameless fascination impelled her to remain.

Even when the snake-charmer shot forth a dusky arm and clawed the basket open, she showed no sign of fear, though Fletcher's hold upon her tightened to a grip. They seemed to be the only Europeans in all that throng, but that fact also she had forgotten. She could think of nothing but the crouching native before her, and the basket in which some living, moving thing lay enshrouded.

Ethel M. Dell

Closely she watched the active fingers, alert and sensitive, feeling over the dingy cloth they had exposed. Suddenly, with a movement too swift to be followed, they rent the covering away, and on the instant, rearing upwards, she beheld a huge snake.

A thrill of horror shot through her, so keen that it stabbed every pulse, making her whole body tingle. But there was no escape for her then, nor did she seek it. She had a most unaccountable feeling that this display was for her alone, that in some way it appealed to her individually; and she was no longer so much as conscious of Fletcher's presence at her side.

The charmer continued his crooning noise, and the great cobra swayed its inflated neck to and fro as though to some mysterious rhythm, the native with naked hand and arm seeming to direct it.

"Loathsome!" murmured a voice into Beryl's ear, but she did not hear it. Her whole intelligence was riveted upon the movements of the serpent and its master. It was a hideous spectacle, but it occupied her undivided attention. She had no room for panic.

Suddenly the man's crooning ceased, and on the instant the cobra ceased to sway. It seemed to gather itself together, was rigid for perhaps five seconds, and then - swift as a lightning flash - it struck.

A sharp cry broke from Beryl, but she never knew that she uttered it. All she was aware of was the ghastly struggle that ensued in front of her, the fierce writhing of the snake, the convulsive movements of the old native, and, curiously distinct from everything else, an impression of some stringed instrument thrumming somewhere at the back of the crowd.

It all ended as unexpectedly as it had begun. The great reptile became suddenly inert, a lifeless thing; the monotonous crooning was resumed, proceeding as it were out of the chaos of the struggle, and round his neck and about his body the snake-charmer wound his vanquished foe.

The moment for *backsheesh* had arrived, and Beryl, coming suddenly out of her absorption, felt for her purse and awoke abruptly to the consciousness of a hand that gripped her arm.

She glanced at Fletcher, who at once slackened his hold. "Don't you give the fellow anything," he said, with a touch of peremptoriness, "I will."

She yielded, considering the matter too trivial for argument, and watched his rupee fall with a tinkle upon the tin plate which the snake-charmer extended at the length of his sinewy arm.

Fletcher speedily made a way for her through the now shifting crowd; and after a little they found the *saice*, waiting with the mare under a tree. The animal was tormented by flies and restless. Certainly in this valley district it was very hot.

"We will go back by the hill road," Fletcher said, as he handed her up. "It is rather longer, but I think it is worth it. This blaze is too much for you."

They left the thronged highroad, and turned up a rutty track leading directly into the hills.

Their way lay between great, glaring boulders of naked rock. Here and there tufts of grass grew beside the stony track, but they were brown and scorched, and served only to emphasise the barrenness of the land.

For a while they drove in silence, mounting steadily the whole time.

Suddenly Fletcher spoke. "We shall come to some shade directly. There is a belt of pine trees round the next curve."

Ethel M. Dell

The words were hardly uttered when unexpectedly the mare shied, struck the ground violently with all four feet together, and bolted.

Beryl heard an exclamation from the native groom, and half-turned to see him clinging to the back with a face of terror. She herself was more astonished than frightened. She gripped the rail instinctively, for the cart was jolting horribly as the mare, stretched out like a greyhound, fled at full gallop along the stony way.

She saw Fletcher, with his feet against the board, dragging backwards with all his strength. He was quite white, but exceedingly collected, and she was instantly quite certain that he knew what he was about.

There followed a few breathless moments of headlong galloping, during which they swayed perilously from side to side, and were many times on the verge of being overturned. Then, the ground rising steeply, the mare's wild pace became modified, developed into a spasmodic canter, became a difficult trot, finally slowed to a walk.

Fletcher pulled up altogether, and turned to the silent woman beside him. "Mrs. Denvers, you are splendid!" he said simply.

She laughed rather tremulously. The tension over, she was feeling very weak.

The *saice* was already at the mare's head, and Fletcher let the reins go. He dismounted without another word and went round to her side. Still silent, he held up his hands to her and lifted her down as though she had been a child. He was smiling a little, but he was still very pale.

As for Beryl, the moment her feet touched the ground she felt as if the whole world had turned to liquid and were swimming around her in a gigantic whirlpool of floating impressions.

"Ah, you are faint!" she heard him say.

And she made a desperate and quite futile effort to assure him that she was nothing of the sort. But she knew that no more than a blur of sound came from her lips, and even while she strove to make herself intelligible the floating world became a dream, and darkness fell upon her.

Ethel M. Dell

V

Gradually, very gradually, the mists cleared from Beryl's brain, and she opened her eyes dreamily, and stared about her with a feeling that she had been asleep for years. She was lying propped upon carriage-cushions in the shade of an immense boulder, and as she discovered this fact, memory flashed swiftly back upon her. She had fainted, of course, in her foolish, weak, womanly fashion. But where was Major Fletcher? The heat was intense, so intense that breathing in that prone position seemed impossible. Gasping, she raised herself. Surely she was not absolutely alone in this arid wilderness!

She was not. In an instant she realised this, and wonder rather than fear possessed her.

There, squatting on his haunches, not ten paces from her, was the old snake-charmer. His basket was by his side; his *chuddah* drooped low over his face; he sat quite motionless, save for a certain palsied quivering, which she had observed before. He looked as if he had been in that place and attitude for many years.

Beryl leaned her head upon her hand and closed her eyes. She was feeling spent and sick. He did not inspire her with horror, this old man. She was conscious of a faint sensation of disgust, that was all.

A few seconds later she looked up again, wondering afresh whither her escort could have betaken himself. It seemed to her that the distance between herself and the old native had dwindled somewhat, but she did not bestow much attention upon him. She merely noted how fiercely the sun beat down upon his shrouded head, and wondered how he managed to endure it.

The next time she opened her eyes, there were scarcely three yards between them. The instant her look fell upon him he began to speak in a thin, wiry voice of great humility.

"Let the gracious lady pardon her servant," he said, in perfect English. "He would not harm a hair of her head."

She raised herself to an upright position with an effort. Very curiously she did not feel in the least afraid. By an abrupt intuition, wholly inexplicable, she knew that the man had something to tell her.

"What is it?" she said.

He cringed before her.

"Let my gracious lady have patience. It is no boon that her servant would desire of her. He would only speak a word of warning in the *mem-sahib's* ear."

Beryl had begun to give him her full attention. She had a feeling that she had seen the man somewhere before, but where and under what circumstances she could not recall. It was no moment for retrospection and the phantom eluded her.

"What is it?" she said again, studying him with knitted brows.

He bowed himself before her till he appeared to be no more than a bundle of dirty linen.

"Let the gracious lady be warned by her servant," he said. "Fletcher *sahib* is a man of evil heart."

Beryl's eyes widened. Assuredly this was the last thing she had expected to hear from such a source.

"What do you mean?" she asked.

He grovelled before her, his head almost in the dust.

"*Mem-sahib* he has gone for water, but he will soon return.

And he will lie to the gracious lady, and tell her that the shaft of the carriage is broken so that he cannot take her back. But it is not so, most gracious. The shaft is cracked, indeed, but it is not beyond repair. Moreover, it was cracked by the *saice* at his master's bidding, while the *mem-sahib* was at the fair."

He paused; but Beryl said nothing. She was listening to the whole story in speechless, unfeigned astonishment.

"Also," her informant proceeded, "the *sahib's* mare was frightened, not by an accident, but by a trick. It was the *sahib's* will that she should run away. And he chose this road so that he might be far from habitation, well knowing that for every mile on the lower road there are two miles to be travelled on this. *Mem-sahib*, your servant has spoken, and he prays you to beware. There is danger in your path."

"But - but," gasped Beryl, "how do you know all this? What makes you tell me? You can't know what you are saying!"

She was thoroughly frightened by this time, and heat and faintness were alike forgotten. Incredible as was the story to which she had listened, there was about it a vividness that made it terrifying.

"But I don't understand," she said helplessly, as the snake-charmer remained silent to her questions. "It is not possible! It could not be!"

He lifted his head a little and, from the depths of the *chuddah*, she knew that piercing eyes surveyed her.

"*Mem-sahib*," he said, "your servant knew that this would happen, and he came here swiftly by a secret way to warn you. More, he knows that when Fletcher *sahib* returns, he will speak lightly of the accident, so that the *Mem-sahib* will have no fear. 'A broken shaft is soon mended,' he will say. 'My servant has returned to Farabad - to a man he knows. We will rest under the trees but a furlong from this place till he comes back.' But, most gracious, he will not come back. There is no place at Farabad at this time of the fair where the work could be done. Moreover, the *saice* has his orders, and he will not seek one. He will go back to Kundaghat with the mare, but he will walk all the way. It is fifteen miles from here by the road. He will not reach it ere nightfall. He will not return till after the darkness falls, and then he will miss the road. He will not find Fletcher *sahib* and the gracious lady before the sunrise."

Thus, in brief but telling sentences, the old native revealed to the white-faced woman before him the whole abominable plot. She listened to him in a growing agony of doubt. Could it be? Was it by any means possible that Fletcher, desiring to win her, but despairing of lessening the distance she maintained between them by any ordinary method, had devised this foul scheme of compromising her in the eyes of society in order to force her to accept him?

Her cheeks burned furiously at the intolerable suspicion. It made her wholly forget that the man before her was an evil-looking native of whom she knew nothing whatever.

With sudden impulse she turned and bestowed her full confidence upon him, the paint-smeared face and mumbling beard notwithstanding.

"You must help me," she said imperiously. "You have done so much. You must do more. Tell me how I am to get back to Kundaghat."

He made a deferential gesture.

"The *Mem-sahib* cannot depart before the major *sahib* returns," he said. "Let her therefore be faint once more, and let him minister to her. Let her hear his story, and judge if her servant has spoken truly. Then let the gracious lady go with him into the shade of the pine trees on the hill. When she is there let her discover that she has left behind her some treasure that she values - such as the golden bangle that is on the

Ethel M. Dell

mem-sahib's wrist. Let her show distress, and Fletcher *sahib* shall come back to seek it. Then let her listen for the scream of a jay, and rise up and follow it. It will lead her by a safe and speedy way to Kundaghat. It will be easy for the *Mem-sahib* to say afterwards that she began to wander and lost her way, till at last she met an aged man who guided her."

Yes, quite easy. She assimilated this subtle suggestion, for the first time in her life welcoming craft. Of the extreme risk of the undertaking she was too agitated to think. To get away was her one all-possessing desire.

While she thus desperately reviewed the situation, the snake-charmer began, with much grunting and mowing, to gather himself together for departure. She watched him, feeling that she would have gladly detained him had that been possible. Slowly, with palsied movements, he at length arose and took up his basket, doubled himself up before her with an almost ludicrous excess of deference, and finally hobbled away.

VI

There fell a step upon the parched earth, and with a start Beryl turned her head. She had seated herself again, but it was impossible to feign limpness with every pulse at the gallop. She looked up at Fletcher with a desperate smile.

He wore a knotted handkerchief on his head to protect it from the sun, and in his hat, which he balanced with great care in both hands, he carried water.

"I am glad to see you looking better," he said as he reached her. "I am afraid there isn't much more than a cupful left. I had to go nearly half a mile to get it, and it has been running out steadily all the way back."

He knelt down before her, deep concern on his sunburnt face. Reluctantly, out of sheer gratitude, she dipped her handkerchief in the tepid drain, and bathed her face and hands.

"I am so sorry to give you all this trouble," she murmured.

He smiled with raised brows.

"I think I ought to say that. You will never trust yourself to me again after this experience."

She looked at him with a guilty sense of duplicity.

"I - scarcely see how you were to blame for it," she said, rather faintly.

He surveyed her for a moment in silence. Then, "I hardly know how to break it to you," he said. "I am afraid the matter is rather more serious than you think."

She forced a smile. This delicate preparation was far more difficult to endure than the actual calamity to which it paved

Ethel M. Dell

the way.

"Please don't treat me like a coward," she said. "I know I was foolish enough to faint, but it was not so much from fright as from the heat."

"You behaved splendidly," he returned, his dark eyes still intently watching her. "But this is not so much a case for nerve as for resignation. Mrs. Denvers, you will never forgive me, I know. That jump of the mare's damaged one of the shafts. The wonder is it didn't break altogether. I have had to send the *saice* back to Farabad to try and get it patched up, and there is very little chance of our getting back to Kundaghat for two or three hours to come."

All the time that he was communicating this tragic news, Beryl's eyes were upon his face. She paid no heed to his scrutiny. Simply, with absolute steadiness, she returned it.

And she detected nothing - nothing but the most earnest regret, the most courteous anxiety regarding her welfare. Could it all be a monstrous lie, she asked herself. And yet it was to the smallest detail the story she had been warned to expect.

"But surely," she said, at last, "we cannot be so very far from Kundaghat?"

"No great distance as the crow flies," said Fletcher, "but a good many miles by road. I am afraid there is nothing for it but to wait till the mischief is repaired. My only comfort is that you will feel the heat less in returning later in the day. There are some pine trees on the other side of the rise where you can rest. If I had only brought something to eat I should have less cause to blame myself. As it is, do you think you will be able to hold out?"

She smiled at that.

"Oh, I am not starving yet," she said, with more assurance;

"but I do not see the use of sitting still under the circumstances. I am quite rested now. Let us walk back to Farabad, and we might start on foot along the lower road for Kundaghat, and tell your man to overtake us."

Notwithstanding the resolution she infused into her voice, she made the proposal somewhat breathlessly, for she knew - in her heart she knew - that it would be instantly negatived.

And so it was. His face expressed sharp surprise for a second, developing into prompt remonstrance.

"My dear Mrs. Denvers, in this heat! You have not the least idea of what it would mean. You simply have not the strength for such a venture."

But Beryl was growing bolder in the face of emergency. She coolly set his assurance aside.

"I do not quite agree with you," she said. "I am a better walker than you seem to imagine, and the walk into Farabad certainly would not kill me. We might be able to hire some conveyance there - a *tonga* or even a bullock-cart" - she laughed a little - "would be better than nothing."

But Fletcher persistently shook his head.

"I am sorry - horribly sorry, but it would be downright maness to attempt it."

"Nevertheless," said Beryl very quietly, "I mean to do so."

She saw his brows meet for a single instant, and she was conscious of a sick feeling at her heart that made her physically cold. Doubt was emerging into deadly conviction.

Suddenly he leaned towards her, and spoke very earnestly.

"Mrs. Denvers, please believe that I regret this mischance every whit as much as you do. But, after all, it is only a mischance, and we may be thankful it was no worse. Shall we not treat it as such, and make the best of it?"

He was looking her straight in the face as he said it, but, steady as was his gaze, she was not reassured. Quick as lightning came the thought - it was almost like an inner voice warning her - that he must not suspect the fact. Whatever happened she must veil her uneasiness, which she feared had been already far too obvious.

Quietly she rose and expressed her willingness to go with him into the shade of the trees.

They stood grouped on the side of a hill, a thick belt through which the scorching sun-rays slanted obliquely, turning the straight brown trunks to ruddiest gold. There was more air here than in the valley, and it was a relief to sit down in the shade and rest upon a fallen tree.

Fletcher threw himself down upon the ground. "We can watch the road from here," he remarked. "We should see the dog-cart about a mile away."

This was true. Barren, stony, and deserted, the road twisted in and out below them, visible from that elevation for a considerable distance. Beryl looked over it in silence. Her heart was beating in great suffocating throbs, while she strove to summon her resolution. Could she do this thing? Dared she? On the other hand, could she face the alternative risk? Her face burned fiercely yet again as she thought of it.

Furtively she began to study the man stretched out upon the ground close to her, and a sudden, surging regret went through her. If only it had been Lord Ronald lounging there beside her, how utterly different would have been her attitude! Foolish and inept he might be - he was - but, as he himself had comfortably remarked, a man might be worse. She trusted him implicitly, every one trusted him. It was impossible to do otherwise.

Had any one accused him of laying a trap for her, she would have treated the suggestion as too contemptible for notice. A sharp sigh escaped her. Why had he taken her so promptly at her word? He could never have seriously cared for her. Probably it was not in him to care.

"You are not comfortable?" said Fletcher.

She started at the sound of his voice, and with desperate impulse took action before her courage could fail her.

"Major Fletcher, I - have lost the bangle you gave me. It slipped off down by that big rock when I was feeling ill. And I must have left it there. Should you very much mind fetching it for me?"

She felt her face grow crimson as she made the request, and she could not look at him, knowing too well what he would think of her confusion. She felt, indeed, as if she could never look him in the face again.

Fletcher sat quite still for a few seconds. Then, "But it's of no consequence, is it?" he said. "I will fetch it for you, of course, if you like, but I could give you fifty more like it. And in any case we can find it when Subdul comes with the dog-cart."

He was reluctant to leave her. She saw it instantly, and tingled at the discovery. With a great effort she made her final attempt.

"Please," she said, with downcast eyes, "I want it now."

He was on his feet at once, looking down at her. "I will fetch it with the greatest pleasure," he said.

And, not waiting for her thanks, he turned and left her.

VII

For many seconds after his departure Beryl sat quite rigid, watching his tall figure pass swiftly downwards through the trees. She did not stir till he had reached the road, then, with a sudden deep breath, she rose.

At the same instant there sounded behind her, high up the hillside among the pine trees, the piercing scream of a jay.

It startled her, for she had not been listening for it. All her thoughts had been concentrated upon the man below her. But this distant cry brought her back, and sharply she turned.

Again came the cry, unmusical, insistent. She glanced nervously around, but met only the bright eyes of a squirrel on a branch above her.

Again it came, arrogantly this time, almost imperiously. It seemed to warn her that there was no time for indecision. She felt as though some mysterious power were drawing her, and, gathering her strength, she began impetuously to mount the hill that stretched up behind her, covered with pine trees as far as she could see. It was slippery with pine needles, and she stumbled a good deal, but she faltered no longer in her purpose. She had done with indecision.

She had climbed some distance before she heard again the guiding signal. It sounded away to her right, and she turned aside at once to follow it. In that instant, glancing downwards through the long, straight stems, she saw Fletcher far below, just entering the wood. Her heart leapt wildly at the sight. She almost stopped in her agitation. But the discordant bird-call sounded yet again, louder and more compelling than before, and she turned as a needle to a magnet and followed.

The growth of pine trees became denser as she proceeded. It seemed to close her in and swallow her. But only once again did fear touch her, and that was when she heard Fletcher's voice, very far away but unmistakable, calling to her by name.

With infinite relief, still following her unseen guide, at last she began to descend. The ground sloped sharply downwards, and creeping undergrowth began to make her progress difficult. She pressed on, however, and at length, hearing the tinkle of running water, realised that she was approaching one of the snow-fed mountain streams that went to swell the sacred waters that flowed by the temple at Farabad.

She plunged downwards eagerly, for she was hot and thirsty, coming out at last upon the brink of a stream that gurgled over stones between great masses of undergrowth.

"Will the *Mem-sahib* deign to drink?" a deferential voice asked behind her.

She looked round sharply to see the old snake-charmer, bent nearly double with age and humility, meekly offering her a small brass drinking-vessel.

His offer surprised her, knowing the Hindu's horror of a stranger's polluting touch, but she accepted it without question. Stooping, she scooped up a cupful of the clean water and drank.

The draught was cold as ice and refreshed her marvellously. She thanked him for it with a smile.

"And now?" she said.

He bowed profoundly, and taking the cup he washed it very carefully in the stream. Then, deprecatingly, he spoke.

"*Mem-sahib*, it is here that we cross the water."

She looked at the rushing stream with dismay. It was not very wide but she saw at once that it was beyond a leap. She fancied that the swirling water in the middle indicated depth.

"Do you mean I must wade?" she asked.

He made a cringing gesture.

"There is another way, most gracious."

She gazed at him blankly.

"Another way?"

Again he bent himself.

"If the *Mem-sahib* will so far trust her servant."

"But - but how?" she asked, somewhat breathlessly. "You don't mean - you can't mean -"

"*Mem-sahib*," he said gently, "it will not be the first time that I have borne one of your race in my arms. I may seem old to you, most gracious, but I have yet the vigour of manhood. The water is swift but it is not deep. Let the *Mem-sahib* watch her servant cross with the snake-basket, and she will see for herself that he speaks the truth. He will return for the *Mem-sahib*, with her permission, and will bear her in safety to the farther bank, whence it is but an hour's journey on foot to Kundaghat."

There was a coaxing touch about all this which was not lost upon Beryl. He was horribly ugly, she thought to herself, with that hideous red smear across his dusky face; but in spite of this she felt no fear. Unprepossessing he might be, but he was in no sense formidable.

As she stood considering him he stooped and, lifting his basket, stepped with his sandalled feet into the stream. His long white garment trailed unheeded upon the water which rose above his knees as he proceeded.

Reaching the further bank, he deposited his burden and at once turned back. Beryl was waiting for him. For some reason unknown even to herself, she had made up her mind to trust this old man.

"If the most gracious will deign to rest her arm upon my shoulder," he suggested, in his meek quaver.

And without further demur she complied.

The moment he lifted her she knew that his strength was fully equal to the venture. His arms were like steel springs. He grunted a little to himself as he bore her across, but he neither paused nor faltered till he set her upon the bank.

"The *Mem-sahib* will soon see the road to Kundaghat," he observed then. "She has but three miles yet to go."

"Only three miles to Kundaghat!" she ejaculated in amazement.

"Only three miles, most gracious." For the first time a hint of pride was mingled with the humility in his reedy voice. "The *Mem-sahib* has travelled hither by a way that few know."

Beryl was fairly amazed at the news. She had believed herself to be many miles away. She began to wonder if her friend in need would consider the few rupees she had left adequate reward for his pains. Since she had parted with Fletcher's gift, she reflected that she had nothing else of value to bestow.

The way now lay uphill, and all undergrowth soon ceased. They came out at last through thinning pine trees upon the crest of the rise, and from here, a considerable distance below, Beryl discerned the road along which she had travelled with Fletcher that morning.

White and glaring it stretched below her, till at last a grove of mango trees, which she remembered to be less than a mile from Kundaghat, closed about it, hiding it from view.

"The *Mem-sahib* will need her servant no more," said her guide, pausing slightly behind her while she studied the landscape at her feet with the road that wound through the valley.

She took out her purse quickly, and shook its contents into her hand. He had been as good as his word, but she knew she had but little to offer him unless he would accompany her all the way to Kundaghat. She stopped to count the money before she turned - two rupees and eight annas. It did not seem a very adequate reward for the service he had rendered her.

With this thought in her mind she slowly turned.

"This is all I have with me -" she began to say, and broke off with the words half-uttered.

She was addressing empty air! The snake-charmer had vanished!

She stood staring blankly. She had not been aware of any movement. It was as if the earth had suddenly and silently gaped and swallowed him while her back was turned.

In breathless astonishment she moved this way and that, searching for him among the trees that seemed to grow too sparsely to afford a screen. But she searched in vain. He had clean gone, and had taken his repulsive pet with him.

Obviously, then, he had not done this thing for the sake of reward.

A sense of uneasiness began to possess her, and she started at last upon her downward way, feeling as if the place were haunted.

With relief she reached the road at length, and commenced the last stage of the return journey. The heat was terrific. She was intensely weary, and beginning to be footsore. At a turn in the road she paused a moment, looking back at the pine-clad hill from which she had come; and as she did so, distinct, though far away behind her, there floated through the midday silence the curious note of a jay. It sounded to her bewildered senses like a cracked, discordant laugh.

Ethel M. Dell

VIII

On the following afternoon Major Fletcher called, but he was not admitted. Beryl was receiving no one that day, and sent him an uncompromising message to that effect. He lingered to inquire after her health, and, on being told that she had overtired herself and was resting, expressed his polite regret and withdrew.

After that, somewhat to Beryl's surprise, he came no more to the bungalow.

She remained in seclusion for several days after her adventure, so that fully a week passed before they met.

It was while out riding one morning with Mrs. Ellis that she first encountered him. The meeting was unexpected, and, conscous of a sudden rush of blood to her cheeks, she bestowed upon him her haughtiest bow. His grave acknowledgment thereof was wholly without effrontery, and he made no attempt to speak to her.

"Have you quarrelled with the Major?" asked Nina, as they rode on.

"Of course not," Beryl answered, with a hint of impatience.

But she knew that if she wished to appear at her ease she must not be too icy. She felt a very decided reluctance to take her friend into her confidence with regard to the Farabad episode. There were times when she wondered herself if she were altogether justified in condemning Major Fletcher unheard, in spite of the evidence against him. But she had no intention of giving him an opportunity to vindicate himself if she could possibly avoid doing so.

In this, however, circumstances proved too strong for her. They were bound to meet sooner or later, and Fate ordained that when this should occur she should be more or less at his mercy.

The occasion was an affair of some importance, being a reception at the palace of the native prince who dwelt at Farabad. It promised to be a function of supreme magnificence; it was, in fact, the chief event of the season, and the Anglo-Indian society of Kundaghat attended it in force.

Beryl went with the Commissioner and his wife, but in the crowd of acquaintances that surrounded her almost from the moment of her arrival she very speedily drifted away from them. One after another claimed her attention, and almost before she knew it she found herself moving unattached through the throng.

She was keenly interested in the brilliant scene about her. Flashing jewels and gorgeous costumes made a glittering wonderland, through which she moved as one beneath a spell. The magic of the East was everywhere; it filled the atmosphere as with a heavy fragrance.

She had withdrawn a little from the stream of guests, and was standing slightly apart, watching the gorgeous spectacle in the splendidly lighted hall, when a tall figure, dressed in regimentals, came quietly up and stood beside her.

With a start she recognised Fletcher. He bent towards her instantly, and spoke.

"I trust that you have now quite recovered from your fatigue, Mrs. Denvers."

She controlled her flush before it had time to overwhelm her.

"Quite, thank you," she replied, speaking stiffly because she could not at the moment bring herself to do otherwise.

He stood beside her for a space in silence, and she wondered greatly what was passing in his mind.

At length, "May I take you to have some supper?" he asked. "Or would you care to go outside? The gardens are worth a visit."

Beryl hesitated momentarily. To have supper with him meant a prolonged *tete-a-tete*, whereas merely to go outside for a few minutes among a host of people could not involve her in any serious embarrassment. She could leave him at any moment if she desired. She was sure to see some of her acquaintances. Moreover, to seem to avoid him would make him think she was afraid of him, and her pride would not permit this possibility.

"Let us go outside for a little, then," she said.

He offered her his arm, and the next moment was leading her through a long, thickly carpeted passage to a flight of marble steps that led downwards into the palace-garden.

He did not speak at all; and she, without glancing at him, was aware of a very decided constraint in his silence. She would not be disconcerted by it. She was determined to maintain a calm attitude; but her heart quickened a little in spite of her. She saw that he had chosen an exit that would lead them away from the crowd.

Dumbly they descended the steps, Fletcher unhesitatingly drawing her forward. The garden was a marvel of many-coloured lights, intricate and bewildering as a maze. Its paths were all carpeted, and their feet made no sound. It was like a dream-world.

Here and there were nooks and glades of deepest shadow. Through one of these, without a pause, Fletcher led her, emerging at length into a wonderful fairyland where all was blue - a twilight haunt, where countless tiny globes of light nestled like sapphires upon every shrub and tree, and a slender fountain rose and fell tinkling in a shallow basin of blue stone.

A small arbour, domed and pillared like a temple, stood beside the fountain, and as they ascended its marble steps a strong scent of sandalwood fell like a haze of incense upon Beryl's senses.

There was no light within the arbour, and on the threshold instinctively she stopped short. They were as much alone as if miles instead of yards separated them from the buzzing crowds about the palace.

Instantly Fletcher spoke.

"Go in, won't you? It isn't really dark. There is probably a couch with rugs and cushions."

There was, and she sat down upon it, sinking so low in downy luxuriance that she found herself resting not far from the floor. But, looking out through the marble latticework into the blue twilight, she was somewhat reassured. Though thick foliage obscured the stars, it was not really dark, as he had said.

Fletcher seated himself upon the top step, almost touching her. He seemed in no hurry to speak.

The only sound that broke the stillness was the babble of the fountain, and from far away the fitful strains of a band of stringed instruments.

Slowly at length he turned his head, just as his silence was becoming too oppressive to be borne.

"Mrs. Denvers," he said, his voice very deliberate and even, "I want to know what happened that day at Farabad to make you decide that I was not a fit escort for you."

It had come, then. He meant to have a reckoning with her. A sharp tingle of dismay went through her as she realised it. She made a quick effort to avert his suspicion.

"I wandered, and lost my way," she said. "And then I met an old native, who showed me a short cut. I ought, perhaps, to have written and explained."

"That was not all that happened," Fletcher responded gravely. "Of course, you can refuse to tell me any more. I am absolutely at your mercy. But I do not think you will refuse. It isn't treating me quite fairly, is it, to keep me in the dark?"

She saw at once that to fence with him further was out of the question. Quite plainly he meant to bring her to book. But she felt painfully unequal to the ordeal before her. She was conscious of an almost physical sense of shrinking.

Nevertheless, as he waited, she nerved herself at length to speak.

"What makes you think that something happened?"

"It is fairly obvious, is it not?" he returned quietly. "I could not very easily think otherwise. If you will allow me to say so, your device was not quite subtle enough to pass muster. Even had you dropped that bangle by inadvertence - which you did not - you would not, in the ordinary course of things, have sent me off post haste to recover it."

"No?" she questioned, with a faint attempt to laugh.

"No," he rejoined, and this time she heard a note of anger, deep and unmistakable, in his voice.

She drew herself together as it reached her. It was to be a battle, then, and instinctively she knew that she would need all her strength.

"Well," she said finally, affecting an assurance she was far from feeling, "I have no objection to your knowing what happened since you have asked. In fact, perhaps, - as you suggest, - it is scarcely fair that you should not know."

"Thank you," he responded, with a hint of irony.

But she found it difficult to begin, and she could not hide it from him, for he was closely watching her.

He softened a little as he perceived this.

"Pray don't be agitated," he said. "I do not for a moment question that your reason for what you did was a good one. I am only asking you to tell me what it was."

"I know," she answered. "But it will make you angry, and that is why I hesitate."

He leaned towards her slightly.

"Can it matter to you whether I am angry or not?"

She shivered a little.

"I never offend any one if I can help it. I think it is a mistake. However, you have asked for it. What happened was this. It was when you left me to get some water. An old man, a native, came and spoke to me. Perhaps I was foolish to listen, but I could scarcely have done otherwise. And he told me - he told me that the accident to the dog-cart was not - not -" She paused, searching for a word.

"Genuine," suggested Fletcher very quietly.

She accepted the word. The narration was making her very nervous.

"Yes, genuine. He told me that the *saice* had cracked the shaft beforehand, that there was no possibility of getting it repaired at Farabad, that he would have to return to Kundaghat and

Ethel M. Dell

might not, probably would not, come back for us before the following morning."

Haltingly, rather breathlessly, the story came from her lips. It sounded monstrous as she uttered it. She could not look at Fletcher, but she knew that he was angry; something in the intense stillness of his attitude told her this.

"Please go on," he said, as she paused. "You undertook to tell me the whole truth, remember."

With difficulty she continued.

"He told me that the mare was frightened by a trick, that you chose the hill-road because it was lonely and difficult. He told me exactly what you would say when you came back. And - and you said it."

"And that decided you to play a trick upon me and escape?" questioned Fletcher. "Your friend's suggestion, I presume?"

His words fell with cold precision; they sounded as if they came through his teeth.

She assented almost inaudibly. He made her feel contemptible.

"And afterwards?" he asked relentlessly.

She made a final effort; there was that in his manner that frightened her.

"Afterwards, he gave a signal - it was the cry of a jay - for me to follow. And he led me over the hill to a stream where he waited for me. We crossed it together, and very soon after he pointed out the valley road below us, and left me."

"You rewarded him?" demanded Fletcher swiftly.

"No; I - I was prepared to do so, but he disappeared."

"What was he like?"

She hesitated.

"Mrs. Denvers!" His tone was peremptory.

"I do not feel bound to tell you that," she said, in a low voice.

"I have a right to know it," he responded firmly.

And after a moment she gave in. The man was probably far away by this time. She knew that the fair was over.

"It was - the old snake-charmer."

"The man we saw at Farabad?"

"Yes."

Fletcher received the information in silence, and several seconds dragged away while he digested it. She even began to wonder if he meant to say anything further, almost expecting him to get up and stalk away, too furious for speech.

But at length, very unexpectedly and very quietly, he spoke.

"Would it be of any use for me to protest my innocence?"

She did not know how to answer him.

He proceeded with scarcely a pause:

"It seems to me that my guilt has been taken for granted in such a fashion that any attempt on my part to clear myself would be so much wasted effort. It simply remains for you to pass sentence."

She lifted her head for the first time, startled out of all composure. His cool treatment of the matter was more disconcerting than any vehement protestations. It was almost as though he acknowledged the offence and swept it aside with the same breath as of no account. Yet it was incredible, this view of the case. There must be some explanation. He would never dare to insult her thus.

Impulsively she rose, inaction becoming unendurable. He stood up instantly, and they faced one another in the weird blue twilight.

"I think I have misunderstood you!" she said breathlessly, and there stopped dead, for something - something in his face arrested her.

The words froze upon her lips. She drew back with a swift, instinctive movement. In one flashing second of revelation unmistakable she knew that she had done him no injustice. Her eyes had met his, and had sunk dismayed before the fierce passion that had flamed back at her.

In the pause that followed she heard her own heartbeats, quick and hard, like the flying feet of a hunted animal. Then - for she was a woman, and instinct guided her - she covered up her sudden fear, and faced him with stately courage.

"Let us go back," she said.

"You have nothing to say to me?" he asked.

She shook her head in silence, and made as if to depart.

But he stood before her, hemming her in. He did not appear to notice her gesture.

"But I have something to say to you!" he said. And in his voice, for all its quietness, was a note that made her tremble. "Something to which I claim it as my right that you should listen."

She faced him proudly, though she was white to the lips.

"I thought you had refused to plead your innocence," she said.

"I have," he returned. "I do. But yet -"

"Then I will not hear another word," she broke in. "Let me pass!"

She was splendid as she stood there confronting him, perhaps more splendid than she had ever been before. She had reached the ripe beauty of her womanhood. She would never be more magnificent than she was at that moment. The magic of her went to the man's head like wine. Till that instant he had to a great extent controlled himself, but that was the turning-point. She dazzled him, she intoxicated him, she maddened him.

The savagery in him flared into a red blaze of passion. Without another word he caught her suddenly to him, and before she could begin to realise his intention he had kissed her fiercely upon the lips.

Ethel M. Dell

IX

The moments that followed were like a ghastly nightmare to Beryl, for, struggle as she might, she knew herself to be helpless. Having once passed the bounds of civilisation, he gave full rein to his savagery. And again and yet again, holding her crushed to him, he kissed her shrinking face. He was as a man possessed, and once he laughed - a devilish laugh - at the weakness of her resistance.

And then quite suddenly she felt his grip relax. He let her go abruptly, so that she tottered and almost fell, only saving herself by one of the pillars of the arbour.

A great surging was in her brain, a surging that nearly deafened her. She was too spent, too near to swooning, to realise what it was that had wrought her deliverance. She could only cling gasping and quivering to her support while the tumult within her gradually subsided.

It was several seconds later that she began to be aware of something happening, of some commotion very near to her, of trampling to and fro, and now and again of a voice that cursed. These things quickly goaded her to a fuller consciousness. Exhausted though she was, she managed to collect her senses and look down upon the spectacle below her.

There, on the edge of the fountain, two figures swayed and fought. One of them she saw at a glance was Fletcher. She had a glimpse of his face in the uncanny gloom, and it was set and devilish, bestial in its cruelty. The other - the other - she stared and gasped and stared again - the other, beyond all possibility of doubt, was the ancient snake-charmer of Farabad.

Yet it was he who cursed - and cursed in excellent English - with a fluency that none but English lips could possibly have achieved. And the reason for his eloquence was not far to seek. For he was being thrashed, thrashed scientifically, mercilessly, and absolutely thoroughly - by the man whom he had dared to thwart.

He was draped as before in his long native garment - and this, though it hung in tatters, hampered his movements, and must have placed him at a hopeless disadvantage even had he not been completely outmatched in the first place.

Standing on the steps above them, Beryl took in the whole situation, and in a trice her own weakness was a thing of the past. Amazed, incredulous, bewildered as she was, the urgent need for action drove all questioning from her mind. There was no time for that. With a cry, she sprang downwards.

And in that instant Fletcher delivered a smashing blow with the whole of his strength, and struck his opponent down.

He fell with a thud, striking his head against the marble of the fountain, and to Beryl's horror he did not rise again. He simply lay as he had fallen, with arms flung wide and face upturned, motionless, inanimate as a thing of stone.

In an agony she dropped upon her knees beside him.

"You brute!" she cried to Fletcher. "Oh, you brute!"

She heard him laugh in answer, a fierce and cruel laugh, but she paid no further heed to him. She was trying to raise the fallen man, dabbing the blood that ran from a cut on his temple, lifting his head to lie in the hollow of her arm. Her incredulity had wholly passed. She knew him now beyond all question. He would never manage to deceive her again.

"Speak to me! Oh, do speak to me!" she entreated. "Ronald, open your eyes! Please open your eyes!"

"He is only stunned." It was Fletcher's voice above her. "Leave him alone. He will soon come to his senses. Serves him right for acting the clown in this get-up."

She looked up sharply at that and a perfect tempest of indignation took possession of her, banishing all fear.

"What he did," she said, in a voice that shook uncontrollably, "was for my sake alone, that he might be able to protect me from cads and blackguards. I refuse to leave him like this, but the sooner you go, the better. I will never - never as long as I live - speak to you again!"

Her blazing eyes, and the positive fury of her voice, must have carried conviction to the most obtuse, and this Fletcher certainly was not. He stood a moment, looking down at her with an insolence that might have frightened her a little earlier, but which now she met with a new strength that he felt himself powerless to dominate. She was not thinking of herself at all just then, and perhaps that was the secret of her ascendancy. His own brute force crumbled to nothing before it, and he knew that he was beaten.

Without a word he bowed to her, smiling ironically, and turned upon his heel.

She drew a great breath of relief as she saw him go. She felt as though a horrible oppression had passed out of the atmosphere. That fairy haunt with its bubbling fountain and sapphire lamps was no longer an evil place.

She bent again over her senseless companion.

"Ronald!" she whispered. "My dear, my dear, can't you hear me? Oh, if only you would open your eyes!"

She soaked her handkerchief in the water and held it to the wound upon his forehead. Even as she did it, she felt him stir, and the next moment his eyes were open, gazing straight up into her own.

"Damn the brute!" said Lord Ronald faintly.

"You are better?" she whispered thankfully.

His hand came upwards gropingly, and took the soaked handkerchief from her. He dabbed his face with it, and slowly, with her assistance, sat up.

"Where is he?" he asked.

"He has gone," she told him. "I - ordered him to go."

"Better late than never," said Lord Ronald thoughtfully.

He leaned upon the edge of the fountain, still mopping the blood from his face, till, suddenly feeling his beard, he stripped it off with a gesture of impatience.

"Afraid I must have given you a nasty shock," he said. "I didn't expect to be mauled like this."

"Please - please don't apologise," she begged him, with a sound that was meant for a laugh, but was in effect more like a sob.

He turned towards her in his slow way.

"I'm not apologising. Only - you know - I've taken something of a liberty, though, on my honour, it was well meant. If you can overlook that -"

"I shall never overlook it," she said tremulously.

He put the *chuddah* back from his head and regarded her gravely. His face was swollen and discoloured, but this fact did not in the smallest degree lessen the quaint self-assurance of his demeanour.

"Yes, but you mustn't cry about it," he said gently. "And you mustn't blame yourself either. I knew the fellow, remember; you didn't."

"I didn't know you, either," she said, sitting down on the edge of the fountain. "I - I've been a perfect fool!"

Silence followed this statement. She did not know quite whether she expected Lord Ronald to agree with her or to protest against the severity of her self-arraignment, but she found his silence peculiarly hard to bear.

She had almost begun to resent it, when suddenly, very softly, he spoke:

"It's never too late to mend, is it?"

"I don't know," she answered. "I almost think it is - at my age."

He dipped her handkerchief again in the fountain, and dabbed his face afresh. Then:

"Don't you think you might try?" he suggested, in his speculative drawl.

She shook her head rather drearily.

"I suppose I shall have to resign myself, and get a companion. I shall hate it, and so will the companion, but -"

"Think so?" said Lord Ronald. He laid his hand quietly on her knee. "Mrs. Denvers," he said, "I am afraid you thought me awfully impertinent when I suggested your marrying me the other day. It wasn't very ingenious of me, I admit. But what can you expect from a nonentity? Not brains, surely! I am not going to repeat the blunder. I know very well that I am no bigger than a peppercorn in your estimation, and we will leave it at that. But, you know, you are too young, you really are too young, to live alone. Now listen a moment. You trust me. You said so. You'll stick to that?"

"Of course," she said, wondering greatly what was coming.

"Then will you," he proceeded very quietly, "have me for a watch-dog until you marry again? I could make you an excellent Sikh servant, and I could go with you practically everywhere. Don't begin to laugh at the suggestion until you have thoroughly considered it. It could be done in such a way that no one would suspect. It matters nothing to any one how I pass my time, and I may as well do something useful for once. I know at first sight it seems impossible, but it is nothing of the sort in reality. It isn't the first time I have faked as a native. I am Indian born, and I have spent the greater part of my life knocking about the Empire. The snake-taming business I picked up from an old bearer of mine - a very old man he's now and in the trade himself. I got him to lend me his most docile cobra. The thing was harmless, of course. But all this is beside the point. The point is, will you put up with me as a retainer, no more, until you find some one more worthy of the high honour of guarding you? I shall never, believe me, take advantage of your kindness. And on the day you marry again I shall resign my post."

She had listened to the amazing suggestion in unbroken silence, and even when he paused she did not at once speak. Her head was bent, almost as though she did not wish him to see her face - he, the peppercorn, the nonentity, whose opinion mattered so little!

Yet as he waited, still with that quiet hand upon her as though to assure her of his solidity, his trustworthiness, she spoke at last, in a voice so small that it sounded almost humble.

"But, Lord Ronald, I - I may never marry again. My late marriage was - was such a grievous mistake. I was so young at the time, and - and -"

"Don't tell me," he said gently.

"But - but - if I never marry again?" she persisted.

"Then - unless, of course, you dismiss me - I shall be with you for all time," he said.

She made a slight, involuntary movement, and he took his hand away.

"Will you think it over before you decide?" he said. "I will come to you, as soon as I am presentable, for your answer. For the present, would you not be wise to go back to your friends? I am too disreputable to escort you, but I will watch you to the palace steps."

He got to his feet as he spoke. He was still absently mopping his face with the scrap of lace he had taken from her.

Beryl stood up also. She wanted to be gracious to him, but she was unaccountably shy. No words would come.

He waited courteously.

At last:

"Lord Ronald," she said with difficulty, "I know you are in earnest. But do you - do you really wish to be taken at your word?"

He raised his eyebrows as if the question slightly surprised him.

"Certainly," he said.

Still she stood hesitating.

"I wish you would tell me why," she said, almost under her breath.

"Why?" he repeated uncomprehendingly.

"Yes, why you wish to safeguard me in this fashion," she explained, in evident embarrassment.

"Oh, that!" he said slowly. "I suppose it is because I happen to care for your safety."

"Yes?" she murmured, still pausing.

He looked at her with his straight grey eyes that were so perfectly true and kind.

"That's all," he said, and smiled upon her reassuringly.

Beryl uttered a sharp sigh and let the matter drop. Nonentity though he might be, she would have given much for a glimpse of his inner soul just then.

Ethel M. Dell

X

For three days after the reception at Farabad Beryl Denvers returned to her seclusion, and during those three days she devoted the whole of her attention to the plan that Lord Ronald Prior had laid before her. It worried her a good deal. There were so many obstacles to its satisfactory fulfilment. She wished he had not been so pleasantly vague regarding his own feelings in the matter. Of course, it was a feather-brained scheme from start to finish, and yet in a fashion it attracted her. He was so splendidly safe, so absolutely reliable; she needed just such a protector. And yet - and yet - there were so many obstacles.

On the fourth day Lord Ronald's card was brought to her. He did not call at the conventional hour, and the reason for this was not hard to fathom. He had come for her final decision, and he desired to see her alone.

She did not know how to meet him or what to say, but it was useless to shirk the interview. She entered her drawing-room with decidedly heightened colour, even while telling herself that it was absurd to feel any embarrassment in his presence.

He was waiting for her on his favourite perch, the music-stool, swinging idly to and fro, with his customary serenity of demeanour. He moved to meet her with a quiet smile of welcome. A piece of strapping-plaster across his left temple was all that remained of his recent disfigurement.

"I hope my visit is not premature," he remarked as he shook hands.

"Oh, no!" she answered somewhat nervously. "I expected you. Please sit down."

He subsided again upon the music-stool, and there followed a silence which she found peculiarly disconcerting.

"You have been thinking over my suggestion?" he drawled at length.

"Yes," she said. "Yes, I have." She paused a moment, then, "I - am afraid it wouldn't answer," she said, with an effort, "though I am very grateful to you for thinking of it. You see, there are so many obstacles."

"But not insurmountable, any of them," smiled Lord Ronald.

"I am afraid so," she said.

He looked at her.

"May I not hear what they are?"

She hesitated.

"For one thing, you know," she said, "one pays one's servants."

"Well, but you can pay me," he said simply. "I shall not ask very high wages. I am easily satisfied. I shouldn't call that an obstacle."

She laughed a little.

"But that isn't all. There is the danger of being found out. It – it would make it rather awkward, wouldn't it? People would talk."

"No one ever talks scandal of me," said Lord Ronald comfortably. "I am considered eccentric, but quite incapable of anything serious. I don't think you need be afraid. There really isn't the smallest danger of my being discovered, and even if I were, I could tell the truth, you know. People always believe what I say."

She smiled involuntarily at his simplicity, but she shook her head.

"It really wouldn't do," she said.

"What! More obstacles?" he asked.

"Yes, one - the greatest of all, in my opinion." She got up and moved across the room, he pivoting slowly round to watch her.

She came to a stand by her writing-table, and began to turn over a packet of letters that lay there. She did it mechanically, with hands that shook a little. Her face was turned away from him.

He waited for a few seconds; then, as she still remained silent, he spoke.

"What is this last obstacle, Mrs. Denvers?"

She answered him with her head bent, her fingers still fluttering the papers before her.

"You," she said, in a low voice. "You yourself."

"Me!" said Lord Ronald, in evident astonishment.

She nodded without speaking.

"But - I'm sorry," he said pathetically, "I'm afraid I don't quite follow you. I am not famed for my wits, as you know."

She laughed at that, unexpectedly and quite involuntarily; and though she was instantly serious again the laugh served to clear away some of her embarrassment.

"Oh, but you are absurd," she said, "to talk like that. No dull-witted person could ever have done what you have been doing lately. Major Fletcher himself told me that day we went to Farabad that it needed sharp wits to pose as a native among natives. He also said -" She paused suddenly.

"Yes?" said Lord Ronald.

She glanced round at him momentarily.

"I don't know why I should repeat it. It is quite beside the point. He also said that it entailed a risk that no one would care to take unless - unless there was something substantial to be gained by it."

"Well, but there was," said Lord Ronald vaguely.

"Meaning my safety?" she questioned.

"Exactly," he said.

She became silent; but she fidgeted no longer with her papers. She was
making up her mind to take a bold step.

"Lord Ronald," she said at last, "I am going to ask you a very direct - a horribly direct - question. Will you answer me quite directly too? And - and - tell me the truth, even if it sounds rather brutal?"

There was an unmistakable appeal in her voice. With an effort she wheeled in her chair, and fully faced him. But she was so plainly distressed that even he could not fail to notice it.

"What is it?" he said kindly. "I will tell you the truth, of course. I always do."

"You promise?" she said, very earnestly.

"Certainly I promise," he said.

"Then - you must forgive my asking, but I must know, and I can't find out in any other way - Lord Ronald, are you - are you in love with me?"

She saw the grey eyes widen in astonishment, and was conscious of a moment of overwhelming embarrassment; and then, slow and emphatic, his answer came, banishing all misgiving.

"But of course I am," he said. "I thought you knew."

She summoned to her aid an indignation she was far from feeling; she had to cloak her confusion somehow. "How could I possibly know?" she said. "You never told me."

"I asked you to marry me," he protested. "I thought you would take the other thing for granted."

She stood up abruptly, turning from him. It was impossible to keep up her indignation. It simply declined to carry her through.

"You - you are a perfect idiot!" she said shakily. And on the words she tried to laugh, but only succeeded in partially smothering a sob.

"Oh, I say!" said Lord Ronald. He got up awkwardly, and stood behind her. "Please don't take it to heart," he urged. "I shouldn't have told you, only - you know - you asked. And it wouldn't make any difference, on my honour it wouldn't. Won't you take my word for it, and give me a trial?"

"No," she said.

"Why not?" he persisted. "Don't you think you are rather hard on me? I shall never take a single inch more than you care to allow."

She turned upon him suddenly. Her cheeks were burning and her eyes were wet, but she no longer cared about his seeing these details.

"What did you mean?" she demanded unexpectedly, "by

saying to me that those fight hardest who fight in vain?"

He was not in the least disconcerted.

"I meant that though you might send me about my business you would not quite manage to shake me off altogether."

"Meaning that you would refuse to go?" she asked, with a quiver that might have been anger in her voice.

"Meaning," he responded quietly, "that though you might deny me yourself, it might not be in your power to deny me the pleasure of serving you."

"And is it not in my power?" she asked swiftly.

He was looking at her very intently.

"No," he said in his most deliberate drawl. "I don't think it is."

"But it is," she asserted, meeting his look with blazing eyes. "You cannot possibly enter my service without my consent. And - and - I am not going to consent to that mad scheme of yours."

"No?" he said.

"No," she repeated with emphasis. "You yourself are the obstacle, as I said before. If - if you had not been in love with me, I might have considered it. But - now - it is out of the question. Moreover," her eyes shot suddenly downwards, as though to hide their fire, "I shall not want that sort of protector now."

"No?" he said again, very softly this time. He was standing straight before her, still closely watching her with that in his eyes that he had never permitted there before.

"No!" she repeated once more, and again brokenly she

laughed; then suddenly raised her eyes to his, and gave him both her hands impetuously, confidingly, yet with a certain shyness notwithstanding. "I - I am going to marry again after all," she said, "if - if you will have me."

"My dear," said Lord Ronald, very tenderly, "I always meant to!"

HER HERO

I

THE AMERICAN COUSIN

"My dear child, it's absurd to be romantic over such a serious matter as marriage - the greatest mistake, I assure you. Nothing could be more suitable than an alliance with this very eligible young man. He plainly thinks so himself. If you are so unreasonable as to throw away this magnificent chance, I shall really feel inclined to give you up in despair."

The soft, drawling accents fell with a gentle sigh through the perfumed silence of the speaker's boudoir. She was an elderly woman, beautiful, with that delicate, china-like beauty that never fades from youth to age. Not even Lady Raffold's enemies had ever disputed the fact of her beauty, not even her stepdaughter, firmly though she despised her.

She sat behind the tea-table, this stepdaughter, dark and inscrutable, a grave, unresponsive listener. Her grey eyes never varied as Lady Raffold's protest came lispingly through the quiet room. She might have been turning over some altogether irrelevant problem at the back of her mind. It was this girl's way to hide herself behind a shield of apparent preoccupation when anything jarred upon her.

"I need scarcely tell you what it would mean to your father," went on the soft voice. "Ever since poor Mortimer's death it has fretted him terribly to think that the estates must pass out of the direct line. Indeed, he hardly feels that the present heir belongs to the family at all. The American branch has always seemed so remote. But now that the young man is actually coming over to see his inheritance, it does seem such a Heaven-sent chance for you. You know, dear, it's your sixth season. You really ought to think seriously of getting settled. I am sure it would be a great weight off my mind to see you suitably married. And this young Cochrane is sure to take a reasonable view of the matter. Americans are so admirably practical. And, of course, if your father could leave all his money to the estates, as this marriage would enable him to do, it would be a very excellent arrangement for all concerned."

The girl at the tea-table made a slight - a very slight - movement that scarcely amounted to a gesture of impatience. The gentle drone of her stepmother's voice was becoming monotonous. But she said nothing whatever, and her expression did not change.

A faintly fretful note crept into Lady Raffold's tone when she spoke again.

"You're so unreasonable, Priscilla. I really haven't a notion what you actually want. You might have been a duchess by this time, as all the world knows, if you had only been reasonable. How is it - why is it - that you are so hard to please?"

Lady Priscilla raised her eyelids momentarily.

"I don't think you would understand, Charlotte, if I were to tell you," she said, in a voice of such deep music that it seemed incapable of bitterness.

"Some ridiculous sentimentality, no doubt," said Lady Raffold.

"I am sure you would call it so."

A faint flush rose in the girl's dark face. She looked at her stepmother no longer, but began very quietly and steadily to make the tea.

Lady Raffold waited a few seconds for her confidence, but she waited in vain. Lady Priscilla had retired completely behind her shield, and it was quite obvious that she had no intention of exposing herself any further to stray shots.

Her stepmother was exasperated, but she found it difficult to say anything more upon the subject in face of this impene-trability. She could only solace herself with the reflection that the American cousin, who had become heir to the earldom and estates of Raffold, would almost certainly take a more common-sense view of the matter, and, if that were so, a little pressure from the girl's father, whom she idolised, would probably be sufficient to settle it according to her desires.

It was so plainly Priscilla's duty to marry the young man. The whole thing seemed to be planned and cut out by Providence. And it was but natural that Ralph Cochrane should see it in the same light. For it was understood that he was not rich, and it would be greatly to his interest to marry Earl Raffold's only surviving child.

So Lady Raffold reasoned to herself as Priscilla poured out the tea in serious silence, and she gradually soothed her own annoyance by the process.

"Come," she said at length, breaking a long silence, "I should think Ralph Cochrane will be in England in ten days at the latest. We must not be too formal with him as he is a relation. Shall we ask him to luncheon on the Sunday after next?"

Priscilla did not at once reply. When at length she looked up, it was with the air of one coming out of a reverie.

"Oh, yes, if you like, Charlotte," she said, in her deep, quiet voice. "No doubt he will amuse you. I know you always enjoy Americans."

"And you, my dear?" said Lady Raffold, with just a hint of sharpness in her tone.

"I?" Again her stepdaughter paused a little, as if collecting her thoughts. "I shall not be here," she said finally. "I have decided to go down to Raffold for midsummer week, and I don't suppose I shall hurry back. It won't matter, will it? I often think that you entertain best alone. And I am so tired of London heat and dust."

There was an unconscious note of wistfulness in the beautiful voice, but its dominant virtue was determination.

Lady Raffold realised at once to her unspeakable indignation that protest was useless.

"Really, Priscilla," was all she found to say, "I am amazed - yes, amazed - at your total lack of consideration."

But Priscilla was quite unimpressed.

"You won't have time to miss me," she said. "I don't think any one will, except, perhaps, Dad; and he always knows where to find me."

"Your father will certainly not leave town before the end of the season," said Lady Raffold, raising her voice slightly.

"Poor dear Dad!" murmured Priscilla.

II

THE ROMANCE OF HER LIFE

"And so I escaped. Her ladyship didn't like it, but it was worth a tussle."

Priscilla leaned back luxuriously in the housekeeper's room at Raffold Abbey, and laughed upon a deep note of satisfaction. She had discarded all things fashionable with her departure from London in the height of the season. The crumpled linen hat she wore was designed for comfort and not for elegance. Her gown of brown holland was simplicity itself. She sat carelessly with her arm round the neck of an immense mastiff who had followed her in.

"I've cut everything, Froggy," she declared, "including the terrible American cousin. In fact, it was almost more on his account than any other that I did it. For I can't and won't marry him, not even for the sake of the dear old Abbey! Are you very shocked, I wonder?"

Froggy the housekeeper - so named by young Lord Mortimer in his schoolboy days - looked up from her work and across at Priscilla, her brown, prominent eyes, to which she owed her *sobriquet*, shining lovingly behind her spectacles. Her real name was Mrs. Burrowes, but Priscilla could not remember a time when she had ever called her anything but Froggy. The old familiar name had become doubly dear to both of them now that Mortimer was dead.

"I should be very shocked, indeed, darling, if it were otherwise," was Froggy's answer.

And Priscilla breathed a long sigh of contentment. She knew that there was no need to explain herself to this, her oldest friend.

She laid her cheek comfortably against the great dog's ear.

"No, Romeo," she murmured. "Your missis isn't going to be thrown at any man's head if she knows it. But it's a difficult world, old boy; almost an impossible world, I sometimes think. Froggy, I know you can be sentimental when you try. What should you do if you fell in love with a total stranger without ever knowing his name? Should you have the fidelity to live in single blessedness all your life for the sake of your hero?"

Froggy looked a little startled at the question, lightly as it was put. She felt that it was scarcely a problem that could be settled offhand. And yet something in Priscilla's manner seemed to indicate that she wanted a prompt reply.

"It is a little difficult to say, dear," she said, after brief reflection. "I can understand that one might be strongly attracted towards a stranger, but I should think it scarcely possible that one could go so far as to fall in love."

Priscilla uttered a faint, rueful laugh.

"Perhaps you couldn't, Froggy," she admitted. "But you know there is such a thing as loving at first sight. Some people go so far as to say that all true love begins that way."

She rose quietly and went to her friend's side.

"Oh, Froggy, it's very difficult to be true to your inner self when you stand quite alone," she said, "and every one else is thinking what a fool you are!" The words had an unwonted ring of passion in them, and, having uttered them, she knelt down by Froggy's side, and hid her face against the ample shoulder. "And I sometimes think I'm a fool myself," she ended, in muffled accents.

Froggy's arms closed instantly and protectingly around her.

"My darling, who is it, then?" whispered her motherly voice.

Priscilla did not at once reply. It was a difficult confidence to make. At last, haltingly, words came:

"It was years ago - that summer we went to New York, Dad and I. He was from the South, so I heard afterwards. He stayed at the same hotel with us, one of those quiet, unobtrusive, big men - not big physically, but - you understand. I might not have noticed him - I don't know - but one day a man in the street threw down a flaming match just as I was coming out of the hotel. I had on a muslin dress, and it caught fire. Of course, it blazed in a moment, and I was terrified. Dad wasn't there. But the man was in the balcony just overhead, and he swung himself down, I never saw how, and caught me in his arms. He had nothing to put it out with. He simply threw me down and flung himself on the top, beating out the flames in all directions with his hands. I was dreadfully upset, of course, but I wasn't much hurt. He was - horribly. One of his hands was all charred.

"He carried me back into the hotel and told me not to be frightened. And he stayed with me till I felt better, because somehow I wanted him to. He was so strong, Froggy, and so kind. He had a voice like a woman's. I've thought since that he must have thought me very foolish and uncontrolled. But he seemed to understand just how I felt. And - do you know - I never saw him again! He went right away that very afternoon, and we never found out who he was. And I never thanked him even for saving my life. I don't think he wanted to be thanked.

"But I have never forgotten him. He was the sort of man you never could forget. I've never seen any one in the least like him. He was somehow so much greater than all the other men I know. Am I a fool, Froggy? I suppose I am. They say every woman will meet her mate if she waits long enough, but it can't be true. I suppose I might as well marry the Yankee heir, only I can't - I can't!"

The low voice ceased, and there fell a silence. Froggy's arms were folded very closely about the kneeling girl, but she had no words of comfort or counsel to offer. She was, in fact, out of her depth, though not for worlds would she have had Priscilla know it.

"You must just follow your own heart, dearest," she said at last. "And I think you will find happiness some day. God grant it!"

Priscilla lifted her head and kissed her. She knew quite well that she had led whither Froggy could not follow. But the knowledge did not hurt her.

She called Romeo, and went out into the summer sunshine, with a smile half tender and half humorous at the corners of her mouth. Poor Froggy!

III

THE PICNIC IN THE GLEN

"I think we will go for a picnic, Romeo," said Priscilla.

It was a Saturday afternoon, warm and slumbrous, and Saturday was the day on which Raffold Abbey was open to the public when the family were away. Priscilla's presence was, as it were, unofficial, but though she was quite content to have it so, she was determined to escape from sight and hearing of the hot and dusty crowd that thronged the place on a fine day from three o'clock till six.

Half a mile or more from the Abbey, a brown stream ran gurgling through a miniature glen, to join the river below the park gates. This stream had been Priscilla's great delight for longer than she could remember. As children, she and her brother Mortimer had spent hours upon its mossy banks, and since those days she had dreamed many dreams, aye, and shed many tears, within sound of its rushing waters. She loved the place. It was her haven of solitude. No one ever disturbed her there.

The walk across the park made them both hot, and it was a relief to sit down on her favourite tree-root above the stream and yield herself to the luxury of summer idleness. A robin was chirping far overhead, and from the grass at her feet there came the whir of a grasshopper. Otherwise, save for the music of the stream, all was still. An exquisite, filmy drowsiness crept over her, and she slept.

A deep growl from her bodyguard roused her nearly an hour later, and she awoke with a start.

Romeo was sitting very upright, watching something on the farther side of the stream. He growled again as Priscilla sat up.

Ethel M. Dell

She looked across in the same direction, and laid a hasty hand upon his collar.

What she saw surprised her considerably. A man was lying face downwards on the brink of the stream, fishing about in the water, with one arm bared to the shoulder. He must have heard Romeo's warning growl, but he paid not the slightest attention to it. Priscilla watched him with keen interest. She could not see his face.

Suddenly he clutched at something in the clear water, and immediately straightened himself, withdrawing his arm. Then, quite calmly, he looked across at her, and spoke in a peculiar, soft drawl like a woman's.

"You'll forgive me for disturbing you, I know," he said, "when I tell you that all my worldly goods were at the bottom of this ditch."

He displayed his recovered property as if to verify his words - a brown leather pocketbook with a silver clasp. Priscilla gazed from it to its owner in startled silence. Her heart was beating almost to suffocation. She knew this man.

The water babbled on between them, singing a little tinkling song all its own. But the girl neither saw nor heard aught of her surroundings. She was back in the heat and whirl of a crowded New York thoroughfare, back in the fierce grip of this man's arms, hearing his quiet voice above her head, bidding her not to be frightened.

Gradually the vision passed. The wild tumult at her heart died down. She became aware that he was waiting for her to speak, and she did so as one in a dream.

"I am glad you got it back," she said.

His brown, clean-shaven face smiled at her, but there was no hint of recognition in his eyes. He had totally forgotten her, of course, as she had always told herself he would. Did not men always forget? And yet - and yet - was he not still her hero - the man for whose sake all other men were less than naught to her?

Again Romeo growled deeply, and she tightened her hold upon him. The stranger, however, appeared quite unimpressed. He stood up and contemplated the stream that divided them with a measuring eye.

"Have I your permission to come across?" he asked her finally, in his soft Southern drawl.

She laughed a little nervously. He was not without audacity, notwithstanding his quiet manner.

"You can cross if you like," she said. "But it's all private property."

He paused, looking at her intently.

"It belongs to Earl Raffold, I have been told?"

She bent her head, and her answer leapt out with an ease that astonished her. She felt it to be an inspiration.

"It does. But the family are in town for the season. I am staying with the housekeeper. She is allowed to have her friends when the family are away."

It was rather breathlessly spoken, but he did not seem to notice.

"I see," he said. "Then one more or less can't make much difference."

With the words he took a single stride forward and bounded into the air. He landed lightly almost at her feet, and Romeo sprang up with an outraged snarl. It choked in his throat almost instantly, however, for the stranger laid a restraining hand upon him, and spoke with soothing self-assurance.

"It's an evil brute that kills a friend, eh, old fellow? You couldn't do it if you tried."

Romeo's countenance changed magically. He turned his hostility into an ardent welcome, and the girl at his side laughed again rather tremulously.

"It's a good thing you weren't afraid. I couldn't have held him."

"I saw that," said the Southerner, speaking softly, his face on a level with the great head he was caressing. "But I knew it would be all right. You see, I - kind of like dogs."

He turned to her after a moment, a faintly quizzical expression about his eyes.

"I won't intrude upon you," he said. "I can go and trespass elsewhere, you know."

Priscilla was not as a rule reckless. A long training in her stepmother's school had made her cautious and far-seeing in all things social. She knew exactly the risk that lay in unconventionality. But, then, had she not fled from town to lead a free life? Why should she submit to the old, galling chain here in this golden world where its restraint was not known? Her whole being rose up in revolt at the bare idea, and suddenly, passionately, she decided to break free. Even the flowers had their day of riotous, splendid life. She would have hers, wherever its enjoyment might lead her, whatever it might cost!

And so she answered him with a lack of reserve at which her London friends would have marvelled.

"You don't intrude at all. If you have come to see the Abbey, I should advise you to wait till after six o'clock."

"When it will be closed to the public?" he questioned, still looking quizzical.

She looked up at him, for the first time deliberately meeting his eyes. Yes it was plain that he did not know her; but on the whole she was glad, it made things easier. She had been so foolish and hysterical upon that far-off day when he had saved her life.

"I will take you over it myself, if you care to accept my guidance," she said, "after the crowd have gone."

He glanced at his watch.

"And you are prepared to tolerate my society till six?" he said. "That is very generous of you."

She smiled, with a touch of wistfulness.

"Perhaps I don't find my own very inspiring."

He raised his eyebrows, but made no comment.

"Perhaps I had better tell you my name," he said, after a pause. "I am in a fashion connected with this place - a sort of friend of the family, if it isn't presumption to put it that way. My name is Julian Carfax, and Ralph Cochrane, the next-of-kin, is a pal of mine, a very great pal. He was coming over to England. Perhaps you heard. But he's a very shy fellow, and almost at the last moment he decided not to face it at present. I was coming over, so I undertook to explain. I spoke to Lady Raffold in town over the telephone, and told her. She seemed to be rather affronted, for some reason. Possibly it was my fault. I'm not much of a diplomatist, anyway."

He seated himself on a mossy stone below her with this reflection, and began to cast pebbles into the brown water.

Priscilla watched him gravely. What he had told her interested her considerably, but she had no intention of giving herself away by betraying it.

There was a decided pause before she made up her mind how to pursue the subject.

"I had no idea that an American could be shy," she said then.

Carfax turned with his pleasant smile.

"No? We're a pushing race, I suppose. But I think Cochrane had some excuse for his timidity this time."

"Yes?" said Priscilla.

He began to laugh quietly.

"You see, it turned out that he was expected to marry the old maid of the family - Lady Priscilla. Naturally he kicked at that."

Priscilla bent sharply over Romeo, and began to examine one of his huge paws. Her face was a vivid scarlet.

"It wasn't surprising, was it?" said Carfax, tossing another pebble into the stream. "It was more than enough, in my opinion, to make any fellow feel shy."

Priscilla did not answer. The colour was slow to fade from her face.

"I wonder if you have ever seen the lady?" Carfax pursued. "She was out of town when I was there."

"Yes; I have seen her."

Priscilla spoke with her head bent.

"You have? What is she like?"

He glanced round with an expression of amused interest. Priscilla looked up deliberately.

"She is quite old and ugly. But I don't think Mr. Ralph Cochrane need be afraid. She doesn't like men. I am rather sorry for her myself."

"Sorry for her? Why?"

Carfax became serious.

"I think she is rather lonely," the girl said, in a low voice.

"You know her well?"

"Can any one say that they really know any one? No. But I think that she feels very deeply, and that her life has always been more or less of a failure. At least, that is the sort of feeling I have about her."

Again, but more gradually, the colour rose in her face. She took up her basket, and began to unpack it.

Carfax turned fully round.

"You go in for character-study," he said.

"A little," she owned. "I can't help it. Now let me give you some tea. I have enough for two."

"I shall be delighted," he said courteously. "Let me help you to unpack."

Priscilla could never recall afterwards how they spent the golden hours till six o'clock. She was as one in a dream, to which she clung closely, passionately, fearing to awake. For in her dream she was standing on the threshold of her paradise, waiting for the opening of the gates.

IV

ON THE THRESHOLD

Raffold Abbey was huge and rambling, girt with many memories. They spent nearly two hours wandering through the house and the old, crumbling chapel.

"There is a crypt below," Priscilla said, "but we can't go down without a lantern. Another day, if you cared -"

"Of course I should, above all things," declared Carfax. "I was just going to ask when I might come again."

Their intimacy had progressed wonderfully during those hours of companionship. The total absence of conventionality had destroyed all strangeness between them. They were as children on a holiday, enjoying the present to the full, and wholly careless of the future.

Not till Carfax had at length taken his leave did Priscilla ask herself what had brought him there. Merely to view his friend's inheritance seemed a paltry reason. Perhaps he was a journalist, or a writer of guide-books. But she soon dismissed the matter, to ask herself a more personal question. Was it possible that he knew her? Had he found out her name after the New York episode, and come at last to seek her? She could not honestly believe this, though her heart leapt at the thought. That affair had taken place four long years before. Of course, he had forgotten it. It could have made no more than a passing impression upon him. Had it been otherwise, would he not have claimed her at once as an old acquaintance?

Yes, it was plain that her first conviction must be correct. He did not know her. The whole incident had passed completely from his memory, crowded out, no doubt, and that speedily, by more absorbing interests. She had flashed across his life, attaining to no more importance than a bird upon the wing.

Ethel M. Dell

He had saved her life at a frightful risk, and then forgotten her very existence. She had always realised it must be so, but, strangely, she had never resented it. In spite of it, with a woman's queer, inexplicable faithfulness, she yet loved her hero, yet cherished closely, fondly, the memory that she doubted not had faded utterly from his mind.

She went to the village church with Froggy on the following day, though fully alive to the risk she ran of being pointed out to the ignorant as Lady Priscilla from the Abbey. She knew by some deep-hidden instinct that he would be there, and she was not disappointed. He came in late, and stood quite still just inside the little building, searching it up and down with keen, quiet eyes that never faltered in their progress till they lighted upon her. She fancied there was a faintly humorous expression about his mouth. His look did not dwell upon her. He stepped aside to a vacant chair close to the door, and Priscilla, in her great, square pew near the pulpit, saw him no more. When she left the church at the end of the service he had already disappeared.

Froggy went out to tea that afternoon with much solicitous regret, which Priscilla treated in a spirit of levity. She packed her tea-basket again as soon as she was alone, selecting her provisions with care. And soon after three, accompanied by Romeo, she started for the glen, not sauntering idly, but stepping briskly through the golden sunshine, as one with a purpose. She felt as if she were going to a trysting-place, though no word of a tryst had passed between them.

He was there before her, bareheaded and alert, quite obviously awaiting her. He did not express his pleasure in words as he took her hand in his. Only there was an indescribable look in his brown eyes that made her very glad that she had come. He had brought an enormous basket of strawberries, which he presented with that drawling ease of manner which she had come to regard as peculiarly his own, and they settled down to the afternoon's enjoyment in a harmony as complete as the summer peace about them.

No spoken confidences passed between them. Their intimacy was such as to make words seem superfluous. Both seemed to feel that the present was all-sufficing.

Only once did Priscilla challenge Carfax's memory. The impulse was irresistible at the moment, though she regretted it later. He was holding out to her the biggest strawberry he could find. It lay on a leaf on the palm of his hand, and as she took it she suddenly saw a long, terrible scar extending upwards from his wrist till his sleeve hid it from view.

"Why," she exclaimed, with a start; then, seeing his questioning look, "surely that's a burn?"

"It is," said Carfax.

He turned his hand over to hide it. His manner seemed to indicate that he did not wish to pursue the subject. But Priscilla, suddenly reckless, ignored the hint.

"But how did you do it?" she asked.

Carfax hesitated for a second, then:

"It was years ago," he said, rather unwillingly. "A lady's dress caught fire. It fell to me to put it out."

"How brave!" murmured Priscilla. Her eyes were shining. Had he looked up then he must have read her secret.

But he did not look up. For the first time he seemed to be labouring under some spell of embarrassment.

"It wasn't brave at all," he said, after a moment. "I could have done no less."

There was almost a vexed note in his voice. Yet she persisted.

"What was she like? Wasn't she very grateful?"

"I don't know at all. I don't suppose she enjoyed the situation any more than I did."

He plucked a tuft of moss and tossed it from him, as if therewith dismissing the subject. And Priscilla felt a little hurt, though not for worlds would she have suffered him to see it.

It fell to him to break the silence a few seconds later, and he did so without a hint of difficulty.

"When am I going to see the crypt?"

Priscilla laughed a little.

"Are you writing a book about the place?"

He laughed back at her quite openly.

"Not at present. When I do, it will be a romance, with you for heroine."

"Oh, no; not me!" she protested. "I am a mere nobody. Lady Priscilla ought to be your heroine."

He raised his eyebrows. She had begun to associate that look of his with protest rather than surprise.

"I have yet to be introduced to Lady Priscilla," he said. "And as she doesn't like men, I almost think I shall forego the pleasure and keep out of her way."

"Perhaps I have given you a wrong impression about her," Priscilla said, speaking with a slight effort. "It is only the idle, foppish men about town she has no use for."

"She is fastidious, apparently," he returned, lying down abruptly at her feet.

"Don't you like women to be fastidious?" Priscilla demanded boldly.

He lay quite motionless for several seconds, then turned in a leisurely fashion upon his side to survey her.

"You are fastidious?" he asked.

"Of course I am!" Priscilla's words came rather breathlessly. "Don't you think me so?"

Again he was silent for seconds. Then, in a baffling drawl, his answer came:

"If you will allow me to say so, I think you are just the sweetest woman I ever met."

Priscilla met his eyes for a single instant, and looked away. She was burning and throbbing from head to foot. She could find naught to say in answer; no word wherewith to turn his deliberate sentence into a jest. Perhaps in her secret heart she did not desire to do so, for a voice within her, a voice long stifled, cried out that she had met her mate. And, since surrender was inevitable, why should she seek to delay it?

But Carfax said no more. Possibly he thought he had said too much. At least, after a long, quiet pause, he looked away from her; and the spell that bound her passed.

V

THE OPENING GATES

That evening Priscilla found a letter from her stepmother awaiting her - a briefly worded, urgent summons.

"Your cousin has not arrived, after all," it said. "Your father and I are greatly disappointed. Would it not be as well for you to return to town? You can scarcely, I fear, afford to waste your time in this fashion. Young Lord Harfield was asking for you most solicitously only yesterday. Such a charming man, I have always thought!"

"That - chicken!" said Priscilla, and tossed her letter aside.

Later, she went up to the top of the Abbey, and out on to a part of the roof that had been battlemented, to dream her dream again under the stars and to view her paradise yet more closely from before the opening gates.

It was very late when she returned lightfooted to Froggy's sitting-room, and, kneeling by her friend's side, interposed her dark head between the kind, bulging eyes and the open Bible that lay upon the table.

"Froggy," she whispered softly, "I'm so happy, dear - so happy!"

And so kneeling, she told Froggy in short, halting sentences of the sudden splendour that had glorified her life.

Froggy was greatly astonished, and even startled. She was also anxious, and showed it. But Priscilla hastened to smooth this away.

"Yes, I know it's sudden. But sometimes, you know, love is like that. Don't be anxious, Froggy. I am much more cautious

- but what a ridiculous word! - than you think. He doesn't know who I am yet. I pretended to him that I was a relation of yours. And he isn't to know at present. You will keep that in mind, won't you? And in a day or two I shall bring him in here to tea, and you will be able to judge of him for yourself. No, dear, no; of course he hasn't spoken. It is much too soon. You forget that though I have known him so long, he has only known me for two days. Oh, Froggy, isn't it wonderful to think of - that he should have come at last like this? It is almost as if - as if my love had drawn him."

VI

WITHIN HER PARADISE

Priscilla's reply to her stepmother's summons, written several days later, was a highly unsatisfactory epistle indeed, in the opinion of its recipient. She found it quite impossible to tear herself away from the country while the fine weather lasted, she wrote. She was enjoying herself immensely, and did not feel that she could ever endure the whole of a London season in one dose again.

It was not a well-thought-out letter, being written in a haste that made itself obvious between the lines. Carfax had hired a motor-car, and was waiting for her. They went miles that day, and when they stopped at last they were in a country that she scarcely knew - a country of barren downs and great sunlit spaces, lonely, immense.

"This is the place," said Carfax quietly, as he helped her to alight.

Priscilla walked a few paces and stood still. She knew exactly why he had chosen it. Her heart was beating wildly. It seemed to dominate all her other faculties. She felt it to be almost more than she could bear.

Those moments of unacknowledged waiting were terrible to her. She knew she had taken an irrevocable step, and her free instinct clamoured loudly against it. It amounted almost to a panic within her.

There came a quiet step on the turf behind her. She did not turn, but the suspense became suddenly unendurable. With a convulsive movement, she made as if she would go on. At the same instant an arm encircled her, checked her, held her closely.

"So, sweetheart!" said Julian Carfax, his voice soothing, womanly, but possessing withal a note of vitality, of purpose, that she had never heard in it before.

She suffered his hold with a faint but desperate cry.

"You don't know me," she said, with a gasping effort. "You don't -" The words failed. He was pressing her to him ever more closely, and she felt his fingers gently fumbling at her veil. With a sudden passionate movement she put up both hands, and threw it back.

"There!" she said, with a sound, half laugh, half sob, and turned herself wholly to him.

The next instant, as his lips pressed hers, all the anguish of doubt that had come upon her was gone like an evil spirit from her soul. She knew only that they stood alone together in a vast space that was filled to the brim with the noonday sunshine. All her heart was flooded with rejoicing. The gates had opened wide for her, and she had entered in.

Ethel M. Dell

VII

BACK TO EARTH

Priscilla never quite realised afterwards how it was that the whole of that long summer day slipped by and her confession remained still unspoken. She did make one or two attempts to lead round to the subject, but each seemed to be foredoomed to failure, and at last she abandoned the idea - for that day, at least. It seemed, after all, but a paltry thing in face of her great happiness.

They sped homeward at length in the light of a cloudless sunset, smoothly and swiftly as if they swooped through air.

"I will take you to the edge of the park," Carfax said; and when they reached it he took her in his arms, holding her fast, as if he could not bear to let her go.

They parted at last almost in silence, but with the tacit understanding that they would meet in the glen on the following day.

Priscilla walked home through the lengthening shadows with a sense of wonderment and unreality at her heart. He had asked for no pledge, yet she knew that the bond between them was such as might stretch to the world's end and never break. They belonged to each other irrevocably now, whatever might intervene.

She reached the Abbey, walking as in a maze of happiness, with no thought for material things.

Romeo came to greet her with effusion, and an air of having something to tell her. She fondled him, and went on with him into the house. They entered by a conservatory, and so through the shrouded drawing-room into the great hall.

The girl's eyes were dazzled by the sudden gloom she found there. She expected to meet no one, and so it was with a violent start that she saw a man's figure detach itself from the shadows and come towards her.

"Who is it?" she asked sharply; and then in astonishment: "Why, Dad!"

Her father's voice answered her, but not with the gruff kindliness to which she was accustomed. It came to her grim and stern, and she knew instinctively that he hated the errand that had brought him.

"I have come down to fetch you," he said. "I do not approve of your being here alone. It is unusual and quite unnecessary. You are quite well?"

"Yes, I am well," Priscilla said. "But why should you object to my being here?"

She stood still, facing him. She knew who had inspired this interference, and from the bottom of her soul she resented it. Her father did not answer. Thinking it over calmly later, she knew that he was ashamed.

"Be ready to start from here in half an hour," he said. "We shall catch the nine-thirty."

Priscilla made no further protest. Her father had never addressed that tone to her before, and it cut her to the heart.

"Very well," she said; and turned to go.

Her deep voice held no anger, and only Romeo, pressed close against her, knew that the hand that had just caressed him was clenched and quivering.

VIII

HER SIMPLE DUTY

Priscilla left a hastily scribbled note for Carfax in Froggy's keeping. In it she explained that she was obliged to go to town, but that she would meet him there any day before noon at any place that he would appoint. Froggy was to be the medium of his communication also.

She made no mention of Carfax to her father. He had hurt her far too deeply for any confidence to be possible. Moreover, it seemed to her that she had no right to speak until Carfax himself gave her leave.

She did not see her stepmother till the following day. The greeting between them was of the coolest, though Lady Raffold, being triumphant, sought to infuse a little sentiment into hers.

"I am really worn out, Priscilla," she said. "It is my turn now to have a little rest. I am going to leave all the hard work to you. It will be such a relief."

Three days later, however, she relinquished this attitude. Priscilla was summoned to her room, where she was breakfasting, and found her in great excitement.

"My dear child, he has arrived. He has actually arrived, and is staying at the Ritz. He must come and dine with us to-morrow night. It will be quite an informal affair - only thirty - so it can easily be managed. He must take you in, Priscilla; and, oh, my dear, do remember that it is the great opportunity of your life, and it mustn't be thrown away, whatever happens! Your father has set his heart upon it."

"Are you talking about Mr. Cochrane?" asked Priscilla.

"To be sure. Who else? Now don't put on that far-away look, pray! You know what is, after all, your simple duty, and I trust you mean to do it. You can't be going to disappoint your father in this matter. And you really must marry soon Priscilla. It is getting serious. In fact, it worries me perpetually. By the way, here is a letter for you from Raffold. It must have got among mine by mistake. Mrs. Burrowes's handwriting, I imagine."

She was right. It was directed by Froggy, but Priscilla paled suddenly as she took it, realising that it contained an answer to her own urgent note.

Alone in her own room she opened it. The message was even briefer than hers had been: "Sweetheart, - At 11 A.M., on Thursday, under the dome of St. Paul's Cathedral. - I am thine, J. C."

Priscilla stood for long seconds with the note in her hand. It had reached her too late. The appointment had been for the day before. She turned to the envelope, and saw that it must have been lying among her stepmother's correspondence for two days. Doubtless he had waited for her at the trysting-place, and waited in vain.

Only one thing remained to be done, and that was to telegraph to Froggy for Carfax's address. But Froggy's answer, when it came, was only another disappointment:

"Address not known. Did you not receive letter I forwarded?" Reluctantly Priscilla realised that there was nothing for it but patience. Carfax would almost certainly write again through Froggy.

That he had not her address she knew, for Froggy was under a solemn vow to reveal nothing, but she would not believe that he would regard her failure to keep tryst as a deliberate effort to snub him, though the fear that he might do so haunted and grew upon her all through the day.

She went to a theatre that night, and later to a dance, but neither entertainment served to lift the deadening weight from her spirits. She was miserable, and the four hours she subsequently spent in bed brought her no relief.

She rose at last in sheer desperation, and went for an early ride in the Park. She met a few acquaintances, but she shook them off. She wanted to be alone.

When she was returning, however, her youthful admirer, Lord Harfield, attached himself to her, refusing to be discouraged.

"I met your cousin at the Club yesterday," he told her.

"What is he like?" Priscilla asked, without much interest.

"Oh, haven't you seen him yet? A very queer fish, with a twang you could cut with a knife. Don't think you'll like him," said Lord Harfield, who was jealous of every man who so much as bowed to Priscilla.

Priscilla smiled faintly.

"I don't think so, either," she said. "You are coming to dine with us to-night, aren't you? He will be there too."

"Will he? I say, what a bore for you! Yes, I'm coming. I'll do my best to help you," the boy assured her eagerly.

And again Priscilla smiled. She was quite sure that she would be bored, whatever happened, though she was too kind-hearted to say so.

THE COMING OF HER HERO

"I wonder why Priscilla has put on that severely plain attire? It makes her look almost ugly," sighed Lady Raffold. "And how dreadfully pale she is to-night! Really, I have never seen her look more unattractive."

She turned with her most dazzling smile to receive the American Ambassador, and no one could have guessed that under her smile was real anger, because her stepdaughter was gracing the occasion in a robe of sombre black.

All the guests had arrived with the exception of Ralph Cochrane, the heir-apparent, as Priscilla styled him, and Lady Raffold chatted with one eye on the door. It was too bad of the young man to be late.

She was just giving him up in despair, and preparing to proceed to the dining-room without him, when his name was announced. Lord Raffold went forward to meet him. Priscilla, sitting on a lounge with Lord Harfield's mother, caught the sound of a soft, leisurely voice apologising; and something tightened suddenly at her heart, and held its beating. It was a voice she knew.

As through a mist, she looked across the great room, with its many lights, its buzz of careless voices. And suddenly, it seemed to her, she was back in the little village church at Raffold, furtively watching a stranger who stood in the entrance, and searched with level scrutiny quite deliberately and frankly till he found her.

Their eyes met, and her heart thrilled responsively as an instrument thrills to the hand of a skilled player.

Almost involuntarily she rose. There was some mistake. She

knew there must be some mistake. She felt that in some fashion it rested with her to explain and to justify his presence there.

But in that instant his eyes left her, and the magnetism that compelled her died swiftly down. She saw him shake hands with Lady Raffold, and bow to the Ambassador.

Then came her stepmother's quick, beckoning glance, and she moved forward in response to it. She was quivering from head to foot, bewildered, in some subtle fashion afraid.

"My dear, your cousin. He will take you in. Ralph, this is Priscilla."

It was sublimely informal. Lady Raffold had rehearsed that introduction several times. It was half the battle that the young man should feel himself one of the family from the outset.

Priscilla grabbed at her self-control, and managed to bow. But the next instant his hand, strong, warm, reassuring, grasped hers.

"Curious, isn't it?" the quiet voice asked. "We can't be strangers, you and I."

The grip of his fingers was close and intimate. It was as if he appealed for her support.

With an effort she forced herself to respond:

"Of course not. It must be quite five years since our first meeting." He looked at her oddly, quizzically, as he offered his arm.

"Why, yes," he drawled, as they began to move towards the door. "Should auld acquaintance be forgot? It is exactly five years ago to-day."

X

THE STORY OF A FRAUD

"Funny, wasn't it, sweetheart?"

The soft voice reached her through a buzz of other louder voices. Priscilla moved slightly, but she did not turn her head.

"You will have to explain," she said. "I don't understand anything yet."

"Nor I," came the quiet retort. "It's the woman's privilege to explain first, isn't it?"

Against her will, the blood rose in her face. She threw him a quick glance.

"I can't possibly explain anything here," she said.

He met her look with steady eyes.

"Let me tell you the story of a fraud," he said; and proceeded without further preliminary. "There was once a man - a second son, without prospects and without fame - who had the good fortune to do a service to a woman. He went away immediately afterwards lest he should make a fool of himself, for she was miles above his head, anyway. But he never forgot her. The mischief was done, so far as he was concerned."

He broke off, and raised his champagne to his lips as if he drank to a memory.

Priscilla was listening, but her eyes were downcast. She wore the old, absent look that her stepmother always deprecated. The soft drawl at her side continued, every syllable distinct and measured.

Ethel M. Dell

"Years passed, and things changed. The man had belonged to a cadet branch of an aristocratic British family. But one heir after another died, till only he was left to inherit. The woman belonged to the older branch of the family, but, being a woman, she was passed over. A time came when he was invited by the head of the house to go and see his inheritance. He would have gone at once and gladly, but for a hint at the end of the letter to the effect that, if he would do his part, what the French shamelessly call a *mariage de convenance* might be arranged between his cousin and himself - an arrangement advantageous to them both from a certain point of view. He didn't set up for a paragon of morality. Perhaps even, had things been a little different, he might have been willing. As it was, he didn't like the notion, and he jibbed." He paused. "But for all that," he said, his voice yet quieter and more deliberate, "he wanted the woman, if he could make her care for him. That was his difficulty. He had a feeling all along that the thing must be an even greater offence to her than it was to him. He worried it all through, and at last he worked out a scheme for them both. He called himself by an old school *alias*, and came to her as a stranger -

"You're not eating anything, sweetheart. Wouldn't it be as well, just for decency's sake? There's a comic ending to this story, so you mustn't be sad. Who's that boy scowling at me on the other side of the table? What's the matter with the child?"

"Never mind," murmured Priscilla hastily. "He doesn't mean anything. Please go on."

He began to laugh at her with gentle ridicule.

"Impatient for the third act? Well, the scheme worked all right. But it so chanced that the woman decided to be subtle, too. She knew him for an old friend the instant she saw him. But he pretended to have forgotten that old affair in New York. He didn't want her to feel in any way under an obligation. So he played the humble stranger, and she - sweetheart - she played the simple, country maiden, and she did it to perfection. I think, you know, that she was a little afraid her name and title would frighten him away."

"And so he humoured her?" said Priscilla, a slight quiver in her deep voice.

"They humoured each other, sweetheart. That was where it began to be funny. Now I am going to get you to tell me the rest of the story."

She turned towards him again, her face very pale.

"Yes; it's very funny, no doubt - funny for the man, I mean; for the woman, I am not so sure. How does she know that he really cared for her from the beginning; that he was always quite honest in his motive? How can she possibly know this?"

Again for a moment their eyes met. There was no hint of dismay in the man's brown face.

"She does know it, sweetheart," he answered, with confidence. "I can't tell you how. Probably she couldn't, either. He was going to explain everything, you know, under the dome of St. Paul's Cathedral. But for some reason it didn't come off. He spent three solid hours waiting for her, but she didn't come. She had found him out, perhaps? And was angry?"

"Perhaps," said Priscilla, her voice very low.

Again he raised his glass to his lips.

"We will have the end of the story presently," he said; and deliberately turned to his left-hand neighbour.

Ethel M. Dell

XI

THE END OF THE STORY

A musical *soiree* was to follow that interminable dinner, and for a time Priscilla was occupied in helping Lady Raffold to receive the after-dinner guests. She longed to escape before the contingent from the dining-room arrived upstairs, but she soon realised the impossibility of this. Her stepmother seemed to want her at every turn, and when at length she found herself free, young Lord Harfield appeared at her elbow.

It was intolerable. She turned upon him without pity.

"Oh, please," she said, "I've dropped my fan in the dining-room or on the stairs. Would you be so kind -"

He departed, not suspecting her of treachery; and she slipped forthwith into a tiny conservatory behind the piano. It was her only refuge. She could but hope that no one had seen her retire thither. Her need for solitude just then was intense. She felt herself physically incapable of facing the crowd in the music-room any longer. The first crashing chords of the piano covered her retreat. She shut herself softly in, and sank into the only chair the little place contained.

Her mind was a chaos of conflicting emotions. Anger, disappointment, and an almost insane exultation fought together for the mastery. She longed to be rational, to think the matter out quietly and impartially, and decide how to treat it. But her most determined efforts were vain. The music disturbed her. She felt as if the chords were hammering upon her brain. Yet when it suddenly ceased, the unexpected silence was almost harder to bear.

In the buzz of applause that ensued, the door behind her opened, and a man entered.

She heard the click of the key in the lock, and turned sharply to protest. But the words died on her lips, for there was that in his brown, resolute face that silenced her. She became suddenly breathless and quivering before him, as she had been that day on the down when he had taken her into his arms.

He withdrew the key, and dropped it into her lap.

"Open if you will," he said, in the quiet voice, half tender, half humorous, that she had come to know so well. "I am closely followed by the infant with the scowl."

Priscilla sat silent in her chair. What could she say to him?

"Well?" he said, after a moment. "The end of the story - is it written yet?"

She shook her head dumbly. Curiously, the throbbing anger had left her heart at the mere sound of his voice.

He waited for about three seconds, then knelt quietly down beside her.

"Say," he drawled, "I kind of like Raffold Abbey, sweetheart. Wouldn't it be nice to spend our honeymoon there? Do you think they would let us?" He laid his hand upon both of hers. "Wouldn't it be good?" he said softly. "I should think there would be room for two, eh, sweetheart?"

With an effort she sought to withstand him before he wholly dominated her.

"And every one will call it a *mariage de convenance*!"

"Let them!" he answered, with suppressed indifference. "I reckon we shall have the laugh. But it isn't so unusual, you know. Americans always fall in love at first sight."

He was unanswerable. He was sublime. She marvelled that she

Ethel M. Dell

could have ever even attempted to resist him.

With a sudden, tremulous laugh, she caught his hand to her, holding it fast.

"Not Americans only!" she said. And swiftly, passionately, she bent and pressed her lips to the red, seared scar upon her hero's wrist.

THE EXAMPLE

"And the fourth angel poured out his vial upon the sun; and power was given unto him to scorch men with fire. And men were scorched with great heat, and blasphemed the name of God, which hath power over these plagues; and they repented not to give Him glory."

The droning voice quivered and fell silent. Within the hospital tent, only the buzz of flies innumerable was audible. Without, there sounded near at hand the squeak of a sentry's boots, and in the distance the clatter of the camp.

The man who lay dying was in a remote and quite detached sense aware of these things, but his fevered imagination had carried him beyond. He watched, as it were, the glowing pictures that came and went in his furnace of pain. These little details were to him but the distant humming of the spinning-wheel of time from which he was drawing ever farther and farther away. They did not touch that inner consciousness with which he saw his visions.

Now and then he turned his head sharply on the pillow, as an alien might turn at the sound of a familiar voice, but always, after listening intently, it came back to its old position, and the man's restless eyes returned to the crack high up in the tent canvas through which the sun shone upon him like a piercing eye.

The occupant of the bed next to him watched him furtively,

Ethel M. Dell

fascinated but uneasy. He was a young soldier of the simple country type, and the wild words that came now and again from the fevered lips startled him uncomfortably. He wished the dying man would cease his mutterings and let him sleep. But every time the prolonged silence seemed to indicate a final cessation of the nuisance, the droning voice took up the tale once more.

"And men were scorched with great heat - and they repented not - repented not."

A soft-stepping native orderly moved to the bedside and paused. Instantly the wandering words were hushed.

"Bring me some water, Sammy," the same voice said huskily. "If you can't take the sun out of the sky, you can give me a drink."

The native shook his head.

"The doctor will come soon," he said soothingly. "Have patience."

Patience! The word had no meaning for him in that inferno of suffering. He moved his head, that searching spot of sunlight dancing in his eyes, and cursed deep in his throat the man who kept him waiting.

Barely a minute later the doctor came - a quiet, bronzed man, level-eyed and strong. He bent over the stricken figure on the bed, and drew the tumbled covering up a little higher. He had just written "mortally wounded" of this man on his hospital report, but there was nothing in his manner to indicate that he had no hope for him.

"Get another pillow," he said to the native orderly. And to the dying man: "That will take the sun out of your eyes. I see it is bothering you."

"Curse the sun!" the parched lips gasped. "Can't you give me a drink?"

The eyes of the young soldier in the next bed scanned the doctor's face anxiously. He, too, wanted a drink. He thirsted from the depths of his soul. But he knew there was no water to be had. The supply had been cut off hours before.

"No," the doctor said gravely. "I can't give it you yet. By-and-bye, perhaps -"

"By-and-bye!" There was a dreadful sound like laughter in the husky voice.

The doctor laid a restraining hand on the man's chest.

"Hush!" he said, in a lower tone. "It's this sort of thing that shows what a fellow is made of. All these other poor chaps are children. But you, Ford, you are grown up, so to speak. I look to you to help me, - to set the example."

"Example! Man alive!" A queer light danced like a mocking spirit in Private Ford's eyes, and again he laughed - an exceeding bitter laugh. "I've been made an example of all my life," he said. "I've sometimes thought it was what I was created for. Ah, thanks!" he added in a different tone, as the doctor raised him on the extra pillow. "You're a brick, sir! Sit down a minute, will you? I want to talk to you."

The doctor complied, his hand on the wounded man's wrist.

"That's better," Ford said. "Keep it there. And stop me if I rave. It's a queer little world, isn't it? I remember you well, but you wouldn't know me. You were one of the highfliers, and I was always more or less of an earthworm. But you'll remember Rotherby, the captain of the first eleven? A fine chap - that. He's dead now, eh?"

"Yes," the doctor said, "Rotherby's dead."

He was looking with an intent scrutiny at the scarred and bandaged face on the pillow. He had felt from the first that this man was no ordinary ranker. Yet till that moment it had never occurred to him that they might have met before.

"I always liked Rotherby," the husky voice went on. "He was a big swell, and he didn't think much of small fry. But you - you and he were friends, weren't you?"

"For a time," the doctor said. "It didn't last."

There was regret in his voice - the keen regret of a man who has lost a thing he valued.

"No; it didn't last," Ford agreed. "I remember when you chucked him. Or was it the other way round? I saw a good deal of him in those days. I thought him a jolly good fellow, till I found out what a scoundrel he was. And I had a soft feeling for him even then. You knew he was a scoundrel, didn't you?"

"Yes, I knew."

The doctor spoke reluctantly. The hospital tent, the silent row of wounded men, the stifling atmosphere, the flies, all were gone from his inner vision. He was looking with grave, compassionate eyes at the picture that absorbed the man at his side.

"He was good company, eh?" the restless voice went on. "But he had his black moments. I didn't know him so well in the days when you and he were friends."

"Nor I," the doctor said. "But - why do you want to talk of him?"

Again he was searching the face at his side with grave intensity. It did not seem to him that this man could ever have been of the sort that his friend Rotherby would have cared to admit to terms of intimacy. Rotherby - notwithstanding his sins - had been fastidious in many ways.

The answer seemed to make the matter more comprehensible.

"I was with him when he died," the man said. "It was in just such an inferno as this. We were alone together, looking for gold in the Australian desert. We didn't find it, though it was there, mountains of it. The water gave out. We tossed for the last drain - and I won. That was how Rotherby came to die. He hadn't much to live for, and he was going to die, anyhow. A queer chap, he was. He and his wife never lived together after the smash came, and he had to leave the country. Perhaps you knew?"

"Yes," the doctor said again, "I knew."

Ford moved his head restlessly.

"The thought of her used to worry him in the night," he said. "I've known him lie for hours not sleeping, just staring up at the stars, and thinking, thinking. I've sometimes thought that the worst torture on earth can't equal that. You know, after he was dead, they found her miniature on him - a thing in a gold case, with their names engraved inside. He used to wear it round his neck like a charm. It was by that they identified him - that and his signet-ring, and one or two letters. Scamp though I was, I had the grace not to rob the dead. They sent the things to his wife. I've often wondered what she did with them."

"I can tell you that," said the doctor quietly. "She keeps them among her greatest treasures."

Ford turned sharply on his pillows, and stifled an exclamation of pain.

"You know her still, then?" he said.

"She is my wife," the doctor answered.

A long silence followed his words. The wounded soldier lay with closed eyes and drawn brows. He seemed to be unconscious of everything save physical pain.

Suddenly he seemed to recover himself, and looked up.

"You," he said slowly, "you are Montagu Durant, the fellow she was engaged to before she married Rotherby."

The doctor bent his head.

"Yes," he said. "I am Montagu Durant."

"Rotherby's friend," Ford went on. "The chap who stuck to him through thick and thin - to be betrayed in the end. I know all about you, you see, though you haven't placed me yet."

"No, I can't place you," Durant said. "I don't think we ever knew each other very well. You will have to tell me who you are."

"Later - later," said Ford. "No, you never knew me very well. It was always you and Rotherby, you and Rotherby. You never looked at any one else, till that row at the 'Varsity when he got kicked out. Yes," with a sudden, sharp sigh, "I was a 'Varsity man too. I admired Leonard Rotherby in those days. Poor old Leo! He knew how to hit a boundary as well as any fellow! You never forgave him, I suppose, for marrying your girl?"

There was a pause, and the fevered eyes sought Durant's face. The answer came at length very slowly.

"I could have forgiven him," Durant said, "if he had stuck to her and made her happy."

"Ah! There came the rub. But did Rotherby ever stick to anything? It was a jolly good thing he died - for all concerned. Yet, you know, he cared for her to the last. Blackguard as he was, he carried her in his heart right up to his death. I tell you

I was with him, and I know."

There was strong insistence in the man's words. Durant could feel the racing pulse leap and quiver under his hand. He leaned forward a little, looking closely into the drawn face.

"I think you have talked enough," he said. "Try to get some rest."

"I haven't raved," said Ford, with confidence. "It has done me good to talk. I can't help thinking of Leo Rotherby. My brain runs on him. He wanted to see you - horribly - before he died. I believe he'd have asked your forgiveness. But you wouldn't have given it to him, I suppose? You will never forgive him in your heart?"

Again the answer did not come at once. Durant was frowning a little - the frown of a man who tries to fathom his own secret impulses.

"I think," he said at last, "that if I had seen him and he had asked for it, I should not have refused my forgiveness."

"No one ever refused Rotherby anything," said the dying man, with a curious, half-humorous twist of his mouth under its dark moustache.

"Except yourself," Durant reminded him, almost involuntarily.

Again the wandering, uneasy eyes sought his. "You mean - that drain of water," Ford said, with a total lack of shame or remorse. "Yes, it's true Rotherby didn't have that. But it didn't make any difference, you know. He was going to die. And the living come before the dead, eh, doctor?"

Durant did not quite understand his tone, but he suffered the words to go unchallenged. He was not there to discuss the higher morality with a dying man. Moreover, he knew that the bare mention of water was a fiery torture to him, disguise it as

Ethel M. Dell

he might.

He sat a little longer, then rose to go. He fancied that there was a shade less of restlessness about this man, whom he knew to be suffering what no other man in the tent could have endured in silence.

In response to a sign he stooped to catch a few, low-spoken words.

"By-and-bye," said Private Ford, with husky self-assurance, "when it's dark - or only moonlight - a man will creep out between the lines and crawl down to the river, to get some water for - the children."

He was wandering again, Durant saw; and his pity mounted high.

"Perhaps, poor fellow; perhaps," he answered gently.

As he went away he heard again the droning, unconscious voice:

"And power was given unto him to scorch men with fire. And men were scorched - with great heat. Eh, Sammy? Is that water you have there? Quick! Give me - what? There is none? Then why the - why the -" There came an abrupt pause; then a brief, dry chuckle that was like the crackling of flame through dead twigs. "Ah, I forgot. I mustn't curse. I've got to set the example to these children. But, O God, the heat and the flies!"

Durant wondered if after all it had been a kindness to call back the passing spirit that had begun to forget.

*　*　*　*　*

Slowly the scorching day wore away, till evening descended in a blaze of gorgeous colouring upon the desolate African wilderness and the band of men that had been surrounded and cut off by a wily enemy.

They were expecting relief. Hourly they expected it, but, being hampered by a score of wounded, it was not possible for them to break through the thickly populated scrub unassisted. And they had no water.

A stream flowed, brown and sluggish, not more than a hundred yards below the camp. But that same stream was flanked on the farther side by a long, black line of thicket that poured forth fire upon any man who ventured out from behind the great rocks that protected the camp.

It had been attempted again and again, for the needs of the wounded were desperate. But each effort had been disastrous, and at last an order had gone forth that no man was to expose himself again to this deadly risk.

So, silent behind their entrenchments, with the hospital tent in their midst, the British force had to endure the situation, waiting with a dogged patience for the coming of their comrades who could not be far away.

Regal to the last, the sun sank away in orange and gold; and night, burning, majestic, shimmering, spread over a cloudless sky. A full moon floated up behind dense forest trees, and shed a glimmering radiance everywhere. The heat did not seem to vary by a breath.

A great restlessness spread like a wave through the hospital tent. Men waked from troubled slumber, crying aloud like children, piteously, unreasoningly, for water.

The doctor went from one to another, restraining, soothing, reassuring. His influence made itself felt, and quiet returned; but it was a quiet that held no peace; it was the silent gripping of an agony that was bound to overcome.

Again and again through the crawling hours the bitter protest

Ethel M. Dell

broke out afresh, like the crying of souls in torment. One or two became delirious and had to be forcibly restrained from struggling forth in search of that which alone could still their torture.

Durant was too fully occupied with these raving patients of his to spare any attention for the bed in the far corner on which they had laid the one man whose injuries were mortal. If he thought of the man at all, it was to reflect that he was probably dead.

But at last a young officer entered the seething tent, and touched him on the shoulder.

"Can you come outside a moment? You're wanted," he said.

Durant turned from a man who was lying exhausted and barely conscious, took up his case, and followed him out. He did just glance at the bed in the corner as he went, but he saw no movement there.

His summoner turned upon him abruptly as they emerged.

"Look here," he said. "There's a water-bag quite full, waiting for those poor beggars in there. Better send one of the orderlies for it."

"Water!" said Durant sharply, as if the news were difficult to believe. Then, recovering himself: "Tell the sentry, will you? I can't spare an orderly."

The young officer complied, and hurried him on.

"The poor chap is breathing his last," he said. "You can't do him any good, but he wants you."

"Who is it?" asked the doctor.

"The man who fetched the water - Ford. He was badly

wounded when he started. He crawled every inch of the way on his stomach, and back again, dragging the bag with him. Heaven knows how he did it! It's taken him hours."

"Ford?" the doctor said incredulously. "Ford? Impossible! How did he get away?"

"Oh, he crawled through somehow; Heaven only knows how! But he's done now, poor beggar - pegging out fast. We got him into shelter, but we couldn't do more, he was in such agony."

The speaker stopped, for Durant had broken into a run. The moonlight showed him a group of men gathered about a prone figure. They separated and stood aside as he reached them; and he, kneeling, found in the prone figure the man who had talked with him in the afternoon of the friend who had played him false.

He was very far gone, lying in a dreadful twisted heap, his head, with its bloodstained bandages, resting on his arm. Yet Durant saw that he still lived, and tried with gentle hands to ease the strain of his position.

With a sharp gasp, Ford opened his eyes.

"Hullo!" he said. "It's you, is it? Did they get the water?"

"They have got it by now," the doctor answered.

"Ah!" The man's lips twisted in a difficult smile. He struggled bravely to keep the mortal agony out of his face. "Gave you the slip that time," he gasped. "Disobeyed orders, too. But it didn't matter - except for example. You must tell them, eh? Dying men have privileges."

"Tell him he'd have had the V. C. for it," whispered the officer in command, over the doctor's shoulder.

Ethel M. Dell

Durant complied, and caught the quick gleam that shot up in the dying eyes at his words.

"The gods were always behind time - with me," came the husky whisper. "I used to think I'd scale Olympus, but - they kicked me down. If - if there's any water to spare, when it's gone round, I - I -"

He broke off with a rending cough. Some one put a tin cup into the doctor's hand, and he held it to the parched lips. Ford drank in great gulps, and, as he drank, the worst agony passed. His limbs relaxed after the draught, and he lay quite still, his face to the sky.

After the passage of minutes he spoke again suddenly. His voice was no longer husky, but clear and strong. His eyes were the eyes of a man who sees a vision.

"Jove!" he said. "What a princely gathering to see me carry out my bat! Don't grin, you fellows. I know it was a fluke - a dashed fine fluke, too. But it's what I always meant, after all. There's good old Monty, yelling himself hoarse in the pavilion. And his girl - waving. Sweet girl, too - the best in the world. I might cut him out there. But I won't, I won't! I'm not such a hound as that, though she's the only woman in the world, bless her, bless her!"

He stopped. Durant was bending over him, listening eagerly, as one might listen to the voice of an old, familiar friend, heard again after many years.

He did not speak. He seemed afraid to dispel the other's dream. But after a moment, the man in his arms made a sudden, impulsive movement towards him. It was almost like a gesture of affection. And their eyes met.

There followed a brief silence that had in it something of strain. Then Ford uttered a shaky laugh. The vision had passed.

"So - you see - he had to die - anyhow," he said. "My love to - your wife, dear old Monty! Tell her - I'm - awfully - pleased!"

His voice ceased, yet for a moment his lips still seemed to form words.

Durant stooped lower over him, and spoke at last with a sort of urgent tenderness.

"Leo!" he said. "Leo, old chap!"

But there came no answer save a faint, still smile. The man he called had passed beyond his reach.

*   *   *   *   *

Relief came to the beleaguered force at daybreak, and the worst incident of the campaign ended without disaster. A casualty list, published in the London papers a few days later, contained an announcement, which concerned nobody who read it, to the effect that Private Ford, of a West African Regiment, had succumbed to his wounds.

Ethel M. Dell

THE FRIEND WHO STOOD BY

"And you will come back, Jim? Promise! Promise!"

"Of course, darling - of course! There! Don't cry! Can't you see it's a chance in a thousand? I've never had such a chance before."

The sound of a woman's low sobbing was audible in the silence that followed; and a man who was leaning on the sea-wall above, started and peered downwards.

He could dimly discern two figures standing in the shadow of a great breakwater below him. More than that he could not distinguish, for it was a dark night; but he knew that the man's arms were about the girl, and that her face was hidden against him.

Realising himself to be an intruder, he stood up and began to walk away.

He had not gone a dozen yards before the sound of flying feet caught his attention, and he turned his head. A woman's light figure was running behind him along the deserted parade. He waited for her under a gas-lamp.

She overtook him and fled past him without a pause. He caught a glimpse of a pale face and fair hair in wild disorder.

Then she was gone again into the night, running swiftly. The darkness closed about her, and hid her from view.

The man on the parade paused for several seconds, then walked back to his original resting-place by the sea-wall.

The band on the pier was playing a jaunty selection from a comic opera. It came in gusts of gaiety. The wash of the sea, as it crept up the beach, was very mysterious and remote.

Below, on the piled shingle, a man stood alone, staring out over the darkness, motionless and absorbed.

The watcher above him struck a match at length and kindled a cigarette. His face was lit up during the operation. It was the face of a man who had seen a good deal of the world and had not found the experience particularly refreshing. Yet, as he looked down upon the silent figure below him, there was more of compassion than cynicism in his eyes. There was a glint of humour also, like the shrewd half-melancholy humour of a monkey that possesses the wisdom of all the ages, and can impart none of it.

Suddenly there was a movement on the shingle. The lonely figure had turned and flung itself face downwards among the tumbling stones. The abandonment of the action was very young, and perhaps it was that very fact that made it so indescribably pathetic. To Lester Cheveril, leaning on the sea-wall, it appealed as strongly as the crying of a child. He glanced over his shoulder. The place was deserted. Then he deliberately dropped his cigarette-case over the wall and exclaimed: "Confound it!"

The prone figure on the shingle rolled over and sat up.

"Hullo!" said Cheveril.

There was a distinct pause before a voice replied: "Hullo! What's the matter?"

Ethel M. Dell

"I've dropped my cigarette-case," said Cheveril. "Beastly careless of me!"

Again there was a pause. Then the man below him stumbled to his feet.

"I've got a match," he said. "I'll see if I can find it."

"Don't trouble," said Cheveril politely. "The steps are close by."

He walked away at an easy pace and descended to the beach. The flicker of a match guided him to the searcher. As he drew near, the light went out, and the young man turned to meet him.

"Here it is," he said gruffly.

"Many thanks!" said Cheveril. "It's so confoundedly dark to-night. I scarcely expected to see it again."

The other muttered an acknowledgment, and stood prepared to depart.

Cheveril, however, paused in a conversational attitude. He had not risked his property for nothing.

"A pretty little place, this," he said. "I suppose you are a visitor here like myself?"

"I'm leaving to-morrow," was the somewhat grudging rejoinder.

"I only came this afternoon," said Cheveril. "Is there anything to see here?"

"There's the sea and the lighthouse," his companion told him curtly - "nothing else."

Cheveril smiled faintly to himself in the darkness.

"Try one of these cigarettes," he said sociably. "I don't enjoy smoking alone."

He was aware, as his unknown friend accepted the offer, that he would have infinitely preferred to refuse.

"Been here long?" he asked him, as they plunged through the shingle towards the sand.

"I've lived here nearly all my life," was the reply. And, after a moment, as if the confidence would not be repressed: "I'm leaving now - for good."

"Ah!" said Cheveril sympathetically. "It's pretty beastly when you come to turn out. I've done it, and I know."

"It's infernal," said the other gloomily, and relapsed into silence.

"Going abroad?" Cheveril ventured presently.

"Yes. Going to the other side of the world." Surliness had given place to depression in the boy's voice. Sympathy, albeit from an unknown quarter, moved him to confidence. "But it isn't that I mind," he said, a moment later. "I should be ready enough to clear out if it weren't for - some one else!"

"A woman, I suppose?" Cheveril said.

He was aware that his companion glanced at him sharply through the gloom, and knew that he was momentarily suspected of eavesdropping.

Then, with impulsive candour, the answer came:

"Yes; the girl I'm engaged to. She has got to stay behind and marry - some one else."

Cheveril's teeth closed silently upon his lower lip. This, also, was one of the things he knew.

"You can't trust her, then?" he said, after a pause.

"Oh, she cares for me - of course!" the boy answered. "But there isn't a chance for us. They are all dead against me, and the other fellow will be on the spot. He hasn't asked her yet, but he means to. And her people will simply force her to accept him when he does. Of course they will! He is Cheveril, the millionaire. You must have heard of him. Every one has."

"I know him well," said Cheveril.

"So do I - by sight," the boy plunged on recklessly - "an undersized little animal with a squint."

"I didn't know he squinted," Cheveril remarked into the darkness. "But, anyhow, they can't make her marry against her will."

"Can't they?" returned the other fiercely. "I don't know what you call it, then. They can make her life so positively unbearable that she will have to give in, if it is only to get away from them. It's perfectly fiendish; but they will do it. I know they will do it. She hasn't a single friend to stand by her."

"Except you," said Cheveril.

They had nearly reached the water. The rush and splash of the waves held something solemn in their harmonies, like the chords of a splendid symphony. Cheveril heard the quick, indignant voice at his side like a cry of unrest breaking through.

"What can I do?" it said. "I have never had a chance till now. I have just had a berth in India offered to me; but I can't possibly hope to support a wife for two years at least. And meanwhile - meanwhile -"

It stopped there; and a long wave broke with a roar, and rushed up in gleaming foam almost to their feet. The younger man stepped back; but Cheveril remained motionless, his face to the swirling water.

Quite suddenly at length he turned, as a man whose mind is made up, and began to walk back to the dimly lighted parade. He marched straight up the shingle, as if with a definite purpose in view, and mounted the rickety iron ladder to the pavement.

His companion followed, too absorbed by his trouble to feel any curiosity regarding the stranger to whom he had poured it out.

Under a flaring gas-lamp, Cheveril stood still.

"Do you mind telling me your name?" he said abruptly.

That roused the boy slightly. "My name is Willowby," he answered - "James Willowby."

He looked at Cheveril with a dawning wonder, and the latter uttered a short, grim laugh. The light streamed full upon his face.

"You know me well, don't you," he said, "by sight?"

Young Willowby gave a great start and turned crimson. He offered neither apology nor excuse.

"I like you for that," Cheveril said, after a moment. "Can you bring yourself to shake hands?"

There was unmistakable friendliness in his tone, and Willowby responded to it promptly. He was a sportsman at heart, however he might rail at circumstance.

As their hands met, he looked up with a queer, mirthless smile.

Ethel M. Dell

"I hope you are going to be good to her," he said.

"I am going to be good to you both," said Lester Cheveril quietly.

In the silence that followed his words, the band on the pier became audible on a sudden gust of wind. It was gaily jigging out the tune of "The Girl I Left Behind Me."

*   *   *   *   *

"What a secluded corner, Miss Harford! May I join you?"

Evelyn Harford looked up with a start of dismay. He was the last person in the world with whom she desired a *tete-a-tete*; but he was dining at her father's house, and she could not well refuse. Reluctantly she laid aside the paper on her knee.

"I thought you were playing bridge," she said, in a chilly tone.

"I cried off," said Cheveril.

He stood looking down at her with shrewd, kindly eyes. But the girl was too intent upon making her escape to notice his expression.

"Won't you go to the billiard-room?" she said. "They are playing pool."

He shook his head.

"I came here expressly to talk to you," he said.

"Oh!" said Evelyn.

She leaned back in her chair, and tried to appear at her ease; but her heart was thumping tumultuously. The man was going to propose, she knew - she knew; and she was not ready for him. She felt that she would break down ignominiously if he pressed his suit just then.

Cheveril, however, seemed in no hurry. He sat down facing her, and there followed a pause, during which she felt that he was studying her attentively.

Growing desperate at length, she looked him in the face, and spoke.

"I am not a very lively companion to-night, Mr. Cheveril," she said. "That is why I came away from the rest."

There was more of appeal in her voice than she intended; and, realising it, she coloured deeply, and looked away again. He was just the sort of man to avail himself of a moment's weakness, she told herself, with rising agitation. Those shrewd eyes of his missed nothing.

But Cheveril gave no sign of having observed her distress. He maintained his silence for some seconds longer. Then, somewhat abruptly, he broke it.

"I didn't follow you in order to be amused, Miss Harford," he said. "The fact is, I have a confession to make to you, and a favour to ask. And I want you to be good enough to hear me out before you try to answer. May I count on this?"

The dry query did more to quiet her perturbation than any solicitude. She was quite convinced that he meant to propose to her, but his absence of ardour was an immense relief. If he would only be businesslike and not sentimental, she felt that she could bear it.

"Yes, I will listen," she said, facing him with more self-possession than she had been able to muster till that moment. "But I shall want a fair hearing, too - afterwards."

A faint smile flickered across Cheveril's face.

Ethel M. Dell

"I shall want to listen to you," he said. "The confession is this: Last night I went down to the parade to smoke. It was very dark. I don't know exactly what attracted me. I came upon two people saying good-bye on the beach. One of them - a woman - was crying."

He paused momentarily. The girl's face had frozen into set lines of composure. It looked like a marble mask. Her eyes met his with an assumption of indifference that scarcely veiled the desperate defiance behind.

"When does the confession begin?" she asked him, with a faint laugh that sounded tragic in spite of her.

He leaned forward, scrutinising her with a wisdom that seemed to pierce every barrier of conventionality and search her very soul.

"It begins now," he said. "She came up on to the parade immediately after, and I waited under a lamp to get a glimpse of her. I saw her face, Miss Harford. I knew her instantly." The girl's eyes flickered a little, and she bit her lip. She was about to speak, but he stopped her with sudden authority. "No, don't answer!" he said. "Hear me out. I waited till she was gone, and then I joined the young fellow on the beach. He was in the mood for a sympathetic listener, and I drew him out. He told me practically everything - how he himself was going to India and had to leave the girl behind, how her people disapproved of him, and how she was being worked upon by means little short of persecution to induce her to marry an outsider on the wrong side of forty, with nothing to recommend him but the size of his banking account. He added that she had not a single friend to stand by and make things easier for her. It was that, Miss Harford, that decided me to take this step. I can't see a woman driven against her will; anything in the world sooner than that. And here comes my request. You want a friend to help you. Let me be that friend. There is a way out of this difficulty if you will but take it. Since I got you into it, it is only fair that I should be the one to help you out. This is not a proposal of marriage, though it may sound like one."

He ended with a smile that was perfectly friendly and kind.

The rigid look had completely passed from the girl's face. She was listening with a curious blend of eagerness and reluctance. Her cheeks were burning; her eyes like stars.

"I am so thankful to hear you say that," she said, drawing a deep breath.

"Shall I go on?" said Cheveril.

She hesitated; and very quietly he held out his hand to her.

"In the capacity of a friend," he said gravely.

And Evelyn Harford put her hand into his with the confidence of a child. It was strange to feel her prejudice against this man evaporate at a touch. It made her oddly unsure of herself. He was the last person in the world to whom she would have voluntarily turned for help.

"Don't be startled by what I am going to say," Cheveril said. "It may strike you as an eccentric suggestion, but there is nothing in it to alarm you. Young Willowby tells me that it will take him two years to make a home for you, and meanwhile your life is to be made a martyrdom on my account. Will you put your freedom in my hands for that two years? In other words, will you consider yourself engaged to me for just so long as his absence lasts? It will save you endless trouble and discomfort, and harm no one. When Willowby comes back, I shall hand you over to him, and your happiness will be secured. Think it over, and don't be scared. You will find me quite easy to manage. In any case, I am a friend you can trust, remember, even though I have got the face of a baboon."

So, with absolute quietness, he made his proposal; and Evelyn,

Ethel M. Dell

amazed and incredulous, heard him out in silence. At his last words she gave a quick laugh that sounded almost hysterical.

"Oh, don't," she said - "don't! You make me feel so ashamed."

Cheveril's face was suddenly quizzical.

"There is nothing to be ashamed of," he said. "I take all the responsibility, and it would give me very great pleasure to help you."

"But I couldn't do such a thing!" she protested. "I couldn't!"

"Listen!" said Cheveril. "I am off for a yachting trip in the Pacific in a week, and I give you my word of honour not to return for nine months, at least. Will that make it easier for you?"

"I am not thinking of myself," she told him, with vehemence. "Of course, it would make everything right for me, so long as Jim knew. But I must think of you, too. I must -"

"You needn't," Cheveril said gently; "you needn't. I have asked to be allowed to stand by you, to have the great privilege of calling myself your friend in need. I am romantic enough to like to see a love affair go the right way. It is for my pleasure, if you care to regard it from that point of view." He paused, and into his eyes there came a queer, watchful expression - the look of a man who hazards much, yet holds himself in check. Then he smiled at her with baffling humour.

"Don't refuse me my opportunity, Miss Harford," he said. "I know I am eccentric, but I assure you I can be a staunch friend to those I like."

Evelyn had risen, and as he ended he also got to his feet. He knew that she was studying him with all her woman's keenness of perception. But the game was in his hands, and he realised it. He was no longer afraid of the issue.

"You offer me this out of friendship?" she said at last.

He watched her fingers nervously playing with a bracelet on her wrist.

"Exactly," he said.

Her eyes met his resolutely.

"Mr. Cheveril," she said (and though she spoke quietly, it was with an effort), "I want you, please, to answer just one question. You have been shown all the cards; but there must - there shall be - fair play, in spite of it."

Her voice rang a little. The bracelet suddenly slipped from her hand and fell to the floor. Cheveril stooped and picked it up. He held it as he made reply.

"Yes," he said, "I like fair play, too."

"Then you will tell me the truth?" she said, holding out her hand for her property. "I want to know if - if you were really going to ask me to marry you before this happened?"

He looked at her with raised eyebrows. Then he took the extended hand.

"Of course I was!" he said simply. She drew back a little, but Cheveril showed no discomfiture. "You see, I'm getting on in life," he said, in a patriarchal tone. "No doubt it was rank presumption on my part to imagine myself in any way suited to you; but I thought it would be nice to have a young wife to look after me. And you know the proverb about 'an old man's darling.' I believe I rather counted on that."

Again he looked quizzical; but the girl was not satisfied.

"That's ridiculous!" she said. "You talk as if you were fifty years older than you are. It may be funny, but it isn't strictly honest."

Cheveril laughed.

"I know what you mean," he said. "But really I'm not being funny. And I am telling you the simple truth when I say that all sentimental nonsense was knocked out of me long ago, when the girl I cared for ran away with a good-looking beast in the Army. Also, I am quite honest when I assure you that I would rather be your trusted friend and accomplice than your rejected suitor. By Jove, I seem to be asking a good deal of you!"

"No, don't laugh," she said quickly, almost as if something in his careless speech had pained her. "We must look at the matter from every stand-point before - before we take any action. Suppose you really did want to marry some one? Suppose you fell in love again? What then?"

"What then?" said Cheveril. And, though he was obligingly serious, she felt that somehow, somewhere, he was tricking her. "I should have to ask you to release me in that event. But I don't think it's very likely that will happen. I'm not so impressionable as I was."

She looked at him doubtfully. Obviously he was not in love with her, yet she was uneasy. She had a curious sense of loss, of disappointment, which even Jim's departure had not created in her.

"I don't feel that I am doing right," she said finally.

"I am quite unscrupulous," said Cheveril lightly. "Moreover, there is no harm to any one in the transaction. Your life is your own. No one else has the right to order it for you. It seems to me that in this matter you need to consider yourself alone."

"And you," she said, in a troubled tone.

He surprised her an instant later by thrusting a friendly hand through her arm.

"Come!" he said, smiling down at her. "Let us go and announce the good news!"

And so she yielded to him, and went.

$$* \quad * \quad * \quad * \quad *$$

The news of Evelyn Harford's engagement to Lester Cheveril was no great surprise to any one. It leaked out through private sources, it being understood that no public announcement was to be made till the marriage should be imminent. And as Cheveril had departed in his yacht to the Pacific very shortly after his proposal, there seemed small likelihood of the union taking place that year.

Meanwhile, her long battle over, Evelyn prepared herself to enjoy her hard-earned peace. Her father no longer poured hurricanes of wrath upon her for her obduracy. Her mother's bitter reproaches had wholly ceased. The home atmosphere had become suddenly calm and sunny. The eldest daughter of the house had done her obvious duty, and the family was no longer shaken and upset by internal tumult.

But the peace was only on the surface so far as Evelyn was concerned. Privately, she was less at peace than she had ever been, and that not on her own account or on Jim Willowby's. Every letter she received from the man who had taken her part against himself stirred afresh in her a keen self-reproach and sense of shame. He wrote to her from every port he touched, brief, friendly epistles that she might have shown to all the world, but which she locked away secretly, and read only in solitude. Her letters to him were even briefer, and she never guessed how Cheveril cherished those scanty favours.

So through all that summer they kept up the farce. In the autumn Evelyn went to pay a round of visits at various country-houses, and it was while staying from home that a letter from Jim Willowby reached her.

He wrote in apparently excellent spirits. He had had an extraordinary piece of luck, he said, and had been offered a very good post in Burmah. If she would consent to go out to him, they could be married at once.

That letter Evelyn read during a solitary ramble over a wide Yorkshire moor, and when she looked up from the boy's signature her expression was hunted, even tragic.

Jim had carefully considered ways and means. The thing she had longed for was within her grasp. All she had ever asked for herself was flung to her without stint.

But - what had happened to her? she wondered vaguely - she realised it all fully, completely, yet with no thrill of gladness. Something subtly potent seemed wound about her heart, holding her back; something that was stronger far than the thought of Jim was calling to her, crying aloud across the barren deserts of her soul. And in that moment she knew that her marriage with Jim had become a final impossibility, and that it was imperative upon her to write at once and tell him so.

She walked miles that day, and returned at length utterly wearied in body and mind. She was facing the hardest problem of her life.

Not till after midnight was her letter to Jim finished, and even then she could not rest. Had she utterly ruined the boy's life? she wondered, as she sealed and directed her crude, piteous appeal for freedom.

When the morning light came grey through her window she was still poring above a blank sheet of notepaper.

This eventually carried but one sentence, addressed to the

friend who had stood by her in trouble; and later in the day she sent it by cable to the other side of the world. The message ran: "Please cancel engagement. - Evelyn." His answering cable was brought to her at the dinner-table. Two words only - "Delighted. - Lester."

Out of a mist of floating uncertainty she saw her host bend towards her.

"All well, I trust?" he said kindly.

And she made a desperate effort to control her weakness and reply naturally.

"Oh, quite, quite," she said. "It is exactly what I expected." Nevertheless, she was trembling from head to foot, as if she had been dealt a stunning blow.

Had she altogether expected so prompt and obliging a reply?

*   *   *   *   *

Some weeks later, on an afternoon of bleak, early spring, Evelyn wandered alone on the shore where she had bidden Jim Willowby farewell. It was raining, and the sea was grey and desolate. The tide was coming in with a fierce roaring that seemed to fill the whole world.

She had a letter from Jim in her hand - his answer to her appeal for freedom; and she had sought the solitude of the shore in which to read it.

She took shelter from the howling sea-wind behind a great boulder of rock. She dreaded his reproaches unspeakably. For the past six weeks she had lived in dread of that moment. Her fingers were shaking as she opened the envelope that bore his boyish scrawl.

An enclosure fell out before she had withdrawn his letter. She caught it up hastily before the wind could take possession. It was an unmounted photograph - actually the portrait of a girl.

Evelyn stared at the roguish, laughing face with a great amazement. Then, with a haste that baffled its own ends, she sought his letter.

It began with astounding jauntiness:

> "DEAR OLD EVE, - What a pair of superhuman idiots we have been! Many thanks for your sweet letter, which did me no end of good. I never loved you so much before, dear. Can you believe it? I am not surprised that you feel unequal to the task of keeping me in order for the rest of our natural lives. Will it surprise you to know that I had my doubts on the matter even when I wrote to suggest it? Never mind, dear old girl, I understand. And may the right man turn up soon and make you happy for the rest of your life!

> "I am sending a photograph of a girl who till three weeks ago was no more than a friend to me, but has since become my *fiancée*. Love is a wonderful thing, Eve. It comes upon you so suddenly and carries you away before you have time to realise what has happened. At least that has been my experience. There is no mistaking the real thing when it actually comes to you.

> "I am getting on awfully well, and like the life. By the way, it was through your friend, Lester Cheveril, that I got this appointment. A jolly decent chap that! I liked him from the first. It isn't every man who will stand being told he squints without taking offence. We are hoping to get married next month. Write - won't you? - and send me your blessing. Much love - Yours ever,

> "JAMES WILLOBY."

Evelyn looked up from the letter with a deep breath of relief. It was so amazingly satisfactory. She almost forgot the emptiness of her own life for the moment in her rejoicing over Jim's happiness.

There was a little puddle of sea-water at her feet; and she climbed up to a comfortable perch on her sheltering rock and turned her face to the sea. Somehow, it did not seem so desolate as it had seemed five minutes before. This particular seat was a favourite haunt of hers in the summer. She loved to watch the tide come foaming up, and to feel the salt spray in her face.

Five minutes later, a great wave came hurling at the rock on which she sat, and, breaking in a torrent of foam, deluged her from head to foot.

She started up in swift alarm. The tide was coming in fast - much faster than she had anticipated. The shore curved inwards in a deep bay just there, and the cliffs rose sheer and unscalable from it to a considerable height.

Evelyn seldom went down to the shore in the winter, and she was not familiar with its dangers. The sea had seemed far enough out for safety when she had rounded the point nearest to the town, barely half an hour before. It was with almost incredulous horror that she saw that the waves were already breaking at the foot of the cliffs she had skirted.

She turned with a sudden, awful fear at her heart to look towards the farther point. It was a full mile away, and she saw instantly that she could not possibly reach it in time. The waves were already foaming white among the scattered boulders at its base.

Again a great wave broke behind her with a sound like the booming of a gun; and she realised that she would be surrounded in less than thirty seconds if she remained where she was. She slipped and slid down the side of the rock with the speed of terror, and plunged recklessly into a foot of water at the bottom. Before another wave broke she was dashing and stumbling among the rocks like a frenzied creature seeking safety from the remorseless, devouring monster that roared behind her.

The next five minutes of her life held for her an agony more terrible than anything she had ever known. Sea, sky, wind, and sudden pelting rain seemed leagued against her in a monstrous array against which she battled vainly with her puny woman's strength. The horror of it was like a leaden, paralysing weight. She fought and struggled because instinct compelled her; but at her heart was the awful knowledge that the sea had claimed her and she could not possibly escape.

She made for the farther point of the bay, though she knew she could not reach it in time. The loose shingle crumbled about her feet; the seaweed trapped her everywhere. She fell a dozen times in that awful race, and each time she rose in agony and tore on. The tumult all about her was like the laughter of fiends. She felt as if hell had opened its mouth, and she, poor soul, was its easy prey.

There came a moment at last when she tripped and fell headlong, and could not rise again. That moment was the culmination of her anguish. Neither soul nor body could endure more. Darkness - a howling, unholy darkness - came down upon her in a thick cloud from which there was no escape. She made a futile, convulsive effort to pray, and lost consciousness in the act.

*   *   *   *   *

Out of the darkness at length she came.

The tumult was still audible, but it was farther away, less overwhelming. She opened her eyes in a strange, unnatural twilight, and stared vaguely upwards.

At the same instant she became aware of some one at her side, bending over her - a man whose face, revealed to her in the dim light, sent a throb of wonder through her heart.

"You!" she said, speaking with a great effort. "Is it really you?"

He was rubbing one of her hands between his own. He paused to answer.

"Yes; it's really me," he said. And she fancied his voice quivered a little. "They told me I might perhaps find you on the shore. Are you better?"

She tried to sit up, and he helped her, keeping his arm about her shoulders. She found herself lying on a ledge of rock high up in the slanting wall of a deep and narrow cave. She knew the place well, and had always avoided it with instinctive aversion. It was horribly eerie. The rocky walls were wet with the ooze and slime of the ages. There was a trickle of spring-water along the ridged floor.

Evelyn closed her eyes dizzily. The marvel of the man's presence was still upon her, but the horror of death haunted her also. She would rather have been drowned outside on the howling shore than here.

"The sea comes in at high tide," she murmured shakily.

Lester Cheveril, crouching beside her, made undaunted reply.

"Yes, I know. But it won't touch us. Don't be afraid!"

The assurance with which he spoke struck her very forcibly; but something held her back from questioning the grounds of his confidence.

"How did you get here?" she asked him instead.

"I saw you from the corner of the bay," he said. "It was before you left your rock. I climbed round the point over the boulders. I thought at the time that there must be some way up the cliff. Then I saw you start running, and I knew you were cut off. I yelled to you, but I couldn't make you hear. So I had to give chase."

His arm tightened a little about her.

"I am sorry you were scared," he said. "Are you feeling better now?"

She could not understand him. He spoke with such entire absence of anxiety. In spite of herself her own fears began to subside.

"Yes, I am better," she said. "But - tell me more. Why didn't you go back when you saw what had happened?"

"I couldn't," he said simply. "Besides, even if they launched the lifeboat, the chances were dead against their reaching you. I thought of a rope, too. But that seemed equally risky. It was a choice of odds. I chose what looked the easiest."

"And carried me here?" she said.

The light, shining weirdly in upon his face, showed her that he was smiling.

"I couldn't stop to consult you," he said. "I saw this hole, and I made for it. I climbed up with you across my shoulder."

"You are wonderfully strong," she said, in a tone of surprise.

He laughed openly.

"Notwithstanding my size," he said. "Yes; I'm fairly muscular, thank Heaven."

Evelyn's mind was still working round the problem of deliverance.

"We shall have to stay here for hours," she said, "even if - if -"

He interrupted her with grave authority.

"There is no 'if,' Miss Harford," he said. "We may have to spend some hours here; but it will be in safety."

"I don't see how you can tell," she ventured to remark, beginning to look around her with greater composure notwithstanding.

"Providence doesn't play practical jokes of that sort," said Cheveril quietly. "Do you know I have come from the other end of the earth to see you?"

She felt the burning colour rush up to her temples, yet she made a determined effort to look him in the face. His eyes, keen and kindly, were searching hers, and she found she could not meet them.

"I - I don't know what brought you," she said, in a very low voice.

She felt the arm that supported her grow rigid, and guessed that he was putting force upon himself as he made reply.

"Let me explain," he said. "You sent me a cablegram which said, 'Please cancel engagement.' Naturally that had but one meaning for me - you and Jim Willowby had got the better of your difficulties, and were going to be married. In the capacity of friend, I received the news with rejoicing. So I cabled back 'Delighted.' Soon after that came a letter from Jim to tell me you had thrown him over. Now, why?"

She answered him with her head bent:

"I found that I didn't care for him quite in that way."

Cheveril did not speak for several seconds. Then, abruptly,

Ethel M. Dell

he said:

"There is another fellow in the business."

She made a slight gesture of appeal, and remained silent.

He leaned forward slowly at length, and laid his hand upon both of hers.

"Evelyn," he said very gently, "will you tell me his name?"

She shook her head instantly. Her lips were quivering, and she bit them desperately.

He waited, but no word came. Outside, the roaring of the sea was terrible and insistent. The great sound sent a shudder through the girl. She shrank closer to the cold stone.

He pulled off his coat and wrapped it round her. Then, as if she had been a child, he drew her gently into his arms, and held her so.

"Tell me - now," he said softly.

But she hid her face dumbly. No words would come.

It seemed a long while before he spoke again.

"That cable of yours was a fraud," he said then. "I was not - I am not - prepared to release you from your engagement except under the original condition."

"I think you must," she said faintly.

He sought for her cold hands and thrust them against his neck. And again there was a long silence, while outside the sea raged fiercely, and far below them in the distance a white streak of foam ran bubbling over the rocky floor.

Soon the streak had become a stream of dancing, storm-tossed water. Evelyn watched it with wide, fascinated eyes. But she made no sign of fear. She felt as if he had, somehow, laid a quieting hand upon her soul.

Higher the water rose, and higher. The cave was filled with dreadful sound. It was almost dark, for dusk had fallen. She felt that but for the man's presence she would have been wild with fear. But his absolute confidence wove a spell about her that no terror could penetrate. The close holding of his arms was infinitely comforting to her. She knew with complete certainty that he was not afraid.

"It's very dark," she whispered to him once; and he pressed her head down upon his breast and told her not to look. Through the tumult she heard the strong, quiet beating of his heart, and was ashamed of her own mortal fear.

It seemed to her that hours passed while she crouched there, listening, as the water rose and rose. She caught the gleam of it now and then, and once her face was wet with spray. She clung closer and closer to her companion, but she kept down her panic. She felt that he expected it of her, and she would have died there in the dark, sooner than have disappointed him.

At last, after an eternity of quiet waiting, he spoke.

"The tide has turned," he said. And his tone carried conviction with it.

She raised her head to look.

A dim, silvery light shone mysteriously in revealing the black walls above them, the tossing water below. It had been within a foot of their resting-place, but it had dropped fully six inches.

Evelyn felt a great throb of relief pass through her. Only then did she fully realise how great her fear had been.

"Is that the moon?" she asked wonderingly.

"Yes," said Cheveril. He spoke in a low voice, even with reverence, she thought. "We shall be out of this in an hour. It will light us home."

"How - wonderful!" she said, half involuntarily.

Cheveril said no more; but the silence that fell between them was the silence of that intimacy which only those who have stood together before the great threshold of death can know. Many minutes passed before Evelyn spoke again, and then her words came slowly, with hesitation.

"You knew?" she said. "You knew that we were safe?"

"Yes," he answered quietly; "I knew. God doesn't give with one hand and take away with the other. Have you never noticed that?"

"I don't know," she answered with a sharp sigh. "He has never given me anything very valuable."

"Quite sure?" said Cheveril, and she caught the old quizzical note in his voice.

She did not reply. She was trying to understand him in the darkness, and she found it a difficult matter.

There followed a long, long silence. The roar of the breaking seas had become remote and vague.

But the moonlight was growing brighter. The dark cave was no longer a place of horror.

"Shall we go?" Evelyn suggested at last.

He peered downwards.

"I think we might," he said. "No doubt your people will be very anxious about you."

They climbed down with difficulty, till they finally stood together on the wet stones.

And there Cheveril reached out a hand and detained the girl beside him.

"That other fellow?" he said, in his quiet, half-humorous voice. "You didn't tell me his name."

"Oh, please!" she said tremulously.

He took her hands gently into his, and stood facing her. The moonlight was full in his eyes. They shone with a strange intensity.

"Do you remember," he said, "how I once said to you that I was romantic enough to like to see a love affair go the right way?"

She did not answer him. She was trembling in his hold.

He waited for a few seconds; then spoke, still kindly, but with a force that in a measure compelled her:

"That is why I want you to tell me his name."

She turned her face aside.

"I - I can't!" she said piteously.

"Then I hold you to your engagement," said Lester Cheveril, with quiet determination.

Her hands leapt in his. She threw him a quick uncertain glance.

Ethel M. Dell

"You can't mean that!" she said.

"I do mean it," he rejoined resolutely.

"But - but -" she faltered. "You don't really want to marry me? You can't!"

He looked grimly at her for a moment. Then abruptly he broke into a laugh that rang and echoed exultantly in the deep shadows behind them.

"I want it more than anything else on earth," he said. "Does that satisfy you?"

His face was close to hers, but she felt no desire to escape. That laugh of his was still ringing like sweetest music through her soul.

He took her shoulders between his hands, searching her face closely.

"And now," he said - "now tell me his name!"

Yet a moment longer she withstood him. Then she yielded, and went into his arms, laughing also - a broken, tearful laugh.

"His name is - Lester Cheveril," she whispered. "But I - I can't think how you guessed."

He answered her as he turned her face upwards to meet his own.

"The friend who stands by sees many things," he said wisely. "And Love is not always blind."

"But you - you weren't in love," she protested. "Not when -"

He interrupted her instantly and convincingly.

"I have always loved you," he said.

And she believed him, because her own heart told her that he had spoken the truth.

Ethel M. Dell

THE RIGHT MAN

I

"He hasn't proposed, then?"

"No; he hasn't." A pause; then, reluctantly: "I haven't given him the opportunity."

"Violet! Do you want to starve?"

The speaker turned in his chair, and looked at the girl bending over the fire, with a quick, impatient frown on his handsome face. They were twins, these two, the only representatives of a family that had been wealthy three generations before them, but whose resources had dwindled steadily under the management of three successive spendthrifts, and had finally disappeared altogether in a desperate speculation which had promised to restore everything.

"You don't seem to realise," the young man said, "that we are absolutely penniless - destitute. Everything is sunk in this Winhalla Railway scheme, up to the last penny. It seemed a gorgeous chance at the time. It ought to have brought in thousands. It would have done, too, if it had been properly supported. But it's no good talking about that. It's just a gigantic failure, or, if it ever does succeed, it will come too late to help us. Just our infernal luck! And now the question is, what is going to be done? You'll have to marry that fellow,

Violet. It's absolutely the only thing for you to do. And I - I suppose I must emigrate."

The girl did not turn her head. There was something tense about her attitude.

"I could emigrate too, Jerry," she said, in a low voice.

"You!" Her brother turned more fully round. "You!" he said again. "Are you mad, I wonder?"

She made a slight gesture of protest.

"Why shouldn't I?" she said. "At least, we should be together."

He uttered a grim laugh, and rose.

"Look here, Violet," he said, and took her lightly by the shoulders. "Don't be a little fool! You know as well as I do that you weren't made to rough it. The suggestion is so absurd that it isn't worth discussion. You'll have to marry Kenyon. It's as plain as daylight; and I only wish my perplexities were as easily solved. Come! He isn't such a bad sort; and, anyhow, he's better than starvation."

The girl stood up slowly and faced him. Her eyes were wild, like the eyes of a hunted creature.

"I hate him, Jerry! I hate him!" she declared vehemently.

"Nonsense!" said Jerry. "He's no worse than a hundred others. You'd hate any one under these abominable circumstances!"

She shuddered, as if in confirmation of this statement.

"I'd rather do anything," she said; "anything, down to selling matches in the gutter."

"Which isn't a practical point of view," pointed out Jerry.

"You would get pneumonia with the first east wind, and die."

"Well, then, I'd rather die." The girl's voice trembled with the intensity of her preference. But her brother frowned again at the words.

"Don't!" he said abruptly. "For Heaven's sake, don't be unreasonable! Can't you see that it's my greatest worry to get you provided for? You must marry. You can't live on charity."

Her cheeks flamed.

"But I can work," she began. "I can -"

He interrupted her impatiently.

"You can't. You haven't the strength, and probably not the ability either. It's no use talking this sort of rot. It's simply silly, and makes things worse for both of us. It's all very well to say you'd rather starve, but when it comes to starving, as it will - as it must - you'll think differently. Look here, old girl: if you won't marry this fellow for your own sake, do it for mine. I hate it just as much as you do. But it's bearable, at least. And - there are some things I can't bear."

He stopped. She was clinging to him closely, beseechingly; but he stood firm and unyielding, his young face set in hard lines.

"Will you do it?" he said, as she did not speak.

"Jerry!" she said imploringly.

He stiffened to meet the appeal he dreaded. But it did not come. Her eyes were raised to his, and she seemed to read there the futility of argument. She remained absolutely still for some seconds, then abruptly she turned from him and burst into tears.

"Don't! don't!" he said.

He stepped close to her, as she leaned upon the mantelpiece, all the hardness gone from his face. Had she known it, the battle at that moment might have been hers; for he would have insisted no longer. He was on the brink of abandoning the conflict. But her anguish of weeping possessed her to the exclusion of everything else.

"Oh, Jerry, go away!" she sobbed passionately. "You're a perfect beast, and I'm another! But I'll do it, I'll do it - for your sake, as I would do anything in the world, though it's quite true that I'd rather starve!"

And Jerry, rather pale, but otherwise complete master of himself, patted her shoulder with a hasty assumption of kindly approval; and told her that he had always known she was a brick.

Ethel M. Dell

II

"Heaven knows I don't aspire to be any particular ornament to society," said Dick Kenyon modestly. "Never have; though I've been pretty well everything else that you can think of, from cow-puncher to millionaire. And I can tell you there's a dashed deal more fun in being the first than the last of those. Still, I think I could make you comfortable if you would have me; though, if you don't want to, just say so, and I'll shunt till further notice."

It was thus that he made his proposal to the girl of his choice; and no one, hearing it, would have guessed that beneath his calm, even phlegmatic, exterior, the man was in a ferment of anxiety. He spoke with a slight nasal twang that seemed to emphasise his deliberation, and his face was mask-like in its composure. Of beauty he had none.

His eyes were extraordinarily blue, but the lids drooped over them so heavily that his expression was habitually drowsy, even stolid. In build, he was short and thick-set, like a bulldog; and there seemed to be something of a bulldog's strength in the breadth of his chest, though there was no hint of energy about him to warrant its development.

The girl he addressed did not look at him. She sat perfectly still, with her hands fast clasped together, and her eyes, wide and despairing, fixed upon the fire in front of her. She was wondering desperately how long she could possibly endure it. Yet his last words were somehow not what she had expected from this man whose manner always seemed to hint that at least half of creation was at his sole disposal. They expressed a consideration on his part that she had been far from anticipating. He waited for an interval of several seconds for her to speak. He was standing up on the hearthrug, his ill-proportioned figure thrown into strong relief by the firelight behind him. At last, as she quite failed to answer him, he drew a pace nearer to her.

"Don't mind me, Miss Trelevan," he said, in a drawl so exaggerated that she thought it must be intentional. "Take your time. There's no hurry. I've always thought it was a bit hard on a woman to expect her to answer an offer of marriage offhand. Perhaps you'd rather write?"

"No," she said, rather breathlessly. "No!" Then, after a pause, still more breathlessly: "Won't you sit down?"

He stepped away from her again, to her infinite relief, and sat down a couple of yards away.

There ensued a most painful silence, during which the battle in the girl's heart raged fiercely. Then at length she took her resolution in both hands, and faced him. He was not looking at her. He sat quite still, and she fancied that his eyes were closed; but when she spoke he turned his head, and she realised that she had been mistaken.

"I can give you your answer now," she said, making the greatest effort of her life. "It is - it is - yes."

She rose with the words, almost as if in preparation for headlong flight. But Dick Kenyon kept his seat. He leaned forward a little, his blue eyes lifted to her face.

"Your final word, Miss Trelevan?" he asked her, in his cool, easy twang.

She wrung her hands together with an unconscious gesture of despair.

"Yes," she said; and added feverishly: "of course."

"You think you've met the right man?" he pursued, his tone one of gentle inquiry, as if he were speaking to a child.

She nodded. She was white to the lips.

"Yes," she said again.

He got up then with extreme deliberation.

"Well," he said, a curious smile flickering about his mouth, "that's about the biggest surprise I've ever had. And I don't mind telling you so. Sure now that you're not making a mistake?"

She uttered a little laugh that sounded hysterical.

"Oh, don't!" she said. "Don't! I have given you my answer!"

"And I'm to take you seriously?" questioned Kenyon. "Very well. I will. But you mustn't be frightened."

He stretched out a steady hand, and laid it on her shoulder. She quivered at his touch, but she did not attempt to resist.

"Don't be scared," he said very gently. "I know I'm as ugly as blazes; at least, I've been told so, but there's nothing else to alarm you if you can once get over that."

There was a note of quaint raillery in his voice. He did not try to draw her to him. Yet she was conscious of a strength that did battle with her half-instinctive aversion - a strength that might have compelled, but preferred to attract.

Unwillingly, at length, she looked at him, meeting his eyes, good-humouredly critical, watching her.

"I am not frightened," she said, with an effort. "It's only that – just at first - till I get used to it - it feels rather strange."

There was unconscious pleading in her voice. He took his hand from her shoulder, looking at her with his queer, speculative smile.

"I don't want to hustle you any," he said. "But if that's all the trouble, I guess I know a remedy."

Violet drew back sharply.

"Oh, no!" she said. "No!"

She was terrified for the moment lest he should desire to put his remedy to the test. But he made no movement in her direction, and another sort of misgiving assailed her.

"Don't be vexed," she said unsteadily. "I - I know I'm despicable. But I shall get over it - if you will give me time."

"Bless your heart, I'm not vexed," said Kenyon. "I'm only wondering, don't you know, how you brought yourself to say 'Yes' to me. But no matter, dear. I'm grateful all the same."

He held out his hand to her, and she laid hers nervously within it. She could not meet his eyes any longer.

Kenyon stooped and put his lips to her cold fingers.

"Jove!" he said softly. "I'm in luck to-day."

And after that he sat down again, and began to behave like an ordinary visitor.

Ethel M. Dell

III

"Great Scotland!" said Jerry.

He looked up from a letter, and gazed at his sister with starting eyes.

"Oh, what?" she exclaimed in alarm.

He sprang up impetuously, and went round the table to her. They were breakfasting in the tiny flat which was theirs for but three short months longer.

"Guess!" he said. "No, don't! I can't wait. It's the family luck, old girl, turned at last! It's the original gorgeous chance again with a practical dead certainty pushing behind. It's the Winhalla Railway turning up trumps just in time."

And, with a whoop that might have been heard from garret to basement, Jerry swept his sister from her chair, and waltzed her giddily round the little room till she cried breathlessly for mercy.

"Oh, but do tell me!" she gasped, when he set her down again. "I want to understand, Jerry. Don't be so mad. Tell me exactly what has happened!"

"I'll tell you," said Jerry, sitting down on the tablecloth. "It's a letter from Gardner - my broker and man of business generally - written last night to tell me that one of these swaggering capitalists has got hold of the Winhalla Railway scheme, and is going to make things hum. Shares are going up already; and they'll run sky high by the end of the week. It's bound to be all right. It was always sound enough. It only wanted capital. He doesn't tell me the bounder's name, but that's no matter. I don't want to go into partnership. I shall sell, sell, sell, at the top of the boom. Gardner's to be trusted. He'll know - and then - and then -"

"Yes; what does it mean?" the girl broke in. "I want to know exactly, Jerry!"

"Mean?" he echoed, his hands upon her shoulders. "It means emancipation, wealth, everything we've lost back again, and more to it! Now do you understand?"

She gasped for breath. She had turned very pale.

"Oh, Jerry!" she said tragically. "Jerry, why didn't this happen before?"

He stared at her for a moment. Then, as understanding came to him, he frowned with swift impatience.

"Oh, that must be broken off!" he said. "You can't marry that fellow now. Why should you?"

Violet shook her head hopelessly.

"I've promised," she said; "promised to marry him at the end of next month."

Jerry jumped up impulsively.

"But that's soon arranged," he declared. "Leave it to me. I'll explain."

"How can you?" questioned Violet.

"I shall put it on a purely business footing," he returned airily. "Don't you worry yourself. He isn't the sort of chap to take it to heart. You know that as well as I do. Perhaps it might be as well to wait till the end of the week and make sure of things, though, before I say anything."

But at this point Violet gave him the biggest surprise he had ever known. She sprang to her feet with flashing eyes.

"Indeed you won't, Jerry!" she exclaimed. "You will tell him to-day - this morning - and end it definitely. Never mind what happens afterwards. I won't carry the dishonourable bargain to that length. I've little enough self-respect left, but what there is of it I'll keep!"

"Heavens above!" ejaculated Jerry, in amazement. "What's the matter now? I was only thinking of you, after all."

"I know you were," she answered passionately. "But you're to think of something greater than my physical welfare. You're to think of my miserable little rag of honour, and do what you can for that, if you really want to help me!"

And with that she went quickly from the room and left him to breakfast alone.

He marvelled for a little at her agitation, and then the contents of the letter absorbed him again. He had better go and see Gardner, he reflected; and then, if the thing really seemed secure, he would take Dick Kenyon on his way back - perhaps lunch with him, and explain matters in a friendly way. There was certainly nothing for Violet to make a fuss about. He was quite fully convinced that the fellow wouldn't care. Marriage was a mere incident to men of his stamp.

So, cheerily at length, having disposed of his breakfast, he rose, collected his correspondence, which consisted for the most part of bills, and, whistling light-heartedly, took his departure.

IV

"Now," said Dick Kenyon, in his easy, self-assured accents, "sit down right there, sonny, and tell me what's on your mind."

He pressed Jerry into his most comfortable chair with hospitable force.

Jerry submitted, because he could not help himself, rather than from choice. Patronage from Dick Kenyon was something of an offence to his ever-ready pride.

As for Dick, he had not apparently the smallest suspicion of any latent resentment of this nature in his visitor's mind. He brought out a box of choice cigars, and set them at Jerry's elbow. They had just lunched together at Kenyon's rooms; and it had been quite obvious to the latter that Jerry had been preoccupied throughout the meal.

Having furnished his guest with everything he could think of to ensure his comfort, he proceeded deliberately to provide for his own.

Jerry was not quite at his ease. He sat with the unlighted cigar between his fingers, considering with bent brows. Kenyon looked at him at last with a faint smile.

"If I didn't know it to be an impossibility," he said, "I should say you were shying at something."

Jerry turned towards him with an air of resolution.

"Look here, Kenyon," he said, in his slightly superior tones, "I have really come to talk to you about your engagement to my sister."

He paused, aware of a change in Kenyon's expression, but wholly unable to discover of what it consisted.

Ethel M. Dell

"What about it?" said Kenyon.

He was on his feet, searching the mantelpiece for an ash-tray. His face was turned from Jerry, but could he have seen it fully, it would have told him nothing.

Jerry went on, with a strong effort to maintain his ease of manner:

"We've been thinking it over, and we have come to the conclusion that perhaps, after all, it was a mistake. In short, my sister has thought better of it; and, as she is naturally sensitive on the subject, I undertook to tell you so, I don't suppose it will make any particular difference to you. There are plenty of girls who would jump at the chance of marrying your millions. But, of course, if you wish it, some compensation could be made."

Jerry paused again. He had placed the matter on the most businesslike footing that had occurred to him. Of course, the man must realise that he was a rank outsider, and would understand that it was the best method.

Kenyon heard him out in dead silence. He had found the ash-tray, but he did not turn his head. After several dumb seconds, he walked across the room to the window, and stood there. Finally he spoke.

"I don't suppose," he said, in his calm, expressionless drawl, "that you have ever had a cowhiding in your life, have you?"

"What?" said Jerry.

He stared at Kenyon in frank amazement. Was the man mad?

"Never had a cowhiding in your life, eh?" repeated Kenyon, without moving.

"What do you mean?" exclaimed Jerry.

Kenyon remained motionless.

"I mean," he said calmly, "that I've thrashed a man to a pulp before now for a good deal less than you have just offered me. It's my special treatment for curs. Suits 'em wonderfully. And suits me, too."

Jerry sprang to his feet in a whirl of wrath, but before he could utter a word Kenyon suddenly turned.

"Go back to your sister," he said, in curt, stern tones, "and tell her from me that I will discuss this matter with her alone. If she intends to throw me over, she must come to me herself and tell me so. Go now!"

But Jerry stood halting between an open blaze of passion and equally open discomfiture. He longed to hurl defiance in Kenyon's face, but some hidden force restrained him. There was that about the man at that moment which compelled submission. And so, at length, he turned without another word, and walked straight from the room with as fine a dignity as he could muster. By some remarkable means, Dick Kenyon had managed to get the best of the encounter.

V

Not the next day, nor the next, did Violet Trelevan summon up courage to face her outraged lover, and ask for her freedom. Jerry did not tell her precisely what had passed, but she gathered from the information he vouchsafed that Kenyon had not treated the matter peaceably. She wondered a little how Jerry had approached it, and told herself with a beating heart that she would have to take her own line of action.

Nevertheless, for a full week she did nothing, and at the end of that week the flutter in the Winhalla Railway shares had subsided completely, and all Jerry's high hopes were dead. From day to day he had tried to console himself and her with the reflection that a speculation of that sort was bound to fluctuate, but, in the end, when the shares went down to zero, he was forced to own that he had been too sanguine. It had been but the last flicker before extinction. The capitalist had evidently thought better of risking his money on such a venture.

"And I was a gaping, weak-kneed idiot not to sell for what I could get!" he told his sister. "But it's just our luck. I might have known nothing decent could ever happen to us!"

It was on that evening, when the outlook was at its blackest, that Violet wrote at last, without consulting Jerry, to the man in whose hands lay her freedom.

It was a short epistle, and humbly worded, for she realised that this, at least, was his due.

"I want you," she wrote, "to forgive me, if you can, for the wrong I have done you, and to set me free. I accepted you upon impulse, I am ashamed to say, for the sake of your money. But the shame would be even greater if I did not tell you so. I do not know what view you will take, but my own is that, in releasing me, you will not lose anything that is worth having."

The answer to this appeal came the next day by hand:

"May I see you alone at your flat at five o'clock?"

She had not expected it, and she felt for an instant as if a master hand had touched her, sending the blood tingling through her veins like fire. She sent a reply in the affirmative; and then set herself to face the longest day she had ever lived through.

She sat alone during the afternoon, striving desperately to nerve herself for the ordeal. But strive as she might, the fact remained that she was horribly, painfully frightened. There was something about this man which it seemed futile to resist, something that dominated her, something against which it hurt her to fight.

She heard his ring punctually upon the stroke of five, and she went herself to answer it.

He greeted her with his usual serenity of manner.

"All alone?" he asked, as he followed her into the little drawing-room in which he had proposed to her so short a time before.

She assented nervously.

"Jerry went into the city. He won't be back yet."

"That's kind of you," said Kenyon quietly.

She did not ask him to sit down. They faced each other on the hearthrug. The strong glare of the electric light showed him that she was very pale.

Abruptly he thrust out his hand to her.

"You must forgive me for bullying your brother the other day," he said. Really, he deserved it."

She glanced up quickly.

"Jerry doesn't understand," she said.

He kept his hand outstretched though she did not take it.

"I don't understand, either," he said.

"Do you really want to shake hands with me?" she murmured, her voice very low.

"I want to hold your hand in mine, if I may," he answered simply. "I think it will help to solve the difficulty. Thank you! Yes; I thought you were trembling. Now, why, I wonder?"

She did not answer him. Her head was bent.

"Don't!" he said gently. "There is no cause. Didn't I tell you I would shunt if you didn't want me?"

Still she was silent, her hand lying passive in his.

"Come!" he said. "I want to understand, don't you know. That note of yours. You say in it that you accepted me for the sake of my money. Even so. But I reckon that is more a reason for sticking to me than for throwing me over."

He paused, but her head only drooped a little lower.

"Doesn't that reason still exist?" he asked her, point blank.

She shivered at the direct question, but she answered it.

"Yes; it does. And that's why I'm ashamed to go on."

"Why ashamed?" he asked. "How do you know my reason for

wanting to marry you is as good since I never told you what it was?"

She looked up then, suddenly and swiftly, and caught a curious glint in the blue eyes that watched her.

"I do know," she said, speaking quickly, impulsively. "And that's why - I can't bear - that you should despise me."

"Ah!" he said. "Do you really care what an outsider like myself thinks of you?"

The colour flamed suddenly in her white face, but he went on in his quiet drawl as if he had not seen it:

"If I thought it was for your happiness, believe me, I would set you free. But, so far, you haven't given me any reason that could justify such a step. Can't you think of one? Honestly, now?"

She shook her head. Her eyes were full of blinding tears.

"What is it, then?" urged Kenyon. And suddenly his voice was as soft as a woman's. "Has the right man turned up unexpectedly, after all? Is it for his sake?"

"Oh, don't!" she cried passionately. "Don't! You hurt me!"

And, turning sharply from him, she hid her face, and broke into anguished weeping.

Kenyon stood quite still for perhaps ten seconds; then he moved close to her, and put his arm round the slight, sobbing figure.

She did not start or attempt to resist him.

"There, there!" he whispered soothingly. "I knew there was a reason. Don't cry, dear! It will be all right - all right. Never mind the beastly money. There's going to be a big boom in the Winhalla Railway shares, and you'll make your fortune over it. Yes; I know all about that. A friend told me. There's a big capitalist pushing behind. They have gone down this week, but they are going to rise like a spring tide next. And then - you'll be free to marry the right man, eh, dear? I sha'n't stand in your way. I'll even come and dance at the wedding, if you'll have me."

She uttered a muffled laugh through her tears, and turned slightly towards him within the encircling arm.

"I hope you will," she murmured. "Because - because -" She broke off, and became silent.

Dick Kenyon's arm did not slacken.

"If you could make it convenient to finish that sentence of yours, I'd be real grateful," he observed, at length.

She lifted her face from her hands, and looked him in the eyes. Her own were shining.

"Because," she said unsteadily, "I couldn't marry the right man - if you weren't there."

He looked straight back at her without a hint of emotion in his heavy eyes.

"Quite sure of that?" he asked.

And she laughed again tremulously as she made reply.

"Quite sure, Dick," she said softly, "though I've only just found it out."

* * * * *

Jerry, tearing in a little later, brimful of city news, noticed that his sister's face was brighter than usual, but failed, in his excitement, to perceive a visitor in the room, the visitor not troubling himself to rise at his entrance.

"News, Vi!" he shouted. "Gorgeous news! The Winhalla Railway is turning up trumps! The shares are simply flying up. I told Gardner I'd sell at fifty, but he says they are worth holding on to, for they'll go above that. He vows they're safe. And who do you think is the capitalist that's pushing behind? Why, Kenyon!"

He broke off abruptly at this point as Kenyon himself arose leisurely with a serene smile and outstretched hand.

"Exactly - Kenyon!" he said. "But if you think he's a rank bad speculator like yourself, sonny, you're mistaken. I didn't make my money that way, and I don't reckon to lose it that way either. But Gardner's right. Those shares are safe. They aren't going down again ever any more."

He turned to the girl on his other side, and laid his free hand on her shoulder.

"And I guess you'll forgive me for distressing you," he said, "when I tell you why I did it."

"Well, why, Dick?" she questioned, her face turned to his.

"I just thought I'd like to know, dear," he drawled, "if there wasn't something bigger than money to be got out of this deal. And - are you listening, Jerry? - I found there was!"

Ethel M. Dell

THE KNIGHT ERRANT

I

THE APPEAL

The Poor Relation hoisted one leg over the arm of his chair, and gazed contemplatively at the ceiling.

"Now, I wonder whom I ought to scrag for this," he mused aloud.

A crumpled newspaper lay under his hand, a certain paragraph uppermost that was strongly scored with red ink. He had read it twice already and after a thoughtful pause he proceeded to read it again.

"A marriage has been arranged and will shortly take place between Cecil Mordaunt Rivington and Ernestine, fourth daughter of Lady Florence Cardwell."

"Why Ernestine, I wonder?" murmured the Poor Relation. "Thought she was still in short frocks. Used to be rather a jolly little kid. Wonder what she thinks of the arrangement?"

A faint smile cocked one corner of his mouth - a very plain mouth which he wore no moustache to hide.

"And Lady Florence! Ye gods! Wonder what she thinks!"

The smile developed into a snigger, and vanished at a breath.

"But it's really infernally awkward," he declared. "Ought one to go and apologise for what one hasn't done? Really, I don't know if I dare!"

Again, as one searching for inspiration, he read the brief paragraph.

"It looks to me, Cecil Mordaunt, as if you are in for a very warm time," he remarked at the end of this final inspection. "Such a time as you haven't had since you left Rugby. If you take my advice you'll sit tight like a sensible chap and leave this business to engineer itself. No good ever came of meddling."

With which practical reflection he rose to fill and light a briar pipe, his inseparable companion, before grappling with his morning correspondence.

This lay in a neat pile at his elbow, and after a ruminative pause devoted to the briar pipe, he applied himself deliberately to its consideration.

The first two he examined and tossed aside with a bored expression. The third seemed to excite his interest. It was directed in a nervous, irregular hand that had tried too hard to be firm, and had spluttered the ink in consequence. The envelope was of a pearly grey tint. The Poor Relation sniffed at it, and turned up his nose.

Nevertheless, he opened the missive with a promptitude that testified to a certain amount of curiosity.

"Dear Knight Errant," he read, in the same desperate handwriting. "Do you remember once years ago coming to the rescue of a lady in distress who was chased by a bull? The lady has never forgotten it. Will you do the same again for the same lady to-day, and earn her undying gratitude? If so, will you confirm the statement in the *Morning Post* as often and as convincingly as you can till further notice? I wonder if you will? I do wonder. I couldn't ask you if you were anything but poor and a sort of relation as well. - Yours, *in extremis*,

"ERNESTINE CARDWELL.

"P.S. - Of course, don't do it if you would really rather not."

"Thank you, Ernestine!" said the Poor Relation. "That last sentence of yours might be described as the saving clause. I would very much rather not, if the truth be told; which it probably never will be. As you have shrewdly foreseen, the subtlety of your '*in extremis*' draws me in spite of myself. I have seen you *in extremis* before, and I must admit the spectacle made something of an impression."

He read the letter again with characteristic deliberation, lay back awhile with pale blue eyes fixed unswervingly upon the ceiling, and finally rose and betook himself to his writing-table.

"Dear Lady in Distress," he wrote. "I am pleased to note that even poor relations have their uses. As your third cousin removed to the sixth or seventh degree, I shall be most happy to serve you. Pray regard me as unreservedly at your disposal. Awaiting your further commands. - Your devoted

"KNIGHT ERRANT."

This letter he directed to Miss Ernestine Cardwell and despatched by special messenger. Then, with a serene countenance, he glanced through his remaining correspondence, stretched himself, yawned, looked out of the window, and finally sauntered forth to his club.

II

CONGRATULATIONS

"Ye gods! I should think Lady Florence is feelin' pretty furious. The fellow hasn't a penny, and isn't even an honourable. I thought all her daughters were to be princesses or duchesses or ranees or somethin' imposin'."

Archie Fielding, gossip-in-chief of the Junior Sherwood Club, beat a rousing tattoo on the table, and began to whistle Mendelssohn's "Wedding March."

"Wonder if he will want me to be best man," he proceeded. "It'll be the seventh time this season. Think I shall make a small charge for my services for the future. Not to poor old Cecil, though. He's always hard-up. I wonder what they'll live on. I'll bet Miss Ernestine hasn't been brought up on cheese and smoked herrings."

"Which is Ernestine?" asked another member, generally known at the club as "that ass Bray." "The little one, isn't it; the one that laughs?"

"The cheeky one - yes," said Archie. "I saw her ridin' in the Park with Dinghra the other day. Awful brute, Dinghra, if he is a rajah's son."

"Shocking bounder!" said Bray. "But rich - a quality that covers a multitude of sins."

"Especially in Lady Florence's estimation," remarked Archie. "She's had designs on him ever since Easter. Ernestine is a nice little thing, you know, but somehow she hangs fire. A trifle over-independent, I suppose, and she has a sharp tongue, too - tells the truth a bit too often, don't you know. I don't get on with that sort of girl myself. But I'll swear Dinghra is head over ears, the brute. I'd give twenty pounds to punch his evil mouth."

"Yes, he's pretty foul, certainly. But apparently she isn't for him. I'm surprised that Cecil has taken the trouble to compete. He's kept mighty quiet about it. I've met him hardly anywhere this season."

"Oh, he's a lazy animal! But he always does things on the quiet; it is his nature to. He's the sort of chap that thinks for about twenty years, and then goes straight and does the one and only thing that no one else would dream of doin'. I rather fancy, for all his humdrum ways, he would be a difficult man to thwart. I'd give a good deal to know how he got over Lady Florence, though. He has precious little to recommend him as a son-in-law."

At this point some one kicked him violently, and he looked up to see the subject of his harangue sauntering up the room.

"Are you talking about me?" he inquired, as he came. "Don't let me interrupt, I beg. I know I'm an edifying topic, eh, Archibald?"

"Oh, don't ask me to praise you to your face," said Archie, quite unperturbed. "How are you, old chap? We are all gapin' with amazement over this mornin's news. Is it really true? Are we to congratulate?"

"Are you referring to my engagement?" asked the Poor Relation, pausing in the middle of the group. "Yes, of course it's true. Do you mean to say you were such a pack of dunderheads you didn't see it coming?"

"There wasn't anything to see," protested Archie. "You've been lyin' low, you howlin' hypocrite! I always said you were a dark horse."

The Poor Relation smiled upon him tolerantly.

"Can't you call me anything else interesting? It seems to have hurt your feelings rather, not being in the know. I can't understand your not smelling a rat. Where are your wits, man?"

He tapped Archie's head smartly with his knuckles, and passed on, the smile still wrinkling his pale eyes and the forehead above them from which the hair was steadily receding towards the top of his skull.

Certainly the gods had not been kind to him in the matter of personal beauty, but a certain charm he possessed, notwithstanding, which procured for him a well-grounded popularity.

"You'll let me wish you luck, anyway, Rivington," one man said.

"Rather!" echoed Archie. "I hope you'll ask me to your weddin'."

"All of you," said the Poor Relation generously. "It's going to be a mountainous affair, and Archie shall officiate as best man."

"When is it to take place?" some one asked.

"Oh, very soon - very soon indeed; actual date not yet fixed. St. George's, Hanover Square, of course; and afterwards at Lady Florence Cardwell's charming mansion in Park Lane. It'll be a thrilling performance altogether." The Poor Relation beamed impartially upon his well-wishers. He seemed to be hugely enjoying himself.

"And whither will the happy pair betake themselves after the reception?" questioned Archie.

"That, my dear fellow, is not yet quite decided."

"I expect you'll go for a motor tour," said Bray.

But Rivington at once shook his head.

"Nothing of that sort. Couldn't afford it. No, we shall do something cheaper and more original than that. I've got an old caravan somewhere; that might do. Rather a bright idea, eh, Archie?"

"Depends on the bride," said Archie, looking decidedly dubious.

"Eh? Think so? We shall have to talk it over." The Poor Relation subsided into a chair, and stretched himself with a sigh. "There are such a lot of little things to be considered when you begin to get married," he murmured, as he pulled out his pipe.

"Some one wanting you on the telephone, sir," announced one of the club attendants at his elbow, a few minutes later.

"Eh? Who is it? Tell 'em I can't be bothered. No, don't. I'm coming."

Laboriously he hoisted himself out of his chair, regretfully he knocked the glowing tobacco out of his pipe, heavy-footed he betook him to the telephone.

"Hullo!"

"Oh!" said a woman's voice. "Is that you?"

"Yes. Who do you want?"

"Mr. Rivington - Cecil Mordaunt Rivington." The syllables came with great distinctness. They seemed to have an anxious ring.

"Yes, I'm here," said the owner of the name. "Who are you?"

"I'm Ernestine. Can you hear me?"

"First-rate! What can I do for you?"

There was a pause, then:

"I had your letter," said the voice, "and I'm tremendously grateful to you. I was afraid you might be vexed."

"Not a bit of it," said Rivington genially. "Anything to oblige."

"Thanks so much! It was great cheek, I know, but I've had such a horrid fright. I couldn't think of any other way out, and you were the only possible person that occurred to me. You were very kind to me once, a long time ago. It's awfully decent of you not to mind."

"Please don't!" said Rivington. "That sort of thing always upsets me. Look here, can't we meet somewhere and talk things over? It would simplify matters enormously."

"Yes, it would. That is what I want to arrange. Could you manage some time this afternoon? Please say you can!"

"Of course I can," said Rivington promptly. "What place?"

"I don't know. It must be somewhere right away where no one will know us."

"How would the city do? That's nice and private."

A faint laugh came to his ear. "Yes; but where?"

Rivington briefly considered.

"St. Paul's Cathedral, under the dome, three o'clock. Will that do?"

"Yes, I'll be there. You won't fail?"

"Not if I live," said Rivington. "Anything else?"

"No; only a million thanks! I'll explain everything when we meet."

"All right. Good-bye!"

As he hung up the receiver, a heavy frown drove the kindliness out of his face.

"What have they been doing to the child?" he said. "It's a pretty desperate step for a girl to take. At least it might be, it would be, if I were any one else."

Suddenly the smile came back and drew afresh the kindly, humorous lines about his eyes.

"She seems to remember me rather well," he murmured. "She certainly was a jolly little kid."

III

THE LADY IN DISTRESS

The afternoon sunlight streamed golden through the cathedral as Cecil Rivington passed into its immense silence. He moved with quiet and leisurely tread; it was not his way to hurry. The great clock was just booming the hour.

There were not many people about. A few stray footsteps wandered through the stillness, a few vague whispers floated to and fro. But the peace of the place lay like a spell, a dream atmosphere in which every sound was hushed.

Rivington passed down the nave till he reached the central space under the great dome. There he paused, and gazed straight upwards into the giddy height above him.

As he stood thus calmly contemplative, a light step sounded on the pavement close to him, and a low voice spoke.

"Oh, here you are! It's good of you to be so punctual."

He lowered his eyes slowly as if he were afraid of giving them a shock, and focussed them upon the speaker.

"I am never late," he remarked. "And I am never early."

Then he smiled kindly and held out his hand.

"Hullo, Chirpy!" he said. "It is Chirpy, isn't it?"

"Yes, it is Chirpy. But I never expected you to remember that."

"I remember most things," said Rivington.

His pale eyes dwelt contemplatively on the girl before him. She was very slim and young, and plainly very nervous. There was

Ethel M. Dell

no beauty about Ernestine Cardwell, only a certain wild grace peculiarly charming, and a quick wit that some people found too shrewd. When she laughed she was a child. Her laugh was irresistible, and there was magic in her smile, a baffling, elusive magic too transient to be defined. Very sudden and very fleeting was her smile. Rivington saw it for an instant only as she met his look.

"Do you know," she said, colouring deeply. "I thought you were much older than you are."

"I am fifty," said Rivington.

But she shook her head.

"It is very good of you to say so."

"Not at all," smiled Rivington. "You, I fancy, must be about twenty-one. How long since the bull episode?"

"Oh, do you remember that, too?" She uttered a faint laugh.

"Vividly," said Rivington. "I have a lively memory of the fleetness of your retreat and the violence of your embrace when the danger was over."

She laughed again.

"It was years and years ago - quite six, I should think."

"Quite, I should say," agreed Rivington. "But we have met since then, surely?"

"Oh yes, casually. But we are not in the same set, are we? Some one once told me you were very Bohemian."

"Who was it? I should like to shoot him!" said Rivington.

At which she laughed again, and then threw a guilty

glance around.

"I don't think this is a very good place for a talk."

"Not if you want to do much laughing," said Rivington. "Come along to the tea-shop round the corner. No one will disturb us there."

They turned side by side, and began to walk back. The girl moved quickly as though not wholly at her ease. She glanced at her companion once or twice, but it was not till they finally emerged at the head of the steps that she spoke.

"I am wondering more and more how I ever had the impertinence to do it."

"There's no great risk in asking a poor relation to do anything," said Rivington consolingly.

"Ah, but I did it without asking." There was an unmistakable note of distress in her quick rejoinder. "I was at my wits' end. I didn't know what on earth to do. And it came to me suddenly like an inspiration. But I wish I hadn't now, with all my heart."

Rivington turned his mild eyes upon her.

"My dear child, don't be silly!" he said. "I am delighted to be of use for a change. I don't do much worth the doing, being more or less of a loafer. It is good for me to exercise my ingenuity now and then. It only gets rusty lying by."

She put out her hand impulsively and squeezed his.

"You're awfully nice to me," she said. "It's only a temporary expedient, of course. I couldn't ask you first - there wasn't time. But I'll set you free as soon as I possibly can. Have people been talking much?"

"Rather! They are enjoying it immensely. I have had to go ahead like steam. I've even engaged a best man."

She threw him a startled look.

"Oh, but -"

"No, don't be alarmed," he said reassuringly. "It's best to take the bull by the horns, believe me. The more fuss you make at the outset, the quicker it will be over. People will be taking us for granted in a week."

"You think so?" she said doubtfully. "I can't think what mother will say. I don't dare think."

"Is your mother away, then?"

"Yes, in Paris for a few days. I couldn't have done it if she had been at home. I don't know quite what I should have done." She broke off with a sudden shudder. "I've had a horrid fright," she said again.

"Come and have some tea," suggested Rivington practically.

IV

A COUNCIL OF WAR

They had tea in a secluded corner, well removed from all prying eyes. Gradually, as the minutes passed, the girl's manner became more assured.

When at length he leaned his elbows on the table and said, "Tell me all about it," she was ready.

She leaned towards him, and dropped her voice.

"You know Mr. Dinghra Singh? I'm sure you do. Every one does."

"Yes, I know him. They call him Nana Sahib at the clubs."

She shuddered again.

"I used to like him rather. He has a wicked sort of fascination, you know. But I loathe him now; I abhor him. And - I am terrified at him."

She stopped. Rivington said nothing. There was not much expression in his eyes. Without seeming to scan very closely, they rested on her face.

After a moment, in a whisper, she continued:

"He follows me about perpetually. I meet him everywhere. He looks at me with horrid eyes. I know, without seeing, the instant he comes into the room."

She paused. Rivington still said nothing.

"He is very rich, you know," she went on, with an effort. "He will be Rajah of Ferosha some day. And, of course, every one is very nice to him in consequence. I never was that. Don't think it! But I used to laugh at him. It's my way. Most men don't like it. No Englishmen do that I know of. But he - this man - is, somehow, different from every one else. And - can you believe it? - he is literally stalking me. He sends me presents - exquisite things, jewellery, that my mother won't let me return. I asked him not to once, and he laughed in my face. He has a horrible laugh. He is half-English, too. I believe that makes him worse. If he were an out-and-out native he wouldn't be quite so revolting. Of course, I see my mother's point of view. Naturally, she would like me to be a princess, and, as she says, I can't pick and choose. Which is true, you know," she put in quaintly, "for men don't like me as a rule; at least, not the marrying sort. I rather think I'm not the marrying sort myself. I've never been in love, never once. But I couldn't - I could not - marry Dinghra. But it's no good telling him so. The cooler I am to him the hotter he seems to get, till - till I'm beginning to wonder how I can possibly get away."

The note of distress sounded again in her voice. Very quietly, as though in answer to it, Rivington reached out a hand and laid it over hers.

But his eyes never varied as he said:

"Won't you finish?"

She bent her head.

"You'll think me foolish to be so easily scared," she said, a slight catch in her voice. "Most women manage to take care of themselves. I ought to be able to."

"Please go on," he said. "I don't think you foolish at all."

She continued, without raising her eyes:

"Things have been getting steadily worse. Last week at Lady Villar's ball I had to dance with him four times. I tried to refuse, but mother was there. She wouldn't hear of it. You know" - appealingly - "she is so experienced. She knows how to insist without seeming to, so that, unless one makes a scene, one has to yield. I thought each dance that he meant to propose, but I just managed to steer clear. I felt absolutely delirious the whole time. Most people thought I was enjoying it. Old Lady Phillips told me I was looking quite handsome." She laughed a little. "Well, after all, there seemed to be no escape, and I got desperate. It was like a dreadful nightmare. I went to the opera one night, and he came and sat close behind me and talked in whispers. When he wasn't talking I knew that he was watching me - gloating over me. It was horrible - horrible! Last night I wouldn't go out with the others. I simply couldn't face it. And - do you know - he came to me!" She began to breathe quickly, unevenly. The hands that lay in Rivington's quiet grasp moved with nervous restlessness. "There was no one in the house besides the servants," she said. "What could I do? He was admitted before I knew. Of course, I ought to have refused to see him, but he was very insistent, and I thought it a mistake to seem afraid. So I went to him - I went to him."

The words came with a rush. She began to tremble all over. She was almost sobbing.

Rivington's fingers closed very slowly, barely perceptibly, till his grip was warm and close. "Take your time," he said gently. "It's all right, you know - all right."

"Thank you," she whispered. "Well, I saw him. He was in a dangerous - a wild-beast mood. He told me I needn't try to run away any longer, for I was caught. He said - and I know it was true - that he had obtained my mother's full approval and consent. He swore that he wouldn't leave me until I promised to marry him. He was terrible, with a sort of suppressed violence that appalled me. I tried not to let him see how terrified I was. I kept quite quiet and temperate for a long time. I told him I could never, never marry him. And each time I said it, he smiled and showed his teeth. He was like a tiger. His eyes were fiendish. But he, too, kept quiet for ever so long. He tried persuasion, he tried flattery. Oh, it was loathsome - loathsome! And then quite suddenly he turned savage, and - and threatened me."

She glanced nervously into Rivington's face, but it told her nothing. He looked merely thoughtful.

She went on more quietly.

"That drove me desperate, and I exclaimed, hardly thinking, 'I wouldn't marry you if you were the only man in the world - which you are not!' 'Oh!' he said at once. 'There is another man, is there?' He didn't seem to have thought that possible. And I - I was simply clutching at straws - I told him 'Yes.' It was a lie, you know - the first deliberate lie I think I have ever told since I came to years of discretion. There isn't another man, or likely to be. That's just the trouble. If there were, my mother wouldn't be so angry with me for refusing this chance of marriage, brilliant though she thinks it. But I was quite desperate. Do you think it was very wrong of me?"

"No," said Rivington deliberately, "I don't. I lie myself - when necessary."

"He was furious," she said. "He swore that no other man should stand in his way. And then - I don't know how it was; perhaps I wasn't very convincing - he began to suspect that I had lied. That drove me into a corner. I didn't know what to say or do. And then, quite suddenly, in my extremity, I thought of you. I really don't know what made me. I didn't so much as know if you were in town. And in a flash I thought of sending that announcement to the paper. That would convince him if nothing else would, and it would mean at least a temporary respite. It was a mad thing to do, I know. But I thought you were elderly and level-headed and a confirmed bachelor and - and a sort of cousin as well -"

"To the tenth degree," murmured Rivington.

"So I told him," she hurried on, unheeding, "that we were engaged, and it was just going to be announced. When he heard that, he lost his head. I really think he was mad for the moment. He sprang straight at me like a wild beast, and I - I simply turned and fled. I'm pretty nimble, you know, when - when there are mad bulls about." Her quick smile flashed across her face and was gone. "That's all," she said. "I tore up to my room, and scribbled that paragraph straight away. I dared not wait for anything. And then I wrote to you. You had my letter with the paper this morning."

"Yes, I had them." Rivington spoke absently. She had a feeling that his eyes were fixed upon her without seeing her. "So that's all, is it?" he said slowly.

Again nervously her hands moved beneath his.

"I've been very headlong and idiotic," she said impulsively. "I've put you in an intolerable position. You must write at once and contradict it in the next issue."

"Do you mind not talking nonsense for a minute?" he said mildly. "I shall see my way directly."

She dropped into instant silence, sitting tense and mute, scarcely even breathing, while the pale blue eyes opposite remained steadily and unblinkingly fixed upon her face.

After a few moments he spoke.

"When does your mother return?"

"To-morrow morning." She hesitated for a second; then, "Of course she will be furious," she said. "You won't be able to argue with her. No one can."

Rivington's eyes looked faintly quizzical.

"I don't propose to try," he said. "She is, as I well know, an

278   Ethel M. Dell

adept in the gentle art of snubbing. And I am no match for her there. She has, moreover, a rooted objection to poor relations, for which I can hardly blame her - a prejudice which, however, I am pleased to note that you do not share."

He smiled at her with the words, and she flashed him a quick, answering smile, though her lips were quivering.

"I am not a bit like my mother," she said. "I was always dad's girl - while he lived. It was he who called me Chirpy. No one else ever did - but you."

"A great piece of presumption on my part," said Rivington.

"No. I like you to. It makes you seem like an old friend, which is what I need just now, more than anything."

"Quite so," said Rivington. "That qualifies me to advise, I suppose. I hope you won't be shocked at what I am going to suggest."

She met his eyes with complete confidence. "I shall do it whatever it is," she said.

"Don't be rash," he rejoined. "It entails a sacrifice. But it is the only thing that occurs to me for the moment. I think if you are wise you will leave London to-night."

"Leave London!" she echoed, looking startled.

"Yes. Just drop out for a bit, cut everything, and give this business a chance to blow over. Leave a note behind for mamma when she arrives, and tell her why. She'll understand."

"But - but - how can I? Dinghra will only follow me, and I shall be more at his mercy than ever in the country."

"If he finds you," said Rivington.

"But mother would tell him directly where to look."

"If she knew herself," he returned drily.

"Oh!" She stared at him with eyes of grave doubt. "But," she said, after a moment, "I have no money. I can't live on nothing."

"I do," said Rivington. "You can do the same."

She shook her head instantly, though she smiled.

"Not on the same nothing, Mr. Rivington."

He took his hand abruptly from hers.

"Look here, Chirpy," he said; "don't be a snob!"

"I'm not," she protested.

"Yes, you are. It's atrocious to be put in my place by a chit like you. I won't put up with it." He frowned at her ferociously. "You weren't above asking my help, but if you are above taking it - I've done with you."

"Oh, not really!" she pleaded. "It was foolish of me, I admit, because you really are one of the family. Please don't scowl so. It doesn't suit your style of beauty in the least, and I am sure you wouldn't like to spoil a good impression."

But he continued to frown uncompromisingly, till she stretched out a conciliatory hand to him across the table.

"Don't be cross, Knight Errant! I know you are only pretending."

"Then don't do it again," he said, relaxing, and pinching her fingers somewhat heartlessly. "I'm horribly sensitive on some points. As I was saying, it won't hurt you very badly to live on nothing for a bit, even if you are a lady of extravagant tastes."

"Oh, but I can work," she said eagerly. "I can change my name, and go into a shop."

"Of course," he said, mildly sarcastic. "You will doubtless find your vocation sooner or later. But that is not the present point. Now, listen! In the county of Hampshire is a little place called Weatherbroom - quite a little place, just a hamlet and a post-office. Just out of the hamlet is a mill with a few acres of farm land attached. It's awfully picturesque - a regular artists' place. By the way, are you an artist?"

"Oh, no. I sketch a little, but -"

"That'll do. You are not an artist, but you sketch. Then you won't be quite stranded. It's very quiet, you know. There's no society. Only the miller and his wife, and now and then the landlord - an out-at-elbows loafer who drifts about town and, very occasionally, plays knight errant to ladies in distress. There isn't even a curate. Can you possibly endure it?"

She raised her head and laughed - a sweet, spontaneous laugh, inexpressibly gay.

"Oh, you are good - just good! It's the only word that describes you. I always felt you were. I didn't know you were a landed proprietor, though."

"In a very small way," he assured her.

"How nice!" she said eagerly. "Yes, I'll go. I shall love it. But" - her face falling - "what of you? Shall you stay in town?"

"And face the music," said the Poor Relation, with his most benign smile. "That is my intention. Don't pity me! I shall enjoy it."

"Is it possible?" Again she looked doubtful.

"Of course it's possible. I enjoy a good row now and then. It keeps me in condition. I'll come down and see you some day, and tell you all about it." He glanced at his watch. "I think we ought to be moving. We will discuss arrangements as we go. I must send a wire to Mrs. Perkiss, and tell her you will go down by the seven-thirty. I will see you into the train at this end, and they will meet you at the other with the cart. It's three miles from the railway."

As they passed out together, he added meditatively, "I think you'll like the old mill, Chirpy. It's thatched."

"I'm sure I shall," she answered earnestly.

V

THE KNIGHT ERRANT TAKES THE FIELD

Rivington returned to his rooms that night, after dining at a restaurant, with a pleasing sense of having accomplished something that had been well worth the doing. He chuckled to himself a little as he walked. It was a decidedly humorous situation.

He was met at the top of the stairs by his servant, a sharp-faced lad of fifteen whom he had picked out of the dock of a police-court some months before, and who was devoted to him in consequence.

"There's a gentleman waitin' for you sir; wouldn't take 'No' for an answer; been 'ere best part of an hour. Name of Sin, sir. Looks like a foreigner."

"Eh?" The blue eyes widened for a moment, then smiled approbation. "Very appropriate," murmured Rivington. "All right, Tommy; I know the gentleman."

He was still smiling as he entered his room.

A slim, dark man turned swiftly from its farther end to meet him. He had obviously been prowling up and down.

"Mr. Rivington?" he said interrogatively.

Rivington bowed.

"Mr. Dinghra Singh?" he returned.

"Have you seen me before?"

"At a distance - several times."

"Ah!" The Indian drew himself up with a certain arrogance, but his narrow black moustache did not hide the fact that his lips were twitching with excitement. His dark eyes shone like the eyes of a beast, green and ominous. "But we have never spoken. I thought not. Now, Mr. Rivington, will you permit me to come at once to business?"

He spoke without a trace of foreign accent. He stood in the middle of the room, facing Rivington, in a commanding attitude.

Rivington took a seat on the edge of the table. He was still faintly smiling.

"Go ahead, sir," he said. "Won't you sit down?"

But Dinghra preferred to stand.

"I am presuming that you are the Mr. Cecil Mordaunt Rivington whose engagement to Miss Ernestine Cardwell was announced in this morning's paper," he said, speaking quickly but very distinctly.

"The same," said Rivington. He added with a shrug of the shoulders, "A somewhat high-sounding name for such a humble citizen as myself, but it was not of my own choosing."

Dinghra ignored the remark. He was very plainly in no mood for trivialities.

"And the engagement really exists?" he questioned.

The Englishman's brows went up.

"Of course it exists."

"Ah!" It was like a snarl. The white teeth gleamed for a moment. "I had no idea," Dinghra said, still with the same feverish rapidity, "that I had a rival."

"Are we rivals?" said Rivington, amiably regretful. "It's the first I have heard of it."

"You must have known!" The green glare suddenly began to flicker with a ruddy tinge as of flame. "Every one knew that I was after her."

"Oh yes, I knew that," said Rivington. "But - pardon me if I fail to see that that fact constitutes any rivalry between us. We were engaged long before she met you. We have been engaged for years."

"For years!" Dinghra took a sudden step forward. He looked as if he were about to spring at the Englishman's throat.

But Rivington remained quite unmoved, all unsuspecting, lounging on the edge of the table.

"Yes, for years," he repeated. "But we have kept it to ourselves till now. Even Lady Florence had no notion of it. There was nothing to be gained by talking. It was a case of -" He dug his hands into his trousers pockets and pulled them inside out with an eloquent gesture. "So, of course, there was nothing for it but to wait."

"Then why have you published the engagement now?" demanded Dinghra.

Rivington smiled.

"Because we are tired of waiting," he said.

"You are in a position to marry, then? You are -"

"I am as poor as a church mouse, if you want to know," said Rivington.

"And you will marry on nothing?"

"I dare say we sha'n't starve," said Rivington optimistically.

"Ah!" Again that beast-like snarl. There was no green glare left in the watching eyes - only red, leaping flame. "And - you like poverty?" asked the Indian in the tone of one seeking information.

"I detest it," said Rivington, with unusual energy.

Dinghra drew a step nearer, noiselessly, like a cat. His lips began to smile. He could not have been aware of the tigerish ferocity of his eyes.

"I should like to make a bargain with you, Mr. Rivington," he said.

Rivington, his hands in his pockets, looked him over with a cool appraising eye. He said nothing at all.

"This girl," said Dinghra, his voice suddenly very soft and persuasive, "she is worth a good deal to you - doubtless?"

"Doubtless," said Rivington.

"She is worth - what?"

Rivington stared uncomprehendingly.

With a slight, contemptuous gesture the Indian proceeded to explain.

"She is worth a good deal to me too - more than you would think. Her mother also desires a marriage between us. I am asking you, Mr. Rivington, to give her up, and to - name your price."

"The devil you are!" said Rivington; but he said it without violence. He still sat motionless, his hands in his pockets, surveying his visitor.

"I am rich," Dinghra said, still in those purring accents. "I am prepared to make you a wealthy man for the rest of your life. You will be able to marry, if you desire to do so, and live in ease and luxury. Come, Mr. Rivington, what do you say to it? You detest poverty. Now is your chance, then. You need never be poor again."

"You're uncommonly generous," said Rivington. "But is the lady to have no say in the matter? Or has she already spoken?"

Dinghra looked supremely contemptuous.

"The matter is entirely between you and me," he said.

"Oh!" Rivington became reflective.

The Indian crossed his arms and waited.

"Well," Rivington said at length, "I will name my price, since you desire it, but I warn you it's a fairly stiff one. You won't like it."

"Speak!" said Dinghra eagerly. His eyes literally blazed at the Englishman's imperturbable face.

Slowly Rivington took his hands from his pockets. Slowly he rose. For a moment he seemed to tower almost threateningly over the lesser man, then carelessly he suffered his limbs to relax.

"The price," he said, "is that you come to me every day for a fortnight for as sound a licking as I am in a condition to administer. I will release Miss Ernestine Cardwell for that, and that alone." He paused. "And I think at the end of my treatment that you will stand a considerably better chance of winning her favour than you do at present," he added, faintly smiling.

An awful silence followed his words. Dinghra stood as though transfixed for the space of twenty seconds. Then, without word or warning of any sort, with a single spring inexpressibly bestial, he leapt at Rivington's throat.

But Rivington was ready for him. With incredible swiftness he stooped and caught his assailant as he sprang. There followed a brief and furious struggle, and then the Indian found himself slowly but irresistibly forced backwards across the Englishman's knee. He had a vision of pale blue eyes that were too grimly ironical to be angry, and the next moment he was sitting on the floor, two muscular hands holding him down.

"Not to-night," said the leisurely voice above him. "To-morrow, if you like, we will begin the cure. Go home now and think it over."

And with that he was free. But he sat for a second too infuriated to speak or move. Then, like lightning, he was on his feet.

They stood face to face for an interval that was too pregnant with fierce mental strife to be timed by seconds. Then, with clenched hands, in utter silence, Dinghra turned away. He went softly, with a gliding, beast-like motion to the door, paused an instant, looked back with the gleaming eyes of a devil - and was gone.

The Poor Relation threw himself into a chair and laughed very softly, his lower lip gripped fast between his teeth.

VI

THE KNIGHT ERRANT'S STRATEGY

It was summer in Weatherbroom - the glareless, perfect summer of the country, of trees in their first verdure, of seas of bracken all in freshest green, of shining golden gorse, of babbling, clear brown streams, of birds that sang and chattered all day long.

And in the midst of this paradise Ernestine Cardwell dwelt secure. There was literally not a soul to speak to besides the miller and his wife, but this absence of human companionship had not begun to pall upon her. She was completely and serenely happy.

She spent the greater part of her days wandering about the woods and commons with a book tucked under her arm which she seldom opened. Now and then she tried to sketch, but usually abandoned the attempt in a fit of impatience. How could she hope to reproduce, even faintly, the loveliness around her? It seemed presumption almost to try, and she revelled in idleness instead. The singing of the birds had somehow got into her heart. She could listen to that music for hours together.

Or else she would wander along the mill-stream with the roar of the racing water behind her, and gather great handfuls of the wild flowers that fringed its banks. These were usually her evening strolls, and she loved none better.

Once, exploring around the mill, she entered a barn, and found there an old caravan that once had been gaily painted and now stood in all the shabbiness of departed glory. She had the curiosity to investigate its interior, and found there a miniature bedroom neatly furnished.

"That's Mr. Rivington's," the miller's wife told her. "He will often run down to fish in the summer, and then he likes it pulled out into the bit of wood yonder by the water, and spends the night there. It's a funny fancy, I often think."

"I should love it," said Ernestine.

She wrote to Rivington that night, her second letter since her arrival, and told him of her discovery. She added, "When are you coming down again? There are plenty of trout in the stream." And she posted the letter herself at the little thatched post-office, with a small, strictly private smile. Oh, no, she wasn't bored, of course! But it would be rather fun if he came.

On the evening of the following day, she was returning from her customary stroll along the stream, when she spied a water-lily, yellow and splendid, floating, as is the invariable custom of these flowers, just out of reach from the bank. She made several attempts to secure it, each failure only serving to increase her determination. Finally, the evening being still and warm, and her desire for the pretty thing not to be denied, she slipped off shoes and stockings and slid cautiously into the stream. It bubbled deliciously round her ankles, sending exquisite cold thrills through and through her. She secured her prize, and gave herself up unreservedly to the enjoyment thereof.

An unmistakable whiff of tobacco-smoke awoke her from her dream of delight. She turned swiftly, the lily in one hand, her skirt clutched in the other.

"Don't be alarmed," said a quiet, casual voice. "It's only me."

"Only you!" she echoed, blushing crimson. "I wasn't expecting anyone just now."

"Oh, but I don't count," he said. He was standing on the bank above her, looking down upon her with eyes so kindly that she found it impossible to be vexed with him, or even embarrassed after that first moment.

Ethel M. Dell

She reached up her hand to him.

"I'm coming out."

He took the small wrist, and helped her ashore. She looked up at him and laughed.

"I'm glad you've come," she said simply.

"Thank you," he returned, equally simply. "How are you getting on?"

"Oh, beautifully! I'm as happy as the day is long."

She began to rub her bare feet in the grass.

"Have my handkerchief," he suggested.

She accepted it with a smile, and sat down.

"Tell me about everything," she said.

Rivington sat down also, and took a long, luxurious pull at the briar pipe.

"Things were quite lively for a day or two after you left," he said. "But they have settled down again. Still, I don't advise you to go back again at present."

"Oh, I'm not going," she said. "I am much happier here. I saw a squirrel this morning. I wanted to kiss it dreadfully, but," with a sigh, "it didn't understand."

"The squirrel's loss," observed Rivington.

She crumpled his handkerchief into a ball, and tossed it at him.

"Of course. But as it will never know what it has missed, it doesn't so much matter. Are you going to live in the caravan? I'll bring you your supper if you are."

"That's awfully good of you," he said.

"Oh, no, it isn't. I want to. I shall bring my own as well and eat it on the step."

"Better and better!" said Rivington.

She laughed her own peculiarly light-hearted laugh.

"I've a good mind to turn you out and sleep there myself. I'm longing to know what it feels like."

"You can if you want to," he said.

She shook her head.

"I daren't, by myself."

"I'll have my kennel underneath," he suggested.

But she shook her head again, though she still laughed.

"No, I mustn't. What would Mrs. Perkiss say? She has a very high opinion of me at present."

"Who hasn't?" said Rivington.

She raised her eyes suddenly and gave him a straight, serious look.

"Are you trying to be complimentary, Knight Errant? Because - don't!"

Rivington blew a cloud of smoke into the air.

"Shouldn't dream of it," he said imperturbably. "I am fully

Ethel M. Dell

aware that poor relations mustn't presume on their privileges."

She coloured a little, and gave her whole attention to fastening her shoe-lace.

"I didn't mean that," she said, after a moment. "Only - don't think I care for that sort of thing, for, candidly, I don't."

"You needn't be afraid," he answered gravely. "I shall never say anything to you that I don't mean."

She glanced up again with her quick smile.

"Is it a bargain?" she said.

He held out his hand to her.

"All right, Chirpy, a bargain," he said.

And they sealed it with a warm grip of mutual appreciation.

"Now tell me what everybody has been saying about me," she said, getting to her feet.

He smiled as he leisurely arose.

"To begin with," he said, "I've seen mamma."

She looked up at him sharply.

"Go on! Wasn't she furious?"

"My dear child, that is but a mild term. She was cold as the nether mill-stone. I am afraid there isn't much chance for us if we persist in our folly."

"Don't be absurd! Tell me everything. Has that announcement been contradicted?"

"Once," said Rivington. "But it has been inserted three times since then."

"Oh, but you didn't -"

"Yes, but I did. It was necessary. I think everyone is now convinced of our engagement, including Lady Florence."

Ernestine laughed a little, in spite of herself.

"I can't think what the end of it will be," she said, with a touch of uneasiness.

"Wait till we get there," said Rivington.

She threw him a glance, half merry and half shy.

"Did you tell mother where I was?"

"On the contrary," said Rivington, "I implored her to tell me."

She drew a sharp breath.

"That was very ingenious of you."

"So I thought," he rejoined modestly.

"And what did she say?"

"She said with scarcely a pause that she had sent you out of town to give you time to come to your senses, and it was quite futile for me to question her, as she had not the faintest intention of revealing your whereabouts."

Ernestine breathed again.

"I said in the note I left behind for her that she wasn't to worry about me. I had gone into the country to get away from my troubles."

Ethel M. Dell

"That was ingenious, too," he commented. "I think, if you ask me, that we have come out of the affair rather well."

"We have all been remarkably subtle," she said, with a sigh. "But I don't like subtlety, you know. It's very horrid, and it frightens me rather."

"What are you afraid of?" he said.

"I don't know. I think I am afraid of going too far and not being able to get back."

"Do you want to get back?" he asked.

"No, no, of course not. At least, not yet," she assured him.

"Then, my dear," he said, "I think, if you will allow me to say so, that you are disquieting yourself in vain."

He spoke very kindly, with a gentleness that was infinitely reassuring.

With an impulsive movement of complete confidence, she slipped her hand through his arm.

"Thank you, Knight Errant," she said. "I wanted that."

She did not ask him anything about Dinghra, and he wondered a little at her forbearance.

VII

HIS INSPIRATION

The days of Rivington's sojourn slipped by with exceeding smoothness. They did a little fishing and a good deal of quiet lazing, a little exploring, and even one or two long, all-day rambles.

And then one day, to Ernestine's amazement, Rivington took her sketching-block from her and began to sketch. He worked rapidly and quite silently for about an hour, smoking furiously the while, and finally laid before her the completed sketch.

She stared at it in astonishment.

"I had no idea you were a genius. Why, it's lovely!"

He smiled a little.

"I did it for a living once, before my father died and left me enough to buy me bread and cheese. I became a loafer then, and I've been one ever since."

"But what a pity!" she exclaimed.

His smile broadened.

"It is, isn't it? But where's the sense of working when you've nothing to work for? No, it isn't the work of a genius. It's the work of a man who might do something good if he had the incentive for it, but not otherwise."

"What a pity!" she said again. "Why don't you take to it again?"

"I might," he said, "if I found it worth while."

Ethel M. Dell

He tapped the ashes from his pipe and settled himself at full length.

"Surely it is worth while!" she protested. "Why, you might make quite a lot of money."

Rivington stuck the empty pipe between his teeth and pulled at it absently.

"I'm not particularly keen on money," he said.

"But it's such a waste," she argued. "Oh, I wish I had your talent. I would never let it lie idle."

"It isn't my fault," he said; "I am waiting for an inspiration."

"What do you mean by an inspiration?"

He turned lazily upon his side and looked at her.

"Let us say, for instance, if some nice little woman ever cared to marry me," he said.

There fell a sudden silence. Ernestine was studying his sketch with her head on one side. At length, "You will never marry," she said, in a tone of conviction.

"Probably not," agreed Rivington.

He lay still for a few seconds, then sat up slowly and removed his pipe to peer over her shoulder.

"It isn't bad," he said critically.

She flashed him a sudden smile.

"Do take it up again!" she pleaded. "It's really wicked of you to go and bury a talent like that."

He shook his head.

"I can't sketch just to please myself. It isn't in me."

"Do it to please me, then," she said impulsively.

He smiled into her eyes.

"Would it please you, Chirpy?"

Her eyes met his with absolute candour.

"Immensely," she said. "Immensely! You know it would."

He held out his hand for the sketch.

"All right, then. You shall be my inspiration."

She laughed lightly.

"Till that nice little woman turns up."

"Exactly," said Rivington.

He continued to hold out his hand, but she withheld the sketch.

"I'm going to keep it, if you don't mind."

"What for?" he said.

"Because I like it. I want it. Why shouldn't I?"

"I will do you something better worth having than that," he said.

"Something I shouldn't like half so well," she returned. "No, I'm going to keep this, in memory of a perfect afternoon and some of the happiest days of my life."

Rivington gave in, still smiling.

"I'm going back to town to-morrow," he said.

"Oh, are you?" Actual dismay sounded in her voice. "Why?"

"I'm afraid I must," he said. "I'm sorry. Shall you be lonely?"

"Oh, no," she rejoined briskly. "Of course not. I wasn't lonely before you came." She added rather wistfully, "It was good of you to stay so long; I hope you haven't been very bored?"

"Not a bit," said Rivington. "I've only been afraid of boring you."

She laughed a little. A certain constraint seemed to have fallen upon her.

"How horribly polite we are getting!" she said.

He laid his hand for an instant on her shoulder.

"I shall come again, Chirpy," he said.

She nodded carelessly, not looking at him.

"Yes, mind you do. I dare say I shan't be having any other visitors at present."

But though her manner was perfectly friendly, Rivington was conscious of that unwonted constraint during the rest of his visit. He even fancied on the morrow that she bade him farewell with relief.

VIII

THE MEETING IN THE MARKET-PLACE

Two days later, Ernestine drove with the miller's wife to market at Rington, five miles distant. She had never seen a country market, and her interest was keen. They started after an early breakfast on an exquisite summer morning. And Ernestine carried with her a letter which she had that day received from Rivington.

> "Dear Chirpy," it ran, "I hasten to write and tell you that now I am back in town again I am most hideously bored. I am, however, negotiating for a studio, which fact ought to earn for me your valued approval. If, for any reason, my presence should seem desirable to you, write or wire, and I shall come immediately. - Your devoted
>
> "KNIGHT ERRANT."

Ernestine squeezed this letter a good many times on the way to Rington. She had certainly been feeling somewhat forlorn since his departure. But, this fact notwithstanding, she had no intention of writing or wiring to him at present. Still, it was nice to know he would come.

They reached the old country town, and found it crammed with market folk. The whole place hummed with people. Ernestine's first view of the market-place filled her with amazement. The lowing of cattle, the bleating of sheep, and the yelling of men combined to make such a confusion of sound that she felt bewildered, even awestruck.

Mrs. Perkiss went straight to the oldest inn in the place and put up the cart. She was there to buy, not to sell.

Ernestine kept with her for the first hour, then, growing weary of the hubbub, wandered away from the market to explore the old town. She sat for a while in the churchyard, and there, to enliven her solitude, re-read that letter of Rivington's. Was he really taking up art again to please her? He had been very energetic. She wondered, smiling, how long his energy would last.

Thus engaged the time passed quickly, and she presently awoke from a deep reverie to find that the hour Mrs. Perkiss had appointed for lunch at the inn was approaching. She rose, and began to make her way thither.

The street was crowded, and her progress was slow. A motor was threading its way through the throng at a snail's pace. The persistence of its horn attracted her attention. As it neared her she glanced at its occupant.

The next moment she was shrinking back into a doorway, white to the lips. The man in the car was Dinghra.

Across the crowded pavement his eyes sought hers, and the wicked triumph in them turned her cold. He made no sign of recognition, and she seemed as though petrified till the motor had slowly passed.

Then a great weakness came over her, and for a few seconds all consciousness of her surroundings went from her. She remembered only those evil eyes and the gloating satisfaction with which they had rested upon her.

"Ain't you well, miss?" said a voice.

With a start she found a burly young farmer beside her. He looked down at her with kindly concern.

"You take my arm," he said. "Which way do you want to go?"

With an effort she told him, and the next moment he was leading her rapidly through the crowd.

They reached the inn, and he put her into the bar parlour and went out, bellowing for Mrs. Perkiss, whom he knew.

When he finally emerged, after finding the miller's wife, a slim, dark man was waiting on the further side of the road. The farmer took no note of him, but the watcher saw the farmer, and with swift, cat-like tread he followed him.

IX

IN FEAR OF THE ENEMY

All the way home the memory of those eyes haunted Ernestine. All the way home her ears were straining to catch the hoot of a motor-horn and the rush of wheels behind them.

But no motor overtook them. Nothing happened to disturb the smiling peace of that summer afternoon.

Back in her little room under the thatch she flung herself face downwards on the bed, and lay tense. What should she do? What should she do? He had seen her. He was on her track. Sooner or later he would run her to earth. And she - what could she do?

For a long while she lay there, too horror-stricken to move, while over and over again there passed through her aching brain the memory of those eyes. Did he guess that she had come there to hide from him? Had he been hunting her for long?

She moved at length, sat up stiffly, and felt something crackle inside her dress. With a little start she realised what it was, and drew forth Rivington's letter.

A great sigh broke from her as she opened and read it once again.

A little later she ran swiftly downstairs with a folded paper in her hand. Out into the blinding sunshine, bareheaded, she ran, never pausing till she turned into the lily-decked garden of the post-office.

She was trembling all over as she handed in her message, but as it ticked away a sensation of immense relief stole over her. She went out again feeling almost calm.

But that night her terrors came back upon her in ghastly array. She could not sleep, and lay listening to every sound. Finally she fell into an uneasy doze, from which she started to hear the dog in the yard barking furiously. She lay shivering for a while, then crept to her window and looked out. The dense shadow of a pine wood across the road blotted out the starlight, and all was very dark. It was impossible to discern anything. She stood listening intently in the darkness.

The dog subsided into a growling monotone, and through the stillness she fancied she caught a faint sound, as if some animal were prowling softly under the trees. She listened with a thumping heart. Nearer it seemed to come, and nearer, and then she heard it no more. A sudden gust stirred the pine tops, and a sudden, overmastering panic filled her soul.

With the violence of frenzy she slammed and bolted her window, and made a wild spring back to the bed. She burrowed down under the blankets, and lay there huddled, not daring to stir for a long, long time.

With the first glimmer of day came relief, but she did not sleep. The night's terror had left her nerves too shaken for repose. Yet as the sun rose and the farmyard sounds began, as she heard the mill-wheel creak and turn and the rush and roar of the water below, common sense came to her aid, and she was able to tell herself that her night alarm might have been due to nothing more than her own startled imagination.

On the breakfast table she found a card awaiting her, which she seized, and read with deepening colour.

> "Expect me by the afternoon train. I shall walk from the station. - K.E."

A feeling of gladness, so intense that it was almost rapture, made her blood flow faster. He was coming in answer to her desperate summons. He would be with her that very day. She was sure that he would tell her what to do.

Ethel M. Dell

She read the card several times in the course of the morning, and came to the conclusion that it would be only nice of her to walk to meet him. The path lay through beech woods. She had gone part of the way with him only three days before. Only three days! It seemed like months. She looked forward to meeting him again as though he had been an old friend.

She started soon after the early dinner. The afternoon was hot and sultry. She was glad to turn from the road into the shade and stillness of the woods. The sun-rays slanting downwards through the mazy, golden aisles made her think of the afternoon on which she had waited for him under the dome of St. Paul's.

The heat as she proceeded became intense. The humming of many insects filled the air with a persistent drone. It was summer at its height.

A heavy languor began to possess her. She remembered that she had not slept all the previous night. She also recalled the panic that had kept her awake, and smiled faintly to herself. She did not feel afraid now that Rivington was coming. She even began to think she had been rather foolish, and wondered if he would think so too.

She began to go more slowly. Her feet felt heavier at every step. A few yards ahead a golden-brown stream ran babbling through the wood. It was close to the path. She would sit down beside it and rest till he arrived.

She reached the stream, sank down upon a bed of moss, then found the heat intolerable, and began impulsively to loosen her shoes. What if he did discover her a second time barefooted? He had not minded before; neither had she. And no one else would come that way. He had even lent her his handkerchief to dry her feet. Perhaps he would again.

Once more a strictly private little smile twitched the corners of her mouth. She slipped off her stockings and plunged her tired feet into the cool, running water.

Leaning back against a tree-trunk she closed her eyes. An exquisite sense of well-being stole over her. He would not be here yet. What did it matter if she dozed? The bubbling of the water lulled her. She rested her feet upon a sunny brown stone. She turned her cheek upon her arm.

And in her sleep she heard the thudding of a horse's hoofs, and dreamed that her knight errant was close at hand.

X

THE TIGER'S PREY

With a start she opened her eyes. Some one was drawing near. It must be later than she had thought.

Again she heard the tramp of a horse's feet, and hastily peered round the trunk of her tree. Surely he had not come on horseback! It must be a stranger. She cast a hasty glance towards her shoes, and gathered her feet under her.

A few yards away she caught sight of a horse's clean limbs moving in the checkered sunlight. Its rider - her heart gave a sudden, sickening throb and stood still. He was riding like a king, with his insolent dark face turned to the sun. She stared at him for one wild moment, then shrank against her tree. It was possible, it was possible even then, that he might pass her by without turning his eyes in her direction.

Nearer he came, and nearer yet. The path wound immediately behind the beech tree that sheltered her. He was close to her now. He had reached her. She cowered down in breathless terror in the moss, motionless as a stone. On went the horse's feet, on without a pause, slow and regular as the beat of a drum. He went by her at a walking pace. Surely he had not seen her!

She did not dare to lift her head, but it seemed to her that the sound of the thudding hoofs died very quickly away. For seconds that seemed like hours she crouched there in the afternoon stillness. Then at last - at last - she ventured to raise herself - to turn and look.

And in that moment she knew the agony that pierces every nerve with a physical anguish in the face of sudden horror. For there, close to her, was Dinghra, on foot, not six paces away, and drawing softly nearer. There was a faint smile on his face.

His eyes were fixed and devilish.

With a gasp she sprang up, and the next moment was running wildly away, away, down the forest path, heedless of the rough ground, of the stones and roots that tore her bare feet, running like a mad creature, with sobbing breath, and limbs that staggered, compel them though she might.

She did not run far. Her flight ended as suddenly as it had begun in a violent, headlong fall. A long streamer of bramble had tripped her unaccustomed feet. She was conscious for an instant of the horrible pain of it as she was flung forward on her hands.

And then came the touch that she dreaded, the sinewy hands lifting her, the sinister face looking into hers.

"You should never run away from destiny," said Dinghra softly. "Destiny can always catch you up."

She gasped and shuddered. She was shaking all over, too crushed, too shattered, for speech.

He set her on her feet.

"We will go back," he said, keeping his arm about her. "You have had a pleasant sleep? I am sorry you awoke so soon."

But she stood still, her wild eyes searching the forest depths.

"Oh, let me go!" she cried out suddenly. "Oh, do let me go!"

His arm tightened, but still he smiled.

"Never again. I have had some trouble to find you, but you are mine now for ever - or at least" - and the snarl of the beast was in his voice - "for as long as I want you."

She resisted him, striving to escape that ever-tightening arm.

Ethel M. Dell

"No!" she cried in an agony. "No! No! No!"

His hold became a vice-like grip. Without a word he forced her back with him along the way she had come. She limped as she went, and he noted it with a terrible smile.

"It would have been better if you hadn't run away," he said.

"Oh, do let me go!" she begged again through her white lips. "Why do you persecute me like this? I have never done you any harm."

"Except laugh at me," he answered. "But you will never do that again, at least."

And then, finding her weight upon him, he stopped and lifted her in his arms.

She covered her face with her hands, and he laughed above her head.

"It is a dangerous amusement," he said, "to laugh at Dinghra. There are not many who dare. There is not one who goes unpunished."

He bore her back to her resting-place. He set her on her feet and drew her hands away, holding her firmly by the wrists.

"Now tell me," he said "it is the last time I shall ever ask you - will you marry me?"

"Never!" she cried.

"Be careful!" he broke in warningly. "That is not your answer. Look at me! Look into my eyes! Do you think you are wise in giving me such an answer as that?"

But she would not meet his eyes. She dared not.

"Listen!" he said. "Your mother has given you to me. She will never speak to you again, except as my promised wife. I have sworn to her that I will make you accept me. No power on earth can take you from me. Ernestine, listen! You are the only woman who ever resisted me, and for that I am going to make you what I have never desired to make any woman before, - my wife - not my servant; my queen - not my slave. I can give you everything under the sun. You will be a princess. You will have wealth, jewels such as you have never dreamed of, palaces, servants, honour -"

"And you!" she cried hysterically. "You!"

"Yes, and me," he said. "But you will have me in one form or another whatever your choice. You won't get away from me. You may refuse to marry me, but -"

"I do!" she burst out wildly. "I do!"

"But -" he said again, very deliberately.

And then, compelled by she knew not what, she lifted her eyes to his. And all her life she shrank and shuddered at the dread memory of what she saw.

For seconds he did not utter a single word. For seconds his eyes held hers, arresting, piercing, devouring. She could not escape them. She was forced to meet them, albeit with fear and loathing unutterable.

"You see!" he said at last, as though concluding an argument. "You are mine! I can do with you exactly as I will - exactly as I will!" He repeated the words almost in a whisper.

But at that she cried out, and began to struggle, like a bird beating its wings against the bars of a cage.

His hold became cruel in an instant. He forced her hands behind her, holding her imprisoned in his arms. He tilted her

Ethel M. Dell

head back. His eyes shone down into hers like the eyes of a tiger that clutches its prey. He quelled her resistance by sheer brutality.

"I have warned you!" he said; and she knew instinctively that he would have no mercy.

"How can I marry you?" she gasped in desperation. "I am engaged to - another man!"

She saw his face change. Instantly she knew that she had made a mistake. The ferocity in his eyes turned to devilish malice.

"You will marry me yet!" he said.

"But you will come to hate me some day!" she cried, clutching at straws. "As - as I hate you to-day!"

His look appalled her, his lips were close to hers.

"If I do," he said, with a fiendish smile, "I shall find a remedy. But so long as you hate me, I shall not grow tired of you!"

And with that he suddenly and savagely pressed his lips to hers.

XI

THE TIGER'S PUNISHMENT

That single kiss was to Ernestine the climax and zenith of horror. It seemed to sear and blister her very soul with an anguish of repulsion that would scar her memory for all time. She retained her consciousness, but she never knew by what lightning stroke she was set free. She was too dazed, too blinded, by her horror to realise. But suddenly the cruel grip that had her helpless was gone. A vague confusion swam before her eyes. Her knees doubled under her. She sank down in a huddled heap, and lay quivering.

There came to her the sound of struggling, the sound of cursing, the sound of blows. But, sick and spent, she heeded none of these things, till a certain monotony of sound began to drum itself into her senses. She came to full understanding to see Dinghra, in the grip of an Englishman, being hideously thrashed with his own horsewhip. He was quite powerless in that grip, but he would fight to the end, and it seemed that the end was not far off. The punishment must have been going on for many seconds. For his face was quite livid and streaked with blood, his hands groped blindly, beating the air, he staggered at each blow.

The whip fell flail-like, with absolute precision and regularity. It spared no part of him. His coat was nearly torn off. In one place, on the shoulder, the white shirt was exposed, and this also was streaked with blood.

Ernestine crouched under the tree and watched. But very soon a new fear sprang up within her, a fear that made her collect all her strength for action. It was something in that awful, livid face that prompted her.

She struggled stiffly to her feet, later she wondered how, and drew near to the two men. The whirling whip continued to

Ethel M. Dell

descend, but she had no fear of that. She came quite close till she was almost under the upraised arm. She laid trembling hands upon a grey tweed coat.

"Let him go!" she said very urgently. "Let him go - while he can!"

Rivington looked down into her white face. He was white himself - white to the lips.

"I haven't done with him yet," he said, and he spoke between his teeth.

"I know," she said. "I know. But he has had enough. You mustn't kill him."

She was strangely calm, and her calmness took effect. Later, she wondered at that also.

Rivington jerked the exhausted man upright.

"Go back!" he said to Ernestine. "Go back! I won't kill him!"

She took him at his word, and went back. She heard Rivington speak briefly and sternly, and Dinghra mumbled something in reply. She heard the shuffling of feet, and knew that Rivington was helping him to walk.

For a little while she watched the two figures, the one supporting the other, as they moved slowly away. Dinghra's head was sunk upon his breast. He slunk along like a beaten dog. Then the trunk of a tree hid them from her sight.

When that happened, Ernestine suffered herself to collapse upon the moss, with her head upon her arms.

Lying thus, she presently heard once more the tread of a horse's feet, and counted each footfall mechanically. They grew fainter and fainter, till at last the forest silence swallowed them, and a great solitude seemed to wrap her round.

Minutes passed. She did not stir. Her strength had gone utterly from her. Finally there came the sound of a quiet footfall.

Close to her it came, and stopped.

"Why, Chirpy!" a quiet voice said.

She tried to move, but could not. She was as one paralysed. She could not so much as utter a word.

He knelt down beside her and raised her to a sitting posture, so that she leaned against him. Holding her so, he gently rubbed her cheek.

"Poor little Chirpy!" he said. "It's all right!"

At sound of the pity and the tenderness of his voice, something seemed to break within her, the awful constriction passed. She hid her face upon his arm, and burst into a wild agony of weeping.

He laid his hand upon her head, and kept it there for a while; then as her sobbing grew more and more violent, he bent over her.

"Don't cry so, child, for Heaven's sake!" he said earnestly. "It's all right, dear; all right. You are perfectly safe!"

"I shall never - feel safe - again!" she gasped, between her sobs.

"Yes, yes, you will," he assured her. "You will have me to take care of you. I shall not leave you again."

"But the nights!" she cried wildly. "The nights!"

"Hush!" he said. "Hush! There is nothing to cry about. I will take care of you at night, too."

She began to grow a little calmer. The assurance of his manner soothed her. But for a long time she crouched there shivering, with her face hidden, while he knelt beside her and stroked her hair.

At last he moved as though to rise, but on the instant she clutched at him with both hands.

"Don't go! Don't leave me! You said you wouldn't!"

"I am not going to, Chirpy," he said. "Don't be afraid!"

But she was afraid, and continued to cling to him very tightly, though she would not raise her face.

"Come!" he said gently, at length. "You're better. Wouldn't you like to bathe your feet?"

"You will stay with me?" she whispered.

"I am going to help you down to the stream," he said.

"Don't - don't carry me!" she faltered.

"Of course not! You can walk on this moss if I hold you up."

But she was very reluctant to move.

"I - I don't want you to look at me," she said, at last, with a great sob. "I feel such a fright."

"Don't be a goose, Chirpy!" he said.

That braced her a little. She dried her tears. She even suffered him to raise her to her feet, but she kept her head bent, avoiding his eyes.

"Look where you are going," said Rivington practically. "Here is my arm. You mustn't mind me, you know. Lean hard!"

She accepted his assistance in silence. She was crying still, though she strove to conceal the fact. But as she sank down once more on the brink of the stream, the sobs broke out afresh, and would not be suppressed.

"I was so happy!" she whispered. "I didn't want him here - to spoil my paradise."

Rivington said nothing. She did not even know if he heard; and if he were aware of her tears he gave no sign. He was gently bathing her torn feet with his hands.

XII

THE KNIGHT ERRANT PLAYS THE GAME

She began to command herself at last, and to be inexpressibly ashamed of her weakness. She sat in silence, accepting his ministrations, till Rivington proceeded to tear his handkerchief into strips for bandaging purposes; then she put out a protesting hand.

"You - you shouldn't!" she said rather tremulously.

He looked at her with his kindly smile.

"It's all right, Chirpy. I've got another."

She tried to laugh. It was a valiant effort.

"I know I'm a horrid nuisance to you. It's nice of you to pretend you don't mind."

"I never pretend," said Rivington, with a touch of grimness. "Do you think you will be able to get your stocking over that?"

"I think so."

"Try!" he said.

She tried and succeeded.

"That's better," said Rivington. "Now for the shoes. I can put them on."

"I don't like you to," she murmured.

"Knights errant always do that," he assured her. "It's part of the game. Come! That's splendid! How does it feel?"

"I think I can bear it," she said, under her breath.

He drew it instantly off again.

"No, you can't. Or, at least, you are not going to. Look here, Chirpy, my dear, I think you must let me carry you, anyhow to the caravan. It isn't far, and I can fetch you some slippers from the mill from there. What? You don't mind, do you? An old friend like me, and a poor relation into the bargain?" The blue eyes smiled at her quizzically, and very persuasively.

But her white face crimsoned, and she turned it aside.

"I don't want you to," she said piteously.

"No, but you'll put up with it!" he urged. "It's too small a thing to argue about, and you have too much sense to refuse."

He rose with the words. She looked up at him with quivering lips.

"You wouldn't do it - if I refused?" she faltered.

The smile went out of his eyes.

"I shall never do anything against your will," he said. "But I don't know how you will get back if I don't."

She pondered this for a moment, then, impulsively as a child, stretched up her arms to him.

"All right, Knight Errant. You may," she said.

And he bent and lifted her without further words.

They scarcely spoke during that journey. Only once, towards the end of it, Ernestine asked him if he were tired, and he scouted the idea with a laugh.

When they reached the caravan, and he set her down upon the step, she thanked him meekly.

"We will have tea," said Rivington, and proceeded to forage for the necessaries for this meal in a locker inside the caravan.

He brought out a spirit-lamp and boiled some water. The actual making of the tea he relegated to Ernestine.

"A woman does it better than a man," he said.

And while she was thus occupied, he produced cups and saucers, and a tin of biscuits, and laid the cloth. Finally, he seated himself on the grass below her, and began with evident enjoyment to partake with her of the meal thus provided.

When it was over, he washed up, she drying the cups and saucers, and striving with somewhat doubtful success to appear normal and unconstrained.

"Do you mind if I smoke?" he asked, at the end of this.

"Of course not," she answered, and he brought out the briar pipe forthwith.

She watched him fill and light it, her chin upon her hand. She was still very pale, and the fear had not gone wholly from her eyes.

"Now I'm going to talk to you," Rivington announced.

"Yes?" she said rather faintly.

He lay back with his arms under his head, and stared up through the beech boughs to the cloudless evening sky.

"I want you first of all to remember," he said, "that what I said a little while ago I meant - and shall mean for all time. I will never do anything, Chirpy, against your will."

He spoke deliberately. He was puffing the smoke upward in long spirals.

"That is quite understood, is it?" he asked, as she did not speak.

"I think so," said Ernestine slowly.

"I want you to be quite sure," he said. "Otherwise, what I am going to say may startle you."

"Don't frighten me!" she begged, in a whisper.

"My dear child, I sha'n't frighten you," he rejoined. "You may frighten yourself. That is what I am trying to guard against."

Her laugh had a piteous quiver in it.

"You think me very young and foolish, don't you?" she said.

He sat up and looked at her.

"I think," he said, "that you stand in very serious need of someone to look after you."

She made a slight, impatient movement.

"Why go over old ground? If you really have any definite suggestion to make, why not make it?"

Rivington clasped his hands about his knees. He continued to look at her speculatively, his pipe between his teeth.

"Look here, Chirpy," he said, after a moment, "I can't help thinking that you would be better off and a good deal happier if you married."

"If I - married!" Her eyes flashed startled interrogation at him. "If I - married!" she repeated almost fiercely. "I would rather die!"

"I didn't suggest that you should marry Dinghra," he pointed out mildly. "He is not the only man in the world."

The hot colour rushed up over her face.

"He is the only one that ever wanted me," she said, in a muffled tone.

"Quite sure of that?" said Rivington.

She did not answer him. She was playing nervously with a straw that she had pulled from the floor of the caravan. Her eyes were downcast.

"What about me?" said Rivington. "Think you could put up with me as a husband?"

She shook her head in silence.

"Why not?" he said gently.

Again she shook her head.

He knelt up suddenly beside her, discarding his pipe, and laid his hand on hers.

"Tell me why not," he said.

A little tremor went through her at his touch. She did not raise her eyes.

"It wouldn't do," she said, her voice very low.

"You don't like me?" he questioned.

"Yes; I like you. It isn't that."

"Then - what is it, Chirpy? I believe you are afraid of me," he said half quizzically.

"I'm not!" she declared, with vehemence. "I'm not such a donkey! No, Knight Errant, I'm only afraid for you."

"I don't quite grasp your meaning," he said.

With an effort she explained.

"You see, you don't know me very well - not nearly so well as I know you."

"I know you well enough to be fond of you, Chirpy," he said.

"That is just because you don't know me," she said, her voice quivering a little. "You wouldn't like me for long, Knight Errant. Men never do."

"More fools they," said the knight errant, with somewhat unusual emphasis. "It's their loss, anyway."

She laughed a little.

"It's very nice of you to say so, but it doesn't alter the fact. Besides -" She paused.

"Besides -" said Rivington.

She looked at him suddenly.

"What about that nice little woman who may turn up some day?"

The humorous corner of Rivington's mouth went up.

"I think she has, Chirpy," he said. "To tell you the honest truth, I've been thinking so for some time."

"You really want to marry me?" Ernestine looked him straight in the eyes. "It isn't - only - a chivalrous impulse?"

He met her look quite steadily.

"No," he said quietly; "it isn't - only - that."

Her eyes fell away from his.

"I haven't any money, you know," she said.

"Never mind about the money," he answered cheerily. "I have a little, enough to keep us from starvation. I can make more. It will do me good to work. It's settled, then? You'll have me?"

"If - if you are sure -" she faltered. Then impulsively, "Oh, it's hateful to feel that I've thrown myself at your head!"

His hand closed upon hers with a restraining pressure.

"You mustn't say those things to me, Chirpy," he said quietly; "they hurt me. Now let me tell you my plans. Do you know what I did when I got back to town the other day? I went and bought a special marriage licence. You see, I wanted to marry you even then, and I hoped that before very long I should persuade you to have me. As soon as I got your telegram, I went off and purchased a wedding-ring. I hope it will fit. But, anyhow, it will serve our present purpose. Will you drive with me into Rington to-morrow and marry me there?"

She was listening to him in wide-eyed amazement.

"So soon?" she said.

"I thought it would save any further trouble," he answered. "But it is for you to decide."

"And - and what should we do afterwards?" she asked, stooping to pick up her straw that had fallen to the ground.

"That, again, would be for you to decide," he answered. "I would take you straight back to your mother if you wished."

She gave a muffled laugh.

"Of course I shouldn't want you to do that."

"Or," proceeded Rivington, "I would hire an animal to draw the caravan, and we would go for a holiday in the forest. Would it bore you?"

"I don't think so," she said, without looking at him. "I - I could sketch, you know, and you could paint."

"To be sure," he said. "Shall we do that, then?"

She began to split the straw with minute care.

"You think there is no danger of - Dinghra?" she said, after a moment.

Rivington smiled grimly, and got to his feet. "Not the smallest," he said.

"He might come back," she persisted. "What if - what if he tried to murder you?"

Rivington was coaxing his pipe back to life. He accomplished his object before he replied. Then:

"You need not have the faintest fear of that," he said. "Dinghra has had the advantage of a public-school education. He has doubtless been thrashed before."

"He is vindictive," she objected.

"He may be, but he is shrewd enough to know when the game is up. Frankly, Chirpy, I don't think the prospect of pestering you, or even of punishing me, will induce him to take the field again after we are married. No" - he smiled down at her - "I think I have cooled his ardour too effectually for that."

She shuddered.

"I shall never forget it."

He patted her shoulder reassuringly.

"I think you will, Chirpy. Or at least you will place it in the same category as the bull incident. You will forget the fright, and remember only with kindness the Knight Errant who had the good fortune to pull you through."

She reached up and squeezed his hand, still without looking at him.

"I shall always do that," she said softly.

"Then that's settled," said Rivington in a tone of quiet satisfaction.

XIII

THE KNIGHT ERRANT VICTORIOUS

"On the 21st of June, quite privately, at the Parish Church, Rington, Hampshire, by the Vicar of the Parish, Cecil Mordaunt Rivington to Ernestine, fourth daughter of Lady Florence Cardwell."

Cecil Mordaunt Rivington, with his pipe occupying one corner of his mouth, and the other cocked at a distinctly humorous angle, sat on the step of the caravan on the evening of the day succeeding that of his marriage, and read the announcement thereof in the paper which he had just fetched from the post-office.

There was considerable complacence in his attitude. A cheerful fire of sticks burned near, over which a tripod supported a black pot.

The sunset light filtered golden through the forest. It was growing late.

Suddenly he turned and called over his shoulder. "I say, Chirpy!"

Ernestine's voice answered from the further end of the caravan that was shut off from the rest by curtains.

"I'm just coming. What is it? Is the pot all right?"

"Splendid. Be quick! I've something to show you."

The curtains parted, and Ernestine came daintily forth.

Rivington barely glanced at her. He was too intent upon the paper in his hand. She stopped behind him, and bent to read the paragraph he pointed out.

After a pause, he turned to view its effect, and on the instant his eyebrows went up in amazement.

"Hullo!" he said.

She was dressed like a gipsy in every detail, even to the scarlet kerchief on her head. She drew back a little, colouring under his scrutiny.

"I hope you approve," she said.

"By Jove, you look ripping!" said Rivington. "How in the world did you do it?"

"I made Mrs. Perkiss help me. We managed it between us. It was just a fancy of mine to fill the idle hours. I didn't think I should ever have the courage to wear it."

He reached up his hand to her as he sat.

"My dear, you make a charming gipsy," he said. "You will have to sit for me."

She laughed, touched his hand with a hint of shyness, and stepped down beside him.

"How is the supper getting on? Have you looked at it?"

He laid aside his paper to prepare for the meal. To her evident relief he made no further comment at the moment upon her appearance. But when supper was over and he was smoking his evening pipe, his eyes dwelt upon her continually as she flitted to and fro, having declined his assistance, and set everything in order after the meal.

The sun had disappeared, and a deep dusk was falling upon the forest. Ernestine moved, elf-like, in the light of the sinking fire. She took no notice of the man who watched her, being plainly too busy to heed his attention.

But her duties were over at last, and she turned from the ruddy firelight and moved, half reluctantly it seemed, towards him. She reached him, and stood before him.

"I've done now," she said. "You can rake out the fire. Good-night!"

He took the little hand in his.

"Are you tired, Chirpy?"

"No, I don't think so." She sounded slightly doubtful.

"Won't you stay with me for a little?" he said. She stood silent. "I was horribly lonely after you went to bed last night," he urged gently.

She uttered a funny little sigh.

"I'm sure you must have been horribly uncomfortable too," she said. "Did you lie awake?"

"No, I wasn't uncomfortable. I've slept in the open heaps of times before. I was just - lonely."

She laid her hand lightly on his shoulder as she stood beside him.

"It was rather awesome," she admitted.

"I believe you were lonely too," he said.

She laughed a little, and said nothing.

He took his pipe from his mouth and laid it tenderly upon the ground.

"Shall I tell you something, Chirpy?"

Her hand began to rub up and down uneasily on his shoulder.

"Well?" she said under her breath.

He looked up at her in the falling darkness.

"I feel exactly as you felt over that squirrel," he said. "Do you remember? You wanted to kiss it, but the little fool didn't understand."

A slight quiver went through Ernestine. Again rather breathlessly, she laughed.

"Some little fools don't," she said.

He moved and very gently slipped his arm about her. "I didn't mean to put it quite like that," he said. "You will pardon my clumsiness, won't you?"

She did not resist his arm, but neither did she yield to it. Her hand still fidgeted upon his shoulder.

"I wish you wouldn't be so horribly nice to me," she said suddenly.

"My dear Chirpy!"

"Yes," she said with vehemence. "Why don't you take what you want? I - I should respect you then."

"But I want you to love me," he answered quietly.

She drew a quick breath, and became suddenly quite rigid, intensely still.

His arm grew a little closer about her.

"Don't you know I am in love with you, Chirpy?" he asked her very softly. "Am I such a dunderhead that I haven't made that plain?"

"Are you?" she said, a sharp catch in her voice. "Are you?" Abruptly she stooped to him. "Knight Errant," she said, and the words fell swift and passionate, "would you have really wanted to marry me - anyway?"

His face was upturned to hers. He could feel her breathing, sharp and short, upon his lips.

"My dear," he said, "I have wanted to marry you ever since that afternoon you met me in St. Paul's."

He would have risen with the words, but she made a quick movement downwards to prevent him, and suddenly she was on her knees before him with her arms about his neck.

"Oh, I'm so glad you told me," she whispered tremulously. "I'm so glad."

He gathered her closely to him. His lips were against her forehead.

"It makes all the difference, dear, does it?"

"Yes," she whispered back, clinging faster. "Just all the difference in the world, because - because it was that afternoon - I began - to want - you too."

And there in the darkness, with the dim forest all about them, she turned her lips to meet her husband's first kiss.

Ethel M. Dell

A QUESTION OF TRUST

I

Pierre Dumaresq stood gazing out to the hard blue line of the horizon with a frown between his brows. The glare upon the water was intense, but he stared into it with fixed, unflinching eyes, unconscious of discomfort.

He held a supple riding-switch in his hands, at which his fingers strained and twisted continually, as though somewhere in the inner man there burned a fierce impatience. But his dark face was as immovable as though it had been carved in bronze. A tropical sun had made him even darker than Nature had intended him to be, a fact to which those fixed eyes testified, for they shone like steel in the sunlight, in curious contrast to his swarthy skin. His hair was black, cropped close about a bullet head, which was set on his broad shoulders with an arrogance that gave him a peculiarly aggressive air. The narrow black moustache he wore emphasised rather than concealed the thin straight line of mouth. Plainly a fighting man this, and one, moreover, accustomed to hold his own.

At the striking of a clock in the room behind him he turned as though a voice had spoken, and left the stone balcony on which he had been waiting. His spurs rang as he stepped into the room behind it. The floor was uncarpeted, and shone like ebony.

He glanced around him as one unfamiliar with his surroundings. It was a large apartment, and lofty, but it contained very little furniture - a couch, two or three chairs, a writing-table; on the walls, several strangely shaped weapons; on the mantelpiece a couple of foils.

He smiled as his look fell upon these, and, crossing the room, he took one of them up, and tested it between his hands.

At the quiet opening of the door he wheeled, still holding it. A woman stood a moment upon the threshold; then slowly entered. She was little more than a girl but the cold dignity of her demeanour imparted to her the severity of more advanced years. Her face was like marble, white, pure, immobile; but there was a touch of pathos about the eyes. They were deeply shadowed, and looked as if they had watched - or wept - for many hours.

Dumaresq bowed in the brief English fashion, instantly straightening himself with a squaring of his broad shoulders that were already so immensely square that they made his height seem inconsiderable.

She gravely inclined her head in response. She did not invite him to sit down, and he remained where he was, with his fierce eyes unwaveringly upon her.

In the middle of the room, full three yards from him, she paused, and deliberately met his scrutiny.

"You wished to see me, Monsieur Dumaresq?" she said in English.

"Yes," said Dumaresq. He turned, and laid the foil back upon the mantelpiece behind him; then calmly crossed the intervening space, and stood before her. "I am grateful to you for granting me an interview, mademoiselle," he said. "I am aware that you have done so against your will."

There was something of a challenge in the words, but she did not seem to hear it. She made answer in a slow, quiet voice that held neither antagonism nor friendliness.

"I supposed that you had some suggestion to make, monsieur, which it was my duty to hear."

"I see," said Dumaresq, still narrowly observing her. "Well, you are right. I have a suggestion to make, one which I beg, for your own sake, that you will cordially consider."

Before the almost brutal directness of his look her own eyes slowly sank. A very faint tinge of colour crept over her pallor, but she made no signs of flinching.

"What is your suggestion, monsieur?" she quietly asked him.

He did not instantly reply. Perhaps he had not altogether expected the calm question. She showed no impatience, but she would not again meet his eyes. In silence she waited.

At length abruptly he began to speak.

"Have you," he asked, "given any thought to your position here? Have you made any plans for yourself in the event of a rising?"

Her eyelids quivered a little, but she did not raise them.

"I do not think," she said, her voice very low, "that the time has yet come for making plans."

Dumaresq threw back his head with a movement that seemed to indicate either impatience or surprise.

"You are living on the edge of a volcano," he told her, with grim force; "and at any moment you may be overwhelmed. Have you never faced that yet? Haven't you yet begun to realise that Maritas is a hotbed of scoundrels - the very scum and rabble of creation - blackguards whom their own countries have, for the most part, refused to tolerate - some of them half-breeds, all of them savages? Haven't you yet begun to ask yourself what you may expect from these devils when they take the law into their own hands? I tell you, mademoiselle, it may happen this very night. It may be happening now!"

She raised her eyes at that - dark eyes that gleamed momentarily and were as swiftly lowered. When she spoke, her low voice held a thrill of scorn.

"Not now, monsieur," she said. "To-night - possibly! But not now - not without you to lead them!"

Pierre Dumaresq made a slight movement. It could not have been called a menace, though it was in a fashion suggestive of violence suppressed - the violence of the baited bull not fully roused to the charge.

"You are not wise, Mademoiselle Stephanie," he said.

She answered him in a voice that quivered, in spite of her obvious effort to control it.

"Nor am I altogether a fool, monsieur. Your sympathies are well known. The revolutionists have looked to you to lead them as long as I have known Maritas."

"That may be, mademoiselle," he sternly responded. "But it is possible, is it not, that they may look in vain?"

Again swiftly her glance flashed upwards.

"Is it possible?" she breathed.

He did not deign to answer.

"I have not come to discuss my position," he said curtly, "but yours. What are you going to do, mademoiselle? How do you propose to escape?"

She was white now, white to the lips; but she did not shrink.

"I beg that you will not concern yourself on my account," she said proudly. "I shall no doubt find a means of escape if I need it."

"Where, mademoiselle?" There was something dogged in the man's voice, his eyes were relentless in their determination. "Are you intending to look to your stepfather for protection?"

Again, involuntarily almost, she raised her eyes, but they held no fear.

"No, monsieur," she responded coldly. "I shall find a better way than that."

"How, mademoiselle?"

The brief question sounded like a threat. She stiffened as she heard it, and stood silent.

"How, mademoiselle?" he said again.

She made a slight gesture of protest.

"Monsieur, it is no one's concern but my own."

"And mine," he said stubbornly.

She shook her head.

"No, monsieur."

"And mine," he repeated with emphasis, "since I presume to make it so. You refuse to answer me merely because you know as well as I do that you are caught in a trap from which you are powerless to release yourself. And now listen to me. There is a way out - only one way, mademoiselle - and if you are wise you will take it, without delay. There is only one man in Maritas who can save you. So far as I know, there is only one man willing to attempt it. That man holds you already in the hollow of his hand. You will be wise to make terms with him while you can."

His tone was curiously calm, almost cynical. His eyes were still fixed unswervingly upon her face. They beat down the haughty surprise with which for a few seconds she encountered them.

"Yes, mademoiselle," he resumed quietly, as though she had spoken. "He is a man whom you despise from the bottom of your soul; but for all that, he is not wholly despicable. Nor is he incapable of deserving your trust if you will bestow it upon him. It is all a question of trust." He smiled grimly at the word. "Whatever you expect from him, that you will receive in full measure. He does not disappoint his friends - or his enemies."

He paused. She was listening with eyes downcast, but her face was a very mask of cold disdain.

"Monsieur," she said, with stately deliberation, "I do not - wholly - understand you. But it would be wasting your time and my own to ask you to explain. As I said before, in the event of a crisis I can secure my own safety."

"Nevertheless," said Pierre Dumaresq with a deliberation even greater than her own, "I will explain, since a clear under-standing seems to me advisable. I am asking you to marry me, Mademoiselle Stephanie, in order to ensure your safety. It is practically your only alternative now, and it must be taken at once. I shall know how to protect my wife. Marry me, and I will take you out of the city to my home on the other side of the island. My yacht is there in readiness, and escape at any time would be easy."

"Escape, monsieur!" Sharply she broke in upon him. Her

coldness was all gone in a sudden flame of indignation kindled by the sheer arrogance of his bearing. "Escape from whom - from what?"

He was silent an instant, almost as if disconcerted. Then:

"Escape from your enemies, mademoiselle," he rejoined sternly. "Escape from the mercy of the mob, which is all you can expect if you stay here."

Her eyes flashed over him in a single, searing glance of the most utter, the most splendid contempt. Then:

"You are more than kind, Monsieur Dumaresq," she said. "But your suggestion does not recommend itself to me. In short, I should prefer - the mercy of the mob."

The man's brows met ferociously. His hands clenched. He almost looked for the moment as though he would strike her. But she did not flinch before him, and very slowly the tension passed. Yet his eyes shone terribly upon her as a sword-blade that is flashed in the sunlight.

"A strange preference, mademoiselle," he remarked at length, turning to pick up his riding-switch. "Possibly you may change your mind - before it is too late."

"Never!" she answered proudly.

And Pierre Dumaresq laughed - a sudden, harsh laugh, and turned to go. It was only what he had expected, after all, but it galled him none the less. He uttered no threat of any sort; only at the door he stood for an instant and looked back at her. And the woman's heart contracted within her as though her blood had turned to ice.

II

When she was alone, when his departing footsteps had ceased to echo along the corridor without, Mademoiselle Stephanie drew a long, quivering breath and moved to a chair by the window. She sank into it with the abandonment of a woman at the end of her strength, and sat passive with closed eyes.

For three years now she had lived in this turbulent island of Maritas. For three years she had watched discontent gradually merge into rebellion and anarchy. And now she knew that at last the end was near.

Her stepfather, the Governor, held his post under the French Government, but France at that time was too occupied with matters nearer home to spare much attention for the little island in the Atlantic and its seething unrest. De Rochefort was considered a capable man, and certainly if treachery and cruelty could have upheld his authority he would have maintained his ascendency without difficulty. But the absinthe demon had gripped him with resistless strength, and all his shrewdness had long since been drained away.

Day by day he plunged deeper into the vice that was destroying him, and Stephanie could but stand by and watch the gradual gathering of a storm that was bound to overwhelm them both.

There was no love between them. They were bound together by circumstance alone. She had gone to the place to be with her dying mother, and had remained there at that mother's request. Madame de Rochefort's belief in her husband had never been shaken, and, dying, she had left her English daughter in his care.

Stephanie had accepted a position that there was no one else to fill, and then had begun the long martyrdom that, she now saw, could have only one ending. She and the Governor were

Ethel M. Dell

doomed. Already the great wave of revolution towered above them. Very soon it would burst and sweep both away into the terrible vortex of destruction.

It was only of late that she had come to realise this, and the horror of the awakening still at times had power to appal her. For she knew she was utterly unprotected. She had tried in vain to rouse the Governor to see the ever-growing danger, had striven desperately to open his eyes to the unmistakable signs of the coming change. He had laughed at her at first, and later, when she had implored him to resign his post, he had brutally refused.

She had never approached him again on the matter, seeing the futility of argument; but on that selfsame day she had provided herself with a means of escape which could not fail her when the last terrible moment arrived. Flight she never contemplated. It would have been an utter impossibility. She was without friends, without money. Her relations in England were to her as beings in another sphere. She had known them in her childhood, but they had since dropped out of her existence. The only offer of help that had reached her was that which she had just rejected from the man whom, of all others, she most hated and desired to avoid.

She shivered suddenly and violently as she recalled the interview. Was it possible that she feared him as well? She had always disliked him, conscious of something in his manner that perpetually excited her antagonism. She had felt his lynx eyes watching her continually throughout the bitter struggle, and she had known always that he was watching for her downfall.

He was the richest man in the island, and as such his influence was considerable. He had not yet made common cause with the revolutionary party, but it was generally felt that his sympathies were on their side, and it was in him that the majority hoped to find a leader when the time for rebellion should be ripe. He had never committed himself to do so, but no one on either side doubted his intentions, Mademoiselle Stephanie, as every one called her, least of all.

She had been accustomed to meeting him fairly often, though he had never been a very frequent guest at the palace. Perhaps he divined her aversion, or perhaps - and this was the more likely supposition - his hatred of the Governor debarred him from enjoying his hospitality.

He was a man of fierce independence and passionate temperament, possessing withal a dogged tenacity that she always ascribed to the fact that he was born of an English mother. But she had never before that day credited him with the desire to exercise a personal influence in her life. She had avoided him by instinct, and till that day he had always seemed to acquiesce.

His offer of marriage had been utterly unexpected. Regarding him as she did, it seemed to her little short of an insult. She hardly knew what motive to ascribe to him for it; but circumstances seemed to point to one, ambition. No doubt he thought that she might prove of use to him when he stepped into the Governor's place.

Well, he had his answer - a very emphatic one. He could scarcely fail to take her at her word. She smiled faintly to herself even while she shivered, as she recalled the scarcely suppressed fury with which he had received his dismissal. She was glad that she had managed to pierce through that immaculate armour of self-complacence just once. She had not been woman otherwise.

III

An intense stillness brooded over the city. The night was starless, the sea black as ink. Stephanie stood alone in the darkness of her balcony, and listened to the silence.

Seven days had elapsed since her interview with Pierre Dumaresq - seven days of horrible, nerve-racking suspense, of anguished foreboding, of ever-creeping, leaden-footed despair. And now at last, though the suspense still held her, she knew that the end had come. Only that evening, as her carriage had been turning in at the palace gates, a bomb had been flung under the wheels. By some miracle it had not exploded. She had passed on unharmed.

But the ghastly incident was to her as the sounding of her own death-knell. Standing there with her face to the sea, she was telling herself that she would never see the daylight again. The very soldiers that guarded them were revolutionists at heart. They were only waiting, so she believed, for a strong man's word of command to throw open the palace doors to frenzied murderers.

No sound came up to her from the motionless sea, no faintest echo of waves upon the shore. The stillness hung like a weight upon the senses. There was something sinister about it, something vaguely terrible. Yet, as she stood there waiting, she was not afraid. Something deeper than fear was in her heart. Pulsing through and through her like an electric current was a deep and passionate revolt against the fate that awaited her.

She could not have said whence it came, this sudden, wild rebellion that tore her quivering heart, but it possessed her to the exclusion of all besides. She had told herself a hundred times before that death, when it came, would be welcome. Yet, now that death was so near her, she longed with all her soul to live. She yearned unspeakably to flee away from this evil place, to go out into the wide spaces of the earth and to feel the sunshine that as yet had never touched her life.

They thought her cold and proud, these people who hated her; but could they have seen the tears that rolled down her face that night there might have been some among them to pity her. But she was the victim of circumstance, bound and helpless, and, though her woman's heart might agonise, there was none to know.

A sudden sound in the night - a sharp sound like the crack of a whip, but louder, more menacing, more nerve-piercing. She turned, every muscle tense, and listened with bated breath.

It had not come from the garden below her. The silence hung there like a pall. Stay! What was that? The sound of a movement on the terrace under her balcony - a muffled, stealthy sound.

There was no sentry there, she knew. The sentries on that side of the palace were posted at the great iron gates that shut off the garden from the road which ran along the shore to the fortress above.

A spasm of fear, sharp as physical pain, ran through her. She stepped quickly back into the room; but there she stopped, stopped deliberately to wrestle with the terror which had swooped so suddenly upon her. She had maintained her self-control admirably a few hours before in the face of frightful danger, but now in this awful silence it threatened to desert her. Desperately, determinedly, she brought it back inch by inch, till the panic in her vanished and her heart began to beat more bravely.

She went at length and opened the door that led into the long corridor outside her apartments. The place was deserted. The silence hung like death. She stood a moment, gathering her courage, then passed out. She must ascertain if the Governor were in his room, and warn him - if he would be warned.

Ethel M. Dell

She had nearly traversed the length of the corridor when again the silence was rent suddenly and terribly by that sound that was like the crack of a whip. She stopped short, all the blood racing back to her heart. She knew it now beyond a doubt. She had known it before in her secret soul. It was the report of a rifle in the palace square.

As she stood irresolute, listening with straining nerves, another sound began to grow out of the night, gathering strength with every instant, a long, fierce roar that resembled nothing that she had ever heard, yet which she knew instinctively for what it was - the raging tumult of an angry crowd. It was like the yelling of a thousand demons.

Suddenly it swelled to an absolute pandemonium of sound, and she shrank appalled. The sudden, paralysing conviction flashed upon her that the palace had been deserted by its guards and was in the hands of murderers. She seemed to hear them swarming everywhere, unopposed, yet lusting for blood, while she, a defenceless woman, stood cowering against a door.

Sheer physical horror seized upon her. The mercy of the mob! The mercy of the mob! The words ran red-hot in her brain. She knew well what she might expect from them. They would tear her limb from limb.

She could not face it. She must escape. Even now surely she could escape. Back in her room, only the length of the corridor away, was deliverance. Surely she could reach it in time! Like a hunted creature she gathered herself together, and, turning, fled along the way she had come.

She rushed at length, panting, into her room, and, without a pause or glance around, fled into the bedroom beyond. It was here, it was here that her deliverance lay, safe hidden in a secret drawer.

The place was in darkness save for the light that streamed after her through the open door. Shaking in every limb, near to fainting, she groped her way across, found - almost fell against - her little writing-table, and sank upon her knees before it - for the moment too spent to move.

But a slight sound that seemed to come from near at hand aroused her. She started up in a fresh panic, pulled out a drawer, that fell with a crash from her trembling hands, and began to feel behind for a secret spring. Oh, she had been a fool, a fool to hide it so securely! She would never find it in the darkness.

Nevertheless, groping, her quivering fingers soon discovered that which they sought. The secret slide opened and she felt for what lay beyond. A moment later she was clasping tightly a little silver flask.

And then, with deliverance actually within her hold, she paused. Kneeling there in the darkness she strove to collect her thoughts, that she might not die in panic. It was not death that she feared just then. She knew that it would come to her swiftly, she believed painlessly. But she would not die before she need. She would wait a little. Perhaps when the wild tumult at her heart had subsided she would be able to pray, not for deliverance from death - there could be no alternative now - but for peace.

So, kneeling alone, she waited; and presently, growing calmer, removed the top of the flask so that she might be ready.

Seconds passed. Her nerves were growing steadier; the mad gallop of her heart was slackening.

She leaned her head on her hand and closed her eyes.

And then, all in a moment, fear seized her again - the sudden consciousness of some one near her, some one watching. With a gasp she started to her feet, and on the instant there came the click of the electric switch by the door, and the room was flooded with light.

Dazzled, almost blinded, she stared across the intervening space, and met the steely, relentless eyes of Pierre Dumaresq!

IV

She stood motionless, staring, as one dazed. He, without apology or word of any sort, strode straight forward. His face expressed stern determination, naught else.

But ere he reached her she awoke to action, stepping sharply backwards so that the table was between them. He came to a stand perforce in front of it, and looked her full and piercingly in the eyes.

"Mademoiselle," he said, and his voice was so curt that it sounded brutal, "you must come at once. The palace is in the hands of murderers. The Governor has been assassinated. In a few seconds more they will be at your door. Come!"

She recoiled from him with a face of horror.

"With you, monsieur? Never!" she cried.

He laid his hand upon the table and leaned forward.

"With me, yes," he said, speaking rapidly, yet with lips that scarcely seemed to move. "I have come for you, and I mean to take you. Be wise, Mademoiselle Stephanie! Come quietly!"

She scarcely heard him. Frenzy had gripped her - wild, unreasoning, all-mastering frenzy. The supreme moment had come for her, and, with a face that was like a death-mask, she raised the silver flask to her lips.

But no drop of its contents ever touched them, for in that instant Pierre vaulted the intervening table and hurled himself upon her. The flask flew from her hand and spun across the room, falling she knew not where; while she herself was caught in the man's arms and held in a grip like iron.

She struggled fiercely to free herself, but for many seconds she struggled in vain. Then, just as her strength was beginning to leave her, he abruptly set her free.

"Come!" he said. "There is no time for childish folly. Find a cloak, and we will go."

His tone was peremptory, but it held no anger. Turning from her, he walked deliberately away into the outer room.

She sank back trembling against the wall, nearer to collapse than she had ever been before. But the momentary respite had its effect, and instinctively she began to gather herself together for fresh effort. He had wrested her deliverance from her, but she would never accept what he offered in exchange. She would never escape with his man. She would sooner - yes, a thousand times sooner - face the mercy of the mob.

"Mademoiselle Stephanie!" Impatiently his voice came to her from the farther room. "Are you coming, or am I to fetch you?"

She did not answer. A sudden wild idea had formed in her brain. If she could slip past him - if she could reach the outer door - he would never overtake her on the corridor. But she must be brave, she must be subtle, she must watch her opportunity.

With some semblance of composure she took out a long travelling-cloak, and walked into the room in which he awaited her. With a start of surprise, she saw him standing by the open window.

"This way, mademoiselle," he said curtly; and she realised that he must have entered from the garden.

"One moment, monsieur," she returned, and quietly crossed the room to the door at the other end.

It was closed. It must have swung to behind her, for she did not remember closing it.

He made no attempt to stop her. He could not surely have guessed her intention, for he remained motionless by the window, watching her. Her heart was thumping as though it would choke her, but yet she controlled herself. He must not suspect till the door was open, till the passage was clear before her, and pursuit of no avail.

She reached out a quivering hand and grasped the ebony knob. Now - now for the last and greatest effort of her life! Sharply she turned the handle, pulled at it, wrenched it with frantic force, finally turned from it and confronted the man at the window with eyes that were hunted, desperate.

"Let me go!" she gasped hoarsely. "How dare you keep me here against my will?"

"I have no desire to keep you here, mademoiselle," he answered. "I am only waiting to take you away."

"I refuse to go with you!" she cried. "I would rather die a thousand times!"

His brows contracted into a single grim line. He left the window and came towards her.

But at his action she sprang away like a mad thing, dodged him, avoided him, then leapt suddenly upon a chair and snatched a rapier from a group of swords arranged in a circle upon the wall. The light fell full upon her ashen face and eyes of horror. She was beside herself.

All her instincts urged her to resistance. She had always shrunk from this man. If she could only hold him at bay for a little - if she could only resist long enough - surely she heard the feet of the murderers upon the corridor already! It would not take them long to batter down the door and take her life!

Ethel M. Dell

As she sprang to the ground again, Pierre spoke. The frown had gone from his face; it wore a faint, ironical smile. His eyes, alert, unblinking, marked her every movement as the eyes of a lynx upon its prey. He did not appear in the least disconcerted. There was even a sort of terrible patience in his attitude, as though he already saw the end of the struggle.

"Would it not be wiser, mademoiselle," he said, "to reserve your steel for an enemy?"

She met his piercing look for an instant as she compelled her white lips to answer. "You are the worst enemy that I have."

He threw back his head with an arrogant gesture very characteristic of him. "By your own choice, mademoiselle," he said.

"Yes," she flung back passionately. "I prefer you as an enemy."

He laughed at that - a fiendish, scoffing laugh that made her shrink in every nerve. Then, with unmoved composure, he walked to the mantelpiece and took up one of the foils that lay there.

"Now," he said quietly, "since you are determined to fight me, so be it! But when you are beaten, Mademoiselle Stephanie, do not ask for mercy!"

But she drew back sharply from his advance. "Take one of those rapiers," she said.

He shook his head, still with that mocking smile upon his lips. "This will serve my purpose better," he said. "Are you ready, mademoiselle? On guard!"

And with that his weapon crossed hers. She knew his purpose the moment she encountered it. It was written in every grim line of his countenance. He meant the conflict to be very short.

She was no novice in the art of fencing, but she was no match for him. Moreover, she could not meet the pitiless eyes that stared straight into hers. They distracted her. They terrified her. Yet every moment seemed to her to be something gained. Through all the wild chaos of her overstrung nerves she was listening, listening desperately, for the sound of feet outside the door. If she could only withstand him for a few short seconds! If only her strength would last!

But she was nearing exhaustion, and she knew it. Her brain had begun to swim. She saw him in a blur before her quivering vision. The hand that grasped the rapier was too numbed to obey her behests. Suddenly there came a tumult in the corridor without - a hoarse yelling and the rush of many feet. It was the sound she had been listening for, but it startled, it unnerved her. And in that instant Pierre thrust through her guard and with a lightning twist of the wrist sent her weapon hurtling through the air.

The sound of its fall was lost in the clamour outside the door - a clamour so sudden and so horrible that it did for Stephanie that which nothing else on earth could have accomplished. It drove her to the man she hated for protection.

As he flung down the foil, she made a swift move towards him. There was no longer shrinking in her eyes. She was simply a trembling, panic-stricken woman, turning instinctively to the stronger power for help. A little earlier she could have died without a tremor, but the wild strife of the past few minutes had broken down her fortitude. Her strength was gone.

"Monsieur!" she panted. "Monsieur!"

He caught her roughly to him. Even in that moment of deadly peril there was a certain fiery exultation about him. He held her fast, his eyes gazing straight down into hers.

"Shall I save you?" he said. "I can die with you - if you prefer it."

"Save me!" she cried piteously. "Save me!"

He bent his head, and suddenly, fiercely, savagely, he kissed her white lips. Then, before she could utter cry or protest, he whirled her across the room to the open window, catching up her cloak as he went; and, almost before the horror of his kiss had dawned upon her, she was out upon the balcony, alone with him in the awful dark.

He kept his hand upon her as he stepped over the stone railing, but all power of independent action seemed to have left her. She was as one stunned or beneath some spell. She stood quite rigid while he groped for and found the ladder by which he had ascended. Then, as he lifted her, she let herself go into his arms without resistance. He clasped her hands behind his neck, and she clung there mechanically as he made the swift descent.

They reached the ground in safety, and he set her on her feet. The terrace on which they found themselves was deserted. But as they stood in the dark they heard the fiends in the corridor burst into the room they had just left. And Pierre Dumaresq, lowering the ladder, laughed to himself a low, fierce laugh, without words.

The next instant there came a rush of feet upon the balcony above them and a torrent of angry shouting. Stephanie shrank against a pillar, but in a moment Pierre's arm encircled her, impelling her irresistibly, and they fled across the terrace through the darkness. The man was still laughing as he ran. There seemed to her something devilish in his laughter.

Down through the palace garden they sped, she gasping and stumbling in nightmare flight, he strongly upholding her, till half a dozen revolver shots pierced the infuriated uproar behind them and something that burned with a red-hot agony struck her left hand. She cried out involuntarily, and Pierre ceased his headlong rush for safety.

"You are hit?" he questioned. "Where?"

But she could not answer him, could not so much as stand. His voice seemed to come from an immense distance. She hardly heard his words. She was sinking, sinking into a void unfathomable.

He did not stay to question further. Abruptly he stooped, gathered her up, slung her across his shoulder, and ran on.

Ethel M. Dell

V

When Stephanie opened her eyes again the sound of the sea was in her ears, and she felt as if she must have heard it for some time. She was lying in a chair amid surroundings wholly strange to her, and some one - a man whose face she could not see - was beside her, bending over a table, evidently engaged upon something that occupied his most minute attention. She watched him dreamily for a little, till the immense breadth of his shoulders struck a quick-growing fear into her heart; then she made a sudden effort to raise herself.

Instantly she was stabbed by a dart of pain so acute that she barely repressed a cry.

"Keep still, mademoiselle!" It was Pierre's voice; he spoke without turning. "I shall not hurt you more than I can help."

She sank back again, shuddering uncontrollably. She knew now what he was doing. It had flashed upon her in that moment of horrible suffering. He was probing for a bullet in her left hand. Dumbly she shut her eyes and set herself to endure.

But the pain was almost insupportable; it seemed to rack her whole body. And the presence of the man she feared, his nearness to her, his touch, added tenfold to the torture. Yet she was helpless, and, spent, exhausted though she was, for very pride she would utter no complaint.

Minutes passed. She was near to fainting again, when abruptly Pierre stood up. She heard him move, and she was conscious of a blessed lessening of the pain. But she dared not stir or open her eyes, lest her self-control should forsake her utterly. She could only lie and wait in quivering suspense.

He bent over her without speaking, and suddenly she felt the rim of a glass against her lips. With a start she looked up. His swarthy face was close to her own, but it was grimly immobile. He seemed to have clad himself from head to foot in an impenetrable armour of reserve. His lips were set in a firm line, as though all speech were locked securely behind them.

Mutely she obeyed his unspoken command and drank. The draught was unlike anything she had ever tasted before. It revived her, renewing her failing strength.

"I thank you, monsieur," she said faintly.

He set down the glass, and busied himself once more with her wounded hand.

"I shall not hurt you any further," he said, as involuntarily she winced.

And he kept his word. The worst of his task was over. He only bathed and bandaged with a gentleness and dexterity at which she marvelled.

At last he looked at her.

"You are better?" he asked.

She met his eyes for an instant. They were absolutely steady, but they told her nothing whatever of his thoughts.

"Yes, I am better," she said, with an effort.

"Can you walk?" he said.

"I think so, monsieur."

"Then come with me," he rejoined, "and I will show you where you can rest."

She sat up slowly. He bent to help her, but she would not accept his help till, rising to her feet, she felt the floor sway beneath her. Then, with a sharp exclamation, she clutched for support and gripped his proffered arm.

"Monsieur!" she gasped.

He held her up, for she was tottering. Her pale face stared panic-stricken up to his.

"Monsieur!" she gasped again. "What is this? Where am I?"

He made answer curtly, in a tone that sounded repressive.

"You are on board my yacht, mademoiselle." She swayed, and he put his arm round her. "You are in safety," he said, in the same brief fashion.

"As - as your prisoner?" she whispered, trying weakly to free herself from his hold.

"As my guest," he said.

By an immense effort she controlled herself, meeting his stern eyes with something like composure. But the memory of that single, scorching kiss was still with her. And in spite of her utmost resolution, she flinched from his direct gaze.

"If I am your guest," she said, her low voice quivering a very little, "I am at liberty to come - and to go - as I will."

"Absolutely!" said Pierre, and she fancied for an instant that he smiled.

"You will take me wherever I desire to go?" she persisted, still battling with her agitation.

"With one exception," he answered quietly. "I will not take you back to Maritas."

She shivered. "Then where, monsieur?"

His expression changed slightly. She had a momentary glimpse of the arrogance she dreaded.

"The world is wide," he said. "And there is plenty of time before us. We need not decide to-night."

She trembled more at the tone than the words. "I did not think you would leave Maritas so soon," she murmured.

"Why not, mademoiselle?" His voice suddenly rang hard; it almost held a threat.

She had withdrawn herself from him, but she was hardly capable of standing alone. She leaned secretly against the chair from which she had just risen.

"Because," she made answer, still desperately facing him, "I thought that Maritas wanted you."

He uttered a brief laugh that sounded savage.

"That was yesterday," he told her grimly. "I have forfeited my popularity since then."

A slow, painful flush rose in Stephanie's drawn face, but she shrank no longer from his look. "And you have gained nothing in exchange," she said, her voice very low.

"Except what I desired to gain," said Pierre Dumaresq.

She made a slight, involuntary movement, and instantly her brows contracted. She closed her eyes with a shudder. The pain was almost intolerable.

A moment later she felt his strong arms lift her and a sudden passion of misery swept over her. Where was the use of feigning strength when he knew so well her utter weakness; of fighting, when she was already so hopelessly beaten; of begging his mercy even when he had warned her so emphatically that she must not expect it?

Despair entered into her. She could resist him no longer by so much as the lifting of a finger. And as the knowledge swept overwhelmingly upon her, the last poor shred of her pride crumbled to nothing in a rush of anguished tears.

Pierre said no more. His hard mouth grew a little harder, his steely eyes a shade more steely - that was all. He bore her unfaltering through the saloon to the state cabin beyond, and laid her down there.

In another second she heard the click of the latch, and his step upon the threshold. Softly the door closed. Softly he went away.

VI

And Stephanie slept. From her paroxysm of weeping she passed into deep, untroubled slumber, and hour after hour slipped over her unconscious head while she lay at rest.

When she awoke at last the evening sun was streaming in through the tiny porthole by the head of her couch, and she knew that she must have slept throughout the day. She was very drowsy still, and for a while she lay motionless, listening to the monotonous beat of the yacht's engines, and watching the white spray as it tossed past.

Very gradually she began to remember what had happened to her. She glanced at her wounded hand, swathed in bandages and resting upon a cushion. Who had arranged it so, she wondered? How had it been done without her waking?

At the back of her mind hovered the answers to both these questions, but she could not bring herself to face them - not yet. She was loth to withdraw herself from the haze of sleep that still hung about her. She shrank intuitively from a full awakening.

And then, while she still loitered on the way to consciousness, there came a soft movement near her, and in a moment all her repose was shattered.

Pierre, his dark face grimly inscrutable, bent over her with a cup of something steaming in his hand.

She shrank at the sight of him. Her whole body seemed to contract. Involuntarily almost she shut her eyes. Her heart leapt and palpitated within her like a chained thing seeking to escape.

Then suddenly it stood still. He was speaking.

"Mademoiselle Stephanie," he said, "I beg you will not agitate yourself. You have no cause for agitation. It is not by my own wish that I intrude upon you. I have no choice."

It was curtly uttered. It sounded rigidly uncompromising. Yet, for some reason wholly inexplicable to herself, she was conscious of relief. She opened her eyes, though she did not dare to raise them.

"How is that, monsieur?" she said faintly.

He was silent for a moment; then:

"There is no woman on board besides yourself," he told her briefly. "Your own people deserted you. I had no time to search for others."

She felt as if his eyes were drawing her own. Against her will she looked up and met them. They told her nothing, but at least they did not frighten her afresh.

"Where are you going to take me?" she asked.

"We will speak of that later," he said. "Will you drink this now? You need it."

"What is it, monsieur?"

For an instant she saw his faint, hard smile.

"It is broth, mademoiselle, nothing more."

"Nothing?" she said, still hesitating. "You - I think you gave me a narcotic before!"

"I did," said Pierre. "And it did you good."

She did not attempt to contradict him. The repression of his manner held her silent. Without further demur she sought to raise herself.

But her head swam the moment she lifted it from the pillow, and she sank down again with closed eyes and drawn brows.

"In a moment," she whispered.

"Permit me," said Pierre quietly; and slipped his arm under her pillow.

She looked up sharply to protest, but the words died on her lips. She saw that he would not be denied.

He supported her with absolute steadiness while she drank, not uttering a word. Finally, he lowered her again, and spoke:

"It is time that your wound was attended to. With your permission I will proceed with it at once."

"Is it serious, monsieur?" she asked.

"I can tell you better when I have seen it," he rejoined, beginning to loosen the bandage. "Does it pain you?" as she winced.

"A little," she acknowledged, with quivering lips.

He glanced at her, and for the first time in all her experience of him he spoke with a hint of kindness.

"It will not take long, Mademoiselle Stephanie. Shut your eyes till it is over."

She obeyed him mutely. Her fear of the man was merging into a curious feeling of reliance. She was beginning to realise that her enforced dependence upon him had in some fashion altered his attitude towards her.

"No," he said at last. "It is not a very serious matter, though it

Ethel M. Dell

may give you some trouble till it is healed. You will need to keep very quiet, mademoiselle, and" - again momentarily she saw his smile - "avoid agitating yourself as much as possible."

"You may rely upon me to do that, monsieur," she returned with dignity; "if I am allowed to do so."

Again for an instant she felt his eyes upon her, and she thought he frowned; but he made no comment.

Quietly he finished his bandaging before he spoke again.

"If there is any other way in which I can serve you," he said then, "you have only to command me."

She turned upon her pillow and faced him. The gradual reviving of her physical strength helped her at least to simulate some of her ancient pride that he had trampled so ruthlessly underfoot.

"What do you mean by that?" she questioned calmly.

He met her look fully and sternly.

"I mean, Mademoiselle Stephanie, precisely what I have said - no more, no less!"

In spite of her utmost effort, she flinched a little. Yet she would not be conquered by a look.

"I am to treat you as my servant, then, monsieur?" she questioned.

He dropped his eyes suddenly from hers.

"If it suits you to do so," he said.

"The situation is not of my choosing," she reminded him.

"Nor mine," he answered drily.

Her heart sank, but with an effort she maintained a fair show of courage.

"Monsieur Dumaresq," she said, "I think that you mean to be kind. I shall act upon that assumption. Since I am thrown upon your hospitality under circumstances which neither of us would have chosen -"

"I did not say that, mademoiselle," he interposed. "I have no quarrel with the gods that govern circumstance. My only regret is that, as my guest, you should be inefficiently served. If you find yourself able to treat me as a servant it will be my pleasure to serve you."

She did not understand his tone. It seemed to her that he was trying in some fashion to warn her. Again the memory of his kiss swept over her; again to the very heart of her she shrank.

"I think," she said slowly, "that I am more your prisoner than your guest, Monsieur Dumaresq."

"It is not always quite wise to express our thoughts," he rejoined, with deliberate cynicism. "I have ventured to point that out to you before."

Again he baffled her. She looked at him doubtfully. He was standing up beside her on the point of departure. He returned her gaze with his steely eyes almost as though he challenged her to penetrate to the citadel they guarded.

With a sharp sigh she abandoned the contest. "I wish I understood you," she said.

He jerked his shoulders expressively.

"You knew me a week ago better than I knew myself," he remarked. "What more would you have?"

She did not answer him. She only moved her head upon the pillow with a gesture of weariness. She knew that she would search those pitiless eyes in vain for the key to the puzzle, and she only longed to be left alone. He could not, surely, refuse to grant her unspoken desire.

Yet for a moment it seemed that he would prolong the interview. He stood above her, motionless, arrogant, frowning downwards as though he had something more to say. Then, while she waited tensely, dreading the very sound of his voice, his attitude suddenly underwent a change. The thin lips tightened sharply. He turned away.

VII

After he was gone, Stephanie sat up and gazed for a long, long time at the scud of water leaping past the porthole.

She felt stunned by the events of the past twenty-four hours. She could only review them with a numbed amazement. The long suspense had ended so suddenly and so terribly. She could hardly begin to realise that it was indeed over, that the storm she had foreseen for so long had burst atlast, sweeping away the Governor in headlong overthrow, and leaving her bruised and battered indeed, but still alive. She had never thought to survive him. She had not loved him, but her lot had been so inextricably bound up with his, that she had never seriously contemplated the possibility of life without him. What would happen to her? she asked herself. How would it end?

There was no denying the fact that, however inexplicable Pierre's treatment might be, she was completely and irretrievably his prisoner.

There was no one to deliver her from him; no one to know or care what became of her. Her importance had crumbled to nothing so far as the world was concerned. She had simply ceased to count. What did he mean to do with her? Why had he refused to discuss the future?

Gradually, with a certain reluctance, her thoughts came down to her recent interview with him, and again the feeling that he had been trying to convey something that she had failed to grasp possessed her. Why had he warned her against attempting to define her position? What had those last words of his meant?

One thing at least was certain. Though he had done little to reassure her, she must make a determined effort to overcome her fear of the man. She must not again shrink openly in his presence. She must feign confidence, though she felt it not.

Ethel M. Dell

Something that he had said a week before on the occasion of his extraordinary proposal of marriage recurred to her at this point with curious force.

"It is all a question of trust," he had said, and she recalled the faint, derisive smile with which he had spoken. "Whatever you expect, that you will receive." The words dwelt in her memory with a strange persistence. She had a feeling that they meant a good deal. It was possible - surely it was possible - that if she trusted him, he might prove himself to be trustworthy. If only her nerves were equal to the task! If only the terrible memory of his kiss could be blotted for ever and ever from her mind!

She rose at last and began to move about the little state cabin. It was furnished luxuriously in every detail - almost, she told herself with a shiver, as though for a bride. Catching sight of her reflection in a mirror, she stared aghast, scarcely recognising herself in the wild-eyed, haggard woman who met her gaze. Small wonder that she had deemed him repressive, she told herself, for she looked like a demented creature.

That astounding glimpse did more for her than any mental effort. Quite calmly she set to work to render her appearance more normal, and, crippled though she was, she succeeded at length in attaining a fairly satisfactory result. At least she did not think that a masculine eye would detect anything amiss.

This achieved, she finally drew her travelling cloak about her and went to the door. It resisted her effort to open, but in a moment she heard a step on the other side and the withdrawal of a bolt.

Pierre opened the door for her, and stood back for her to pass. But she remained on the threshold.

"Monsieur Dumaresq, why did you lock me in?" she asked him, with something of her old stateliness of demeanour, which had made men deem her proud.

His grey eyes comprehended her in a single glance. He made her his curt, British bow.

"You were overwrought, Mademoiselle Stephanie," he said. "I was not sure of your intentions. But I see that the precaution was unnecessary."

She understood him, and a faint flush rose in her pale face.

"Quite," she responded. "I have come to my senses, monsieur, and I know how to value your protection. I shall not seek that means of escape so long as you are safeguarding me."

She smiled with the words, a brave and steadfast smile, and extended her hand to him.

The gesture was queenly, but the instant his fingers closed upon it she quivered uncontrollably from head to foot. A sudden mist descended before her eyes, and she groped out blindly for support. Her overtaxed nerves had betrayed her again.

"Come and sit down, mademoiselle," a quiet voice said; and a steady arm impelled her forward. "There is something of a swell to-night. I am afraid you feel it."

So courteous was the tone that she almost gasped her astonishment. She sank into a chair, and made a desperate effort to regain her self-control.

"You are very kind, monsieur," she said, not very steadily. "No doubt I shall become accustomed to it."

"I do not think you are quite fit for this," he said gravely.

She looked up at him with more confidence.

"I am really stronger than you think," she said. "And I wanted to speak to you on the subject of our destination."

She fancied that he stiffened a little at the words, but he merely said:

"Well, mademoiselle?"

"Will you not sit down," she said, "and tell me where the yacht is going?"

He sat down on the edge of the table. There was undeniable restlessness in his attitude.

"We are running due west at the present moment," he said.

"With what object?" she asked.

"With no object, mademoiselle," he rejoined, "except to keep out of reach of our enemies."

"You have left Maritas for good?" she asked.

He uttered a short laugh.

"Certainly. I have nothing to go back for."

"And you are indifferent," she questioned, with slight hesitation, "as to the direction you take?"

"No, I am not indifferent," he answered curtly.

She was silent. His manner puzzled her, made her afraid in spite of herself.

There followed a short pause, then he turned slightly and looked at her.

"Have you any particular wishes upon the subject?" he asked.

"Yes, monsieur."

Her reply was very low.

"Let me hear them," said Pierre.

"I should like," she said slowly, "if it be possible, to go to England. I have relations there who might help me."

"Help you, mademoiselle?"

His tone sounded harsh.

"To earn my living," she answered simply.

His brows met suddenly.

"It is a far cry to England," he observed.

"I know it," she said. "I am counting upon your kindness."

"I see," said Pierre. "I am to take you there, and - leave you. Is that it?"

She bent her head.

"If you will, monsieur."

"And if I will not?" he said.

She was silent.

He stood up abruptly, and walked to the farther end of the saloon. When he came back his face was set and grim. He halted in front of her.

"I am to do this thing for nothing?" he said. And it seemed to her that, though uttered quietly, his words came through clenched teeth.

Again wild panic was at her heart, but with all her strength she held it back.

"You offered to serve me, monsieur," she reminded him.

"Even a servant expects to be paid," he rejoined curtly.

"But I have nothing to offer you," she said.

She saw the grey eyes glitter as steel in sudden sunshine. Their brightness was intolerable. She turned her own away.

"Does it not occur to you, Mademoiselle Stephanie," he said, "that your life is more my property than your own at the present moment? Have I no claim to be consulted as to its disposal?"

"None, monsieur," she made answer quickly. "None whatever."

"And yet," he said, "you asked me to save you when - had you preferred it - I would have died with you."

She was silent, remembering with bitterness her wild cry for deliverance.

He waited a little. Then:

"You may have nothing to offer me, Mademoiselle Stephanie," he said, "but, by heaven, you shall take nothing away."

She heard a deep menace in his voice that was like the growl of an angry beast. She shuddered inwardly as she listened, but outwardly she remained calm. She even, after a few moments, mustered strength to rise and face him.

"What is it that you want of me, Monsieur Dumaresq?" she asked. "How can I purchase your services?"

He flung back his head abruptly. She thought that he was

going to utter his scoffing laugh. But it did not come. Instead, he looked at her, looked at her long and piercingly, while she stood erect and waited.

At last: "The price for my services," he said deliberately, "is that you marry me as soon as we reach England."

"Marry you!" In spite of her utmost resolution she started, and slightly shrank. "You still desire that?"

"I still desire it," he said.

"And if I refuse?" she questioned, her voice very low.

"You will not refuse," he returned, with conviction. "You dare not refuse."

She stood silent.

"And that being so," said Pierre, with a certain doggedness peculiarly at variance with his fierce and headlong nature, "that being so, Mademoiselle Stephanie, would it not be wiser for you to yield at once?"

"To yield, monsieur?"

Her eyes sought his for the fraction of a second. He was still closely watching her.

"To give me your promise," he said. "It is all I shall ask of you. I shall be satisfied with that."

"And what have you to offer in exchange?" she said.

A strange expression, that was almost a smile, flitted over his hard face.

"I will give you my friendship," he said, "no more, no less."

But still she hesitated, till suddenly, with a gesture wholly arrogant, he held out his hand.

"Trust me," he said, "and I will be trustworthy."

She knew it for a definite promise, however insolently expressed. It was plain that he meant what he said. It was plain that he desired to win her confidence. And in a measure she was reassured. His actions testified to a patience of which she had not deemed him capable.

Slowly, in unconscious submission to his will, she laid her hand in his.

"And afterwards, monsieur?" she said. "Shall I be able to trust you then?"

He leaned slightly towards her, looking more closely into her face.

Then: "All my life, Stephanie," he said, and before she realised his intention he had pressed her hand to his lips with the action of a man who seals an oath.

VIII

From that hour forward, Stephanie was no longer a close prisoner. She was free to wander wherever she would about the yacht, but she never penetrated very far. The vessel was no mere pleasure boat, and there was much that might have interested her, had she been disposed to take an interest therein. But she shrank with a morbid dread from the eyes of the Spanish sailors. She longed unspeakably to hide herself away in unbroken seclusion.

Her wound healed rapidly, so rapidly that Pierre soon ceased to treat it, but it took much longer for her to recover from the effects of that terrible night at Maritas. The horror of it was with her night and day.

Pierre's treatment of her never varied. He saw to her comfort with unfailing vigilance and consideration, but he never attempted to obtrude himself upon her. He seldom spoke to her unless she addressed him. He never by word or look referred to the compact between them. Her fear of him had sunk away into the background of her thoughts. Furtively she studied him, but he gave her no cause for fear. When she sat on the deck, he never joined her. He did not so much as eat with her till one day, not without much inward trepidation, she invited him to do so. And she marvelled, again and again she marvelled, at his forbearance.

Calmly and uneventfully the endless summer days slipped by. Her strength was undoubtedly returning to her, the youth in her reviving. The long rest was taking effect upon her. The overstrung nerves were growing steady again. Often she would sit and ponder upon the future, but she had no definite idea to guide her. At first she shrank unspeakably from the bare thought of the end of the voyage, but gradually she became accustomed to it. It seemed too remote to be terrible, and her reliance upon Pierre's good faith increased daily. Somehow, unaccountably, she had wholly ceased to regard him as an

Ethel M. Dell

enemy. Possibly her fears and even her antagonism were only dormant, but at least they did not torment her. She did not start at the sound of his voice, or shrink from the straight regard of those hard eyes. She knew by that instinct that cannot err that he meant to keep his word.

They left the regions of endless summer behind at last, and the cooler breezes of the north swept the long, blue ridges over which they travelled. They came into a more frequented, less dreamlike sea, but though many vessels passed them, they were seldom near enough for greeting. And Stephanie came to understand that it was not Pierre's desire to hold much converse with the outer world. Yet she knew that they were heading straight for England, and their isolation was bound ere long to come to an end.

It was summer weather even in England just then, summer weather in the blue Atlantic, summer everywhere. She spent many hours of each day in a sheltered corner of the deck, watching the leaping waves, green and splendid, racing from the keel. And a strange content was hers while she watched, born of the unwonted peace which of late had wrapped her round. She was as one come into safe harbourage after long and futile tossing upon the waters of strife. She did not question her security. She only knew that it was there.

But one day there came a change - a grey sky and white-capped waves. Suddenly and inexplicably, as is the way of the northern climate, the sunshine was withdrawn, the summer weather departed, and there came desolation.

Stephanie's corner on deck was empty. She crouched below, ill, shivering with cold and wretchedness. All day long she listened to the howling wind and pitiless, lashing rain, rising above the sullen roar of the waves. All day long the vessel pitched and tossed, flinging her back and forth while she clung in desperation to the edge of her berth.

Pierre waited upon her from time to time, but he could do

little to relieve her discomfort, and he left her for the most part alone.

As evening drew on, the gale increased, and Stephanie, lying in her cabin, could hear the great waves breaking over the deck with a violence that grew more awful with every moment. Her nerves began to give way under the strain. It was a long while since Pierre had been near her, and the loneliness appalled her.

She could endure it no longer at last, and arose with a wild idea of going on deck. The narrow walls of her cabin had become unendurable.

With difficulty, grabbing at first one thing, then another for support, she made her way to the saloon. The place was empty, but a single lamp burned steadily by the door that led to the companion, and guided her halting steps.

The floor was at a steep upward angle when she started, but before she had accomplished half the distance it plunged suddenly downwards, and she was flung forward against the table. Bruised and frightened, she dragged herself up, reached the farther door at a run, only to fall once more against it.

Here she lay for a little, half-stunned, till that terrible slow upheaval began again. Then, with a sharp effort, she recalled her scattered senses and struggled up, clinging to the handle. Slowly she mounted, slowly, slowly, till her feet began to slip down that awful slant. Then at the last moment, when she thought she must fall headlong, there came that fearful plunge again, and she knew that the yacht was deep in the trough of some gigantic wave.

The loneliness was terrible. It seemed like the forerunner of annihilation. She felt that whatever the danger on deck, it must be easier to face than this fearful solitude. And so at last, in a brief lull, she opened the door.

A great swirl of wind and water dashed down upon her on the

instant. The lamp behind her flickered and went out, but there was another at the head of the steps to light her halting progress, and, clinging with both hands to the rail, she began to ascend.

The uproar was deafening. It deprived her of the power to think. But she no longer felt afraid. She found this limbo of howling desolation infinitely preferable to the awful loneliness of her cabin. Slowly and with difficulty she made her way.

She had nearly reached the top when a man's figure in streaming oilskins sprang suddenly into the opening. Above the storm she heard a hoarse yell of warning or of anger, she knew not which, and the next instant Pierre was beside her, holding her imprisoned against the hand-rail to which she clung.

She stood up and faced him, still gripping the rail.

"Take me on deck!" she cried to him. "I shall not be afraid."

She had flung her cloak about her, but the hood had blown back from her head, and her hair hung loose. Pierre looked at her in stern silence, holding her fast. She fancied he was displeased with her for leaving the cabin, and she reiterated her earnest request that he would suffer her to come up just for a little to breathe the fresh air.

"It is so horrible below," she told him. "It frightens me."

Pierre was frowning heavily.

"Do you think you would not be my first care?" he demanded, bracing himself as the vessel plunged to support her with greater security.

She did not answer. There was a touch of ferocity in the question that silenced her. The pitching of the yacht threw her against him the next moment, and her feet slipped from beneath her.

Unconsciously almost she turned and clung to the arms that held her up. They tightened about her to a grip that made her gasp for breath. He lifted her back to the foothold she had lost. His face was more grimly set than she had ever seen it.

She wondered if he was secretly afraid. For they seemed to be sinking down, down, down into the depths of destruction, and only his close holding kept her where she was.

She thought that they were going straight to the bottom, and involuntarily her clinging hands held faster. Involuntarily, too, she raised her eyes to his, seeking, as the human soul is bound to seek, for human comradeship in face of mortal danger.

But the next instant she knew that no thought of danger was in his mind, or if it existed it was obscured by something infinitely greater.

His eyes saw her and her only. The fierce flame of his passion blazed down upon her, searing its terrible way to her soul, dazzling her, hypnotising her, till she could see nought else, could feel nought but the burning intensity of the fire that had kindled so suddenly about her.

A dart of wild dismay went through her as keen as physical pain, but in a moment it was gone. For though he held her caught against his breast and covered her face with kisses that seemed to scorch her, it was not fear that she felt so much as a gasping wonder that she was unafraid.

IX

When Pierre let her go, she fell, half-fainting, against the rail, and must have sunk at his feet had he not sharply stooped and lifted her. Profiting by a brief lull in the tempest, he bore her down the steps and into the dark saloon. She lay quite passive in his arms, dazed, exhausted, but still curiously devoid of fear.

He laid her upon a cushioned locker by the wall, and relighted the lamp. Then, in utter silence, he carried her to her cabin beyond and left her there. She had a single glimpse of his face as he turned away, and it seemed to her that she had looked upon the face of a man in torture. He went away without a word, and she was left alone.

And so for hours she lay, unmindful of the storm, regardless utterly of aught that happened, lying with wide eyes and burning cheeks, conscious only of that ever-growing wonder that was not fear.

At dawn the wind abated and the yacht began to pitch less. When the sun had been up for a few hours, the gale of the night was a thing of the past, and only the white-capped waves were left as a laughing reminder of the storm that had passed over.

The day was brilliant, and Stephanie arose at length with a feeling that she must go up into the sunshine and face the future. The thought of meeting Pierre even could not ultimately detain her below, though it kept her there considerably longer than usual. After all, was she not bound to meet him? Of what use was it to shirk the inevitable?

But when she finally entered the saloon, he was not there. The table was laid for breakfast, and a sailor was at hand to serve her. But of Pierre there was no sign. He evidently had no intention of joining her.

She made no inquiry for him, but as soon as the meal was over she took her cloak and prepared to go on deck. With nervous haste she passed the scene of the previous night's encounter. She almost expected to find Pierre waiting for her at the top of the companion, but she looked for him in vain. And even when she finally stepped upon the deck and crossed to the rail that she might search the whole length of the yacht, she could not discover him.

A vague uneasiness began to trouble her. The suspense was hard to bear. She longed to meet him and have done with it.

But she longed in vain. All through the sunny hours of the morning she sat or paced in solitude. No one came near her till her breakfast attendant appeared with another meal.

By the end of the afternoon she was thoroughly miserable. She longed intensely to inquire for the yacht's master, yet could not bring herself to do so. Eventually it began to rain, and she went below and sat in the saloon, trying, quite ineffectually, to ease her torment of suspense with a book. But she comprehended nothing of what she read, and when the young cabin steward appeared again to set the dinner she looked up in desperation.

She was on the point of questioning him as to his master's whereabouts; the question, indeed, was already half uttered, when her eyes went beyond him and she broke off short.

Pierre himself was quietly entering through the companion door.

He bowed to her in his abrupt way, and signed to the lad to continue his task.

"He understands no English," he said. "You do not object to his presence?"

She replied in the negative, though in her heart she wished he

Ethel M. Dell

had dismissed him. She could not meet his eyes before a third person. It added tenfold to her embarrassment.

But when he seated himself near her, she did venture a fleeting glance at him, and was amazed unspeakably by what she saw. For his face was haggard and drawn like the face of a sick man, and every hint of arrogance was gone from his bearing. He looked beaten.

He began to speak at once, jerkily, unnaturally, almost as if he also were embarrassed. "I have something to say to you," he said, "which I beg you will hear with patience. It concerns your future - and mine."

The strangeness of his manner, his obvious dejection, the amazing humility of his address, combined to endue Stephanie with a composure she had scarcely hoped to attain.

She found herself able to look at him quite steadily, and did so. It was he who - for the first time in her recollection - avoided her eyes.

"What is it, Monsieur Dumaresq?" she asked quietly.

His hands were gripped upon the arms of his chair. He seemed to be holding himself there by force.

"Just this," he said. "I find that your estimate is after all the correct one. You have always regarded me as a blackguard, and a blackguard I am. I am not here to apologise for it, simply to acknowledge my mistake, for, strange as it will seem to you, I took myself for something different. At least when I gave you my word I thought I was capable of keeping it. Well, it is broken, and, that being so, I can no longer hold you to yours. Do you understand, Mademoiselle Stephanie? You are a free woman."

For an instant he looked at her, and an odd thrill of pity ran through her for his humiliation.

She said nothing. She had no words in which to express herself. Moreover, her eyes were suddenly full of unaccountable tears. She could not have trusted her voice.

After a moment he resumed. "There is only one thing left to say. In two days we shall be in British waters. I will land you wherever you wish. But you shall not go from me to earn your own living. You will accept - you shall accept" - she heard the stubborn note she had come to know so well in his voice - "sufficient from me to make you independent for the rest of your life. Yes, from me, mademoiselle!" He looked her straight in the eyes with something of his old arrogance. "You can refuse, of course. No doubt you will refuse. But I can compel you. If you will not have it as a gift, you shall have it as - a bequest."

He ceased, but he continued to sit with his eyes upon her, ready, she knew, to beat down any and every objection she might raise.

She did not speak. She was for the moment too much surprised for speech; but as his meaning dawned upon her, something that was greater than either surprise or pity took possession of her, holding her silent. She only, after several moments, rose and stood with her face turned from him, watching through the porthole the waves that leaped by, all green and amber, in the light of sunset.

"You understand me clearly, Mademoiselle Stephanie?" he asked at length, in a voice that came harshly through the silence.

She moved slightly, but she did not turn.

"I have never understood you, monsieur," she made answer, her voice very low.

He jerked his shoulders impatiently.

"At least you understand me on this point," he said curtly.

She was silent. At length:

"But you do not understand me," she said.

"Better than you fancy, mademoiselle," he answered bitterly. "I do not think your feelings where I am concerned have ever been very complicated."

Again slightly she moved without looking round.

"I wish you would tell your man to go," she said.

"Mademoiselle?" There was a note of surprise in the query.

"Tell him to go!" she reiterated, with nervous vehemence.

There fell an abrupt silence. Then she heard an imperious snap of the fingers from Pierre, followed instantly by the steward's retiring footsteps.

She waited till she heard them no longer, then slowly she turned. Pierre had not moved from his chair. He was gripping the arms as before. She stood with her back to the light, thankful for the dimness that obscured her face.

"I - I have something to say to you, monsieur," she said.

"I am listening, mademoiselle," he responded briefly, not raising his eyes.

"Ah, but you must help me," she said, and her voice shook a little. "It - it is no easy thing that I have to say."

He made a fierce movement of unrest.

"How can I help you? I have given you your freedom. What more can I do?"

"You can spare me a moment's kindness," she answered gently. "You may be angry with yourself, but you need not be angry with me also."

"I am not angry with you," he responded half sullenly. "But I can bear no trifling, I warn you. I am not my own master. If you wish to secure yourself from further insult, you will be wise to leave me alone."

"And if not?" she questioned slowly. "If - for instance - I do not feel myself insulted by what happened last night?"

He glanced up at that so suddenly that she felt as if something pierced her.

"Then," he rejoined harshly, "you are a very strange woman, Mademoiselle Stephanie."

"I begin to think I am," she said, with a rather piteous smile. "Yet, for all that, I will not be trifled with either. A compact such as ours can only be cancelled by mutual consent. I think you are rather inclined to forget that."

"Meaning?" said Pierre abruptly.

She drew a sharp breath. Her heart was beating very fast.

"Meaning," she said, "meaning that I do not - and I will not - agree to your proposal; that if I accept my freedom from you, it will be because you force me to do so, and I will take nothing else - do you hear? - nothing else, either as a gift or as a bequest. You may compel me to accept my freedom - against my will; but nothing else, I swear - I swear!"

Her voice broke suddenly. She pressed her hands against her throat, striving to control her agitation. But she might as well have striven to contend with the previous night's storm; for it shook her, from head to foot it shook her, as a tree is shaken by the tempest.

As for Pierre, before her words were fairly uttered he had leapt to his feet. His hands were clenched. He looked almost as if he would strike her.

"What do you mean?" he thundered.

She could not answer, but still she did not flinch. She only threw out her hands and set them against his breast, holding him from her. Whether or not her eyes spoke for her she never knew, but he became suddenly rigid at her touch, standing motionless, waiting for her with a patience she found well-nigh incredible.

"Tell me," he said at last, and in his voice restraint and passion were strangely mingled, "what is it you are trying to make me understand? In Heaven's name don't be afraid!"

"I am not," she whispered back breathlessly, "believe me, I am not. But, oh, Pierre, it's so hard for a woman to tell a man what is in her heart when - when she doesn't even know that he cares to hear."

"Stephanie!" he said. He unclenched his hands, and slowly, very slowly, took her quivering wrists. His eyes would have searched hers, but she was looking at him no longer. Her head was bent. She was crying softly, like a child that has been frightened.

"Stephanie!" he said again.

She made a little movement towards him, hesitated a moment, then went close and hid her face against his breast.

"Oh, do make it easy for me!" she entreated brokenly. "Do - do try to understand!"

His arms closed about her. He held her tensely against his heart, so that she heard the wild tumult of its beating. But he said nothing whatever. He waited for her still.

And so at last she found strength to turn her face a little upwards and whisper his name.

"Pierre!" And then, with more assurance, "Pierre, it is true I haven't much to offer you. But such as it is - such as it is - and you asked for it once, remember - will you not take it?"

"Meaning?" he said again, and his voice was hoarse and low. It seemed to come through closed lips.

"Meaning," she answered him quickly and passionately, "that revolutionist as you have been, tyrant as you are, you have managed somehow to bind me to you. Oh, I was a fool - a fool - not to marry you long ago at Maritas even though I hated you. I might have known that you would conquer me in the end."

"Has it come to that?" said Pierre, and there was a queer break in his voice that might have been laughter. "And have you never asked yourself what made me a revolutionist - and a tyrant?"

"Never," she murmured.

"Must I tell you?" he said. "Will you believe me if I do?"

She turned her face fully to him, no longer fearing to meet that piercing scrutiny before which she had so often quailed. "Was it for my sake?" she said.

He met her look with eyes that gleamed as steel gleams in red firelight.

"How else could I have saved you?" he said. "How else could I have been in time?"

"Oh, but you should have told me!" she said. "You should have told me!"

Ethel M. Dell

"And if I had," said Pierre, "would you have hated me less? Do you hate me the less now that you know it?"

She was silent.

"Tell me, Stephanie," he persisted.

Her eyes fell before his.

"Have I ever hated you?" she said, her voice very low.

"If I did not make you hate me last night," he said, "then you never have."

"And I never shall," she supplemented under her breath.

"That," said Pierre, "is another matter. You forget that I am a blackguard."

Again she heard in his voice that sound that might have been laughter. It thrilled her strangely, seeming in some fashion to convey a message that was beyond words. She turned in his arms, responding instinctively, and clung closely to him.

"I forget everything," she told him very earnestly, "except that to-morrow - or the next day - you will be - my husband."

His arms grew tense about her. She felt his breathing quicken.

"Be careful!" he muttered. "Be careful! Remember, I am not to be trusted."

But she answered him with that laughter that is without fear and more intimate than speech.

"All that is over," she said, and lifted her face to his. And then, more softly, in a voice that quivered and broke, "I trust you with my whole heart. And Pierre - my Pierre - you will never again - kiss me - against my will!"

WHERE THE HEART IS

"Of course, I know that a quiet, well-meanin' fool like myself hasn't much of a chance with women, but I just thought I'd give you the opportunity of refusin' me, and then we should know where we were."

It was leisurely uttered, and without any hint of agitation. The speaker was lying on his back at the end of a long, green lawn. His hat was over the upper part of his face, leaving only his mouth visible. It was a singularly kindly mouth. Some critics called it weak, though there was no sign of nervousness about it. The clean lips made their statement without faltering, and without apparent effort, and, having spoken, relaxed into a faint smile that was pleasantly devoid of self-consciousness.

The girl at whose side he lay listened with a slight frown between her eyes. She was quivering inwardly with embarrassment, but she would have died sooner than have betrayed it. The shyest child found it hard to be shy with Tots Waring. His full name was Tottenham, but nobody dreamed of using it. From his cradle onwards he had been Tots to all who knew him. His proposal was followed by a very decided pause. Then, still frowning, the girl spoke.

"Is it a joke?"

"Never made a joke in my life," said Tots.

"Then why don't you do it properly?"

There was a decided touch of irritation in the question. The girl was leaning slightly forward, her hands clasped round her knee. Her black brows looked decidedly uncompromising, and there was a faintly contemptuous twist about her upper lip.

"Don't be vexed!" pleaded Tots. "I suppose you know by experience how these things are managed, but I don't. You see, it's my first attempt."

Unwillingly, as it were in spite of itself, the contemptuous curve became a very small smile. The girl's dark eyes dwelt for several seconds upon that portion of her suitor's countenance that was visible under the linen hat. There was a wonderful serenity about the mouth and chin she studied. They did not look in the least as if their owner were taking either himself or her seriously. Her own lips tightened a little, and a sudden gleam shot up behind her black lashes - a gleam that had in it an elusive glint of malice. She suffered her eyes to pass beyond him and to rest upon a distant line of firs. The man stretched out beside her remained motionless.

"Why," she said at last, with slight hesitation, "should you take it for granted that I should refuse you?"

"Eh?" said Tots. He stirred languidly, and removed the hat from his face, but he still maintained his easy attitude. He had heavy-lidded eyes, upon the colour of which most people disagreed - eyes that never appeared critical, and yet were somehow not wholly in keeping with the kindly, half-whimsical mouth. "I'm not takin' it for granted," he said. "I only think it likely. You see, all I have to go upon is this: Every one hereabouts is gettin' married or engaged, except you and me. That, of course, is all right for them, but it isn't precisely excitin' for us. I thought it might be more fun for both of us if we did the same. At least, I thought I'd find out your opinion about it, and act accordin'ly. If we don't see alike about it, of course, there's no more to be said. We'll just go on as we were before, and hope that somethin' else nice will turn up soon."

"To relieve our mutual boredom!" The girl's laugh sounded rather hard. "Don't you think," she asked, after a moment, "that we should bore each other even worse if we got engaged?"

"Oh, I don't know!" Tots laughed too - an easy, tolerant laugh. "Could but try, eh?" he suggested. "I'm tired of this everlastin' lookin' on."

"So am I - horribly tired." The girl rose suddenly, with a movement curiously vehement.

"But I shouldn't have thought you'd care," she said, with a touch of bitterness. "I should have thought a bovine existence suited you."

Tots sat up deliberately and put on his hat. His manner betrayed no resentment.

"Really?" he said, with his pleasant smile. "You see, one never knows."

He reached up a hand to her, and, wondering a little at herself, she gave him her own to assist him to rise.

He got to his feet and stood before her - a loose-limbed, awkward figure that towered above her, making her feel rather small.

"It's done, then, is it?" he questioned, still keeping her hand in his.

She looked up at him with a nervous laugh. Secretly she was wondering how far he was going to carry the joke.

"Why, of course," she said. "Can you imagine any sane woman refusing such a magnificent offer?"

Though she suffered that ring of mockery in her voice, she was

Ethel M. Dell

still thinking as she spoke that it would serve him right if she frightened him well by letting him imagine that she was taking him seriously.

"Good!" said Tots, in the tone of one well pleased with his bargain. "It shall be my business to see that you do not regret it."

And with the words he drew her hand through his arm, laughing back at her with baffling complacence, and led her down the long lawn with the air of one who had taken possession.

*   *   *   *   *

Ruth Carey had been accustomed to fend for herself nearly all her life. Her lot had been cast in a very narrow groove, and it had not contained a single gleam of romance to make it beautiful. The whole of her early girlhood had been spent buried in a country vicarage, utterly out of touch with all the rest of the world. Here she had lived with her grandfather, leading a wild and free existence, wholly independent of society, hewing, as it were, a way for herself in a desert that was very empty and almost unthinkably barren.

Then, when she was eight-and-twenty, a silent, curiously undeveloped woman, the inevitable change had come. Her grandfather had died, and she had gone out at last beyond the sky-line of her desert into the crowded thoroughfares of men.

The gay crowd of cousins with whom she made her home found her unattractive, and took no special pains to discover further. They were all younger than she was, and full to the brim of their own various interests. Of the five girls, three were already engaged, and one was on the eve of marriage.

It was at this juncture that Tots had lounged into Ruth's consideration and proposed himself as a candidate for her favour.

The Swindler and Other Stories   389

Tots was a familiar friend of the family. Every one liked him in a tolerant, joking sort of way. No one took him seriously. He was to act as best man at the forthcoming wedding, being a near friend and the host of the bridegroom.

Uniformly kind to man and beast, he had made himself lazily pleasant to the unattractive cousin. Circumstance had thrown them a good deal together, and he had not quarrelled with circumstance. He had acquiesced with a smile.

He made it appear in some fashion absurd that they should not at least be friends, and then, having gained that much, he astounded her by proposing to her. It was a preposterous situation. Having at length freed herself from him, she escaped to the house to review it with burning cheeks. It was nothing but a joke, of course - of course, however he might repudiate the fact, and she resented it with all her might. She would teach him that such jokes were not to be played upon her with impunity. She had no one to defend her from this species of insult. She would defend herself. She would fool him as he sought to fool her.

But there was a yet more painful ordeal in store for her that night in the billiard-room, had she but known it. The morrow's bridegroom, Fred Danvers, having failed to execute an easy shot, some one accused him of possessing shaky nerves.

"You'll never get through to-morrow if you can't do an easy thing like that," was the laughing remark.

Tots looked up.

"Oh, rot! The bridegroom has no business to suffer with the jumps. That's the best man's privilege. He does all the work, and has all the responsibility. Why, I'm shakin' in my shoes whenever I think of to-morrow, but if it were my own weddin' I shouldn't turn a hair."

Young Danvers guffawed at this.

Ethel M. Dell

"Bet you'll turn the colour of this table when the time comes, if it ever does come, which I doubt!"

"Why?" questioned Tots.

Danvers laughed again, enjoying the joke. Tots was always more or less of a butt to his friends.

"In the first place, you'd never have the courage or the energy to propose. In the second, no girl would ever take you seriously. In the third -"

He broke off, struck silent by a wholly unexpected display of energy on the part of Tots, who had suddenly hurled a piece of chalk at him from the other end of the room. It hit him smartly on the shoulder, leaving a white patch to testify to the excellence of Tots's aim.

"I beg your pardon," said Tots mildly. "But you really shouldn't talk such rot, particularly in the presence of my *fiancee.*"

He turned round to Ruth, who was shrinking into a corner behind him, and with a courtly gesture drew her forward.

"In the first place," he said, addressing the assembled company with a good-humoured smile, "I had the courage and the energy to propose only this afternoon. In the second place, this lady did me the inestimable favour of takin' me seriously. And in the third place, we're goin' to get married as soon as possible."

In the astounded silence that followed these announcements, he stooped, with no exaggeration of reverence, and kissed the icy, trembling hand he held.

*   *   *   *   *

Ruth never knew afterwards how she came through those

terrible moments. She was as one horror-stricken into acquiescence. She scarcely heard the nightmare buzz of congratulation all about her. The only thing of which she was vividly conscious, over and above her dumb anguish of consternation, was the fast grip of Tots's hand. It seemed to hold her up, to sustain her, while the very soul of her was ready to faint with dismay.

She did not even remember later how she effected her escape at last, but she had a vague impression that Tots managed it for her. It was all very dreadful and incomprehensible. She felt as if she were suddenly caught in a trap from which there could never be any escape. And she was terrified beyond all reason.

All the night she lay awake, turning the matter over and over, but in every respect it presented to her a problem too complicated for her solution. When morning came she was tired out physically and mentally, conscious only of an ardent desire to flee from her perplexities.

Her cousin's wedding occupied the minds of all, and she spent the earlier hours in comparative peace in the bustle of preparation. She saw nothing of Tots, and she hoped his responsibilities would keep him too busy to spare her any of his attention.

Vain hope! When she went to her room to don her bridesmaid's dress, she found a small parcel awaiting her. With a sinking heart, she opened it, a jeweller's box with a strip of paper wound about it. The paper contained a message in four words: "With love from Tots."

A wild tumult arose within her, and her fingers shook so that she could scarcely remove the lid of the box. Succeeding at length, she stood motionless, staring with wide, scared eyes at the ring that lay shining in the sunlight, as though she beheld some evil charm. The diamonds flashed in her eyes and dazzled her, making her see nothing but tiny pin-points of intolerable light. Her heart thumped and raced as though it would choke her. Unconsciously she gasped for breath. That ring was to her another bar in the door of her prison-house.

At an urgent call from one of her cousins, she started and almost threw the box, with its contents, into a drawer. Feverishly she began to dress. It was much later than she had realised. When she appeared in the hall with the other bridesmaids, some one remarked upon her deathly pallor, but she shrank away behind the bride, anxious only to screen herself from observation. She would have given all she had to have avoided Tots just then, but there was no escape for her. He was in the church-porch as she entered it, though there was no time for more than a hurried hand-clasp.

The church was very hot, and the crush of guests great. She listened to the marriage service as a prisoner might listen to his death sentence. The irrevocability of it was anguish to her tortured imagination. And all the while she was conscious - vividly, terribly conscious - of Tots's presence, Tots's inscrutable scrutiny, Tots's triumph of possession. He would never let her go, she felt. She was his beyond all dispute. He had asked, and she had bestowed, not understanding what she was doing.

There could be no withdrawal now. She could not picture herself asking for it, and she was sure he would not grant it if she did. He would only laugh.

There fell a sudden silence in the church - a curious, unnatural silence. It seemed to be growing very dark, and she wondered, panting, if it were the darkness that so smothered her. With a sharp movement she lifted her face, gasping as a half-drowned person gasps. And everywhere above, around her, were tiny, dancing points of light.

* * * * *

"That's better," said Tots. "Don't be frightened. It's all right."

He rubbed her cheek softly, reassuringly, and then fell to chafing her weak hands. Ruth lay back against a grave-mound and stared at him. He was wonderfully gentle with her, almost like a woman. On her other side one of her fellow bridesmaids was stooping over her, holding a glass of water.

"You fainted from the heat," she explained. "But you are better now. I shouldn't go back if I were you. It's just over."

With a sense of shame Ruth withdrew her hand from Tots.

"I'm sorry," she murmured.

"Nonsense!" said Tots kindly. "Nobody's blamin' you, my child. It's this infernal heat. You stay quietly here for a bit. I must go back and see that Danvers signs his name all right. But I'll come and fetch you afterwards."

He departed, and Ruth suddenly realised an urgent need for solitude. She turned to her cousin.

"Do please go! I shall be all right. It is cool and shady here. And they will be looking for you in the vestry. Please go! I will wait till - Tots comes back."

Her cousin demurred a little, but it was obvious that her inclination fell in with Ruth's request, and it was also quite obvious that Ruth did not want her. So, after some persuasion, she yielded and went.

During the interval that followed, Ruth sat in the quiet corner just out of sight of the vestry door, bracing herself to meet Tots and implore him to set her free. It was a bad quarter of an hour for her, and when, at the end of it, Tots came, she looked on the verge of fainting again.

"Sorry I couldn't come before," said Tots. "But my responsibilities are over now, thank the gods. I suppose, now, you didn't have time for anything to eat before you came?"

This was the actual truth. Ruth owned it with a feeling of guilt. And suddenly she found that she could not speak then. There was something that made it impossible. Perhaps it was the loud clash of the bells overhead.

"I am very sorry," she said again.

Tots smiled.

"You must manage better at our own weddin'," he said. "There's nothin' like fortifyin' yourself with a good substantial meal for an ordeal of this sort. You're feelin' better, eh? Take my arm."

She obeyed him, still quivering with her fruitless effort to tell him of the miserable deception she had unintentionally practised upon him. She had a feeling that, if she made him angry, the world itself would stop. Surely no one had ever found Tots formidable before.

At the touch of his hand upon hers, she started.

"What's wrong with it?" queried Tots softly. "Doesn't it fit?"

She glanced up in confusion. She was trembling so that she could scarcely stand. He slipped his arm about her reassuringly, comfortably.

"Never mind. We must look at it together. I'll take it back if it isn't right. We'll go through the church, shall we? It's the shortest way."

He led her, unresisting, back into the building, and the clamour of the bells merged into the swelling chords of the organ. As they walked side by side down the empty aisle the strains of Mendelssohn's Wedding March transformed their progress into a triumphant procession, and Tots looked down into the girl's face with a smile....

There was no help for it. She could not tell him to his face. Gradually the conviction dawned upon her through another night of racking thought. And there was only one thing left to do. She must go.

Soon after sunrise she was up, and writing a note to her aunt. She experienced small difficulty in this. It was quite simple to express her thanks for all the kindness shown her, and to explain that she had decided to pay a visit to her old home. She scarcely touched upon the suddenness of her departure. The Careys were all of them sudden in their ways. This move of hers would hardly strike them as extraordinary. She was, moreover, so much a stranger among them that it did not seem to matter in the face of her great need what they thought.

But a note to Tots was a different matter altogether, and she sat for nearly two hours motionless above a sheet of paper, considering. In the end she was again overcome by the almost physical impossibility of putting the intolerable situation into bald words. Simply, she felt utterly incapable of dealing with it. He had told her he was not joking. She had believed the contrary in spite of this assurance. And she had dared to trifle with him, to treat his offer as a jest.

How could she explain, how apologise, for such a mistake as this? The thing was beyond words, and at length she gave up the attempt in despair. She would send him back his ring in silence, and perhaps he would understand. At least, he would know that she was unworthy of that which he had offered her. She took the ring from its hiding-place, and once more the sunlight flashed upon its stones. For a space she stood gazing fixedly, as one fascinated. And then, suddenly, inexplicably, her eyes filled with tears, and she packed up the little box hurriedly with fingers that trembled.

She directed the parcel to Tots, and put it aside with the intention of posting it herself. A tiny strip of paper on the floor attracted her attention as she turned. She picked it up. It was only Tots's simple message in four short words. She caught her breath sharply as she slipped it into her dress....

Home! Ruth Carey stood in the little inn-parlour that smelt of honeysuckle and stale tobacco, and looked across the village street. It looked even narrower than in the old days, and the pond on the green had shrunk to a mere dark puddle. The old grey church on the hill looked like a child's toy, and the quiet that brooded everywhere was the quiet of stagnation. An ancient dog was limping down the road - the only living thing in sight.

The girl turned from the window with a heavy sigh. She was conscious of a great emptiness, of a craving too intense to be silenced, a feverish longing that had in it the elements of a bitter despair. She had fled from captivity to the desert. But she had not found relief. She had escaped indeed. But she was like to perish of starvation in the wilderness.

She slept that night from sheer weariness, but, waking in the early morning, she lay for hours, listening to the cheery pipings of the birds, and wondering what she should do with her life. For there was no one belonging to her in a truly intimate sense. She had no near ties. There was no one who really wanted her, except - The burning colour rushed up to her temples. No; even he did not want her now. And again the loneliness and the emptiness seemed more than she could bear.

Dressing, she told herself suddenly and passionately that her home-coming had been a miserable farce, a sham, and a delusion. And she called bitterly to mind words that she had once either read or heard: "Where the heart is, there is home."

The scent of honeysuckle and stale tobacco was mingled with that of fried bacon as she opened the door of the inn-parlour. It rushed out to greet her in a nauseating wave, and she nearly shut the door again in disgust. But the sight of an immense bunch of roses waiting for her on the table checked the impulse. She went forward into the room and picked it up, burying her face in its fragrance.

There was a tiny strip of paper twisted about one of the stalks which she did not at first perceive. When she did, she unfolded it, wondering. Four words met her eyes, written in minute characters, and it was as if a meteor had flamed suddenly across her sky. They were words that, curiously, had never ceased to ring in her brain since the moment she had first read them: "With love from Tots."

*   *   *   *   *

Fully five minutes passed before Ruth crossed the room to the honeysuckle-draped window, the roses pressed against her thumping heart. Outside, an ancient wooden bench that sagged dubiously in the middle stood against a crumbling stone wall. It was a bench greatly favoured by aged labourers in the summer evenings, but this morning it had but one occupant - a loose-knit, lounging figure with a straw hat drawn well down over the eyes, and a pipe thrust between the teeth.

As Ruth gazed upon this negligent apparition, it suddenly moved, and the next instant it stood up in the sunshine and faced her, hat in one hand, pipe in the other.

"Mornin'" said Tots. "Got somethin' nice for breakfast?" His brown face smiled imperturbably upon her. He looked pleased to see her, but not extravagantly so.

Ruth fell back a step from the window, her roses clutched fast against her. She was for the moment speechless.

Tots continued to smile sociably.

"Nice, quiet little place - this," he said. "There's a touch of the antediluvian about it that I like. Good idea of yours, comin' here. No one to get in the way. It won't be disturbin' you if I sit on the window-sill while you have your breakfast?"

Ruth experienced a sudden, hysterical desire to laugh. He was beyond her, this man - utterly, hopelessly beyond her.

She sat down at the table, not with the idea of eating anything, but from a sense of sheer helplessness. Tots knocked the ashes from his pipe and took his seat on the window-sill. He did not seem to be aware of any strain in the situation.

After a pause, during which Ruth sat motionless, he turned a little to survey her.

"Not begun yet?" he queried.

She looked back at him with a species of desperate courage.

This sort of thing could not go on. She must be brave for once. Unconsciously she was still gripping the roses with both hands.

"Mr. Waring -" she began.

"Tots," he substituted gently.

"Well - Tots," she repeated unwillingly, "I - I want to ask you something."

"Fire away!" said Tots.

"I want to know - I want to know -" She stumbled again, and broke off in distress.

Tots wheeled round as he sat, and brought his long legs into the room.

"Please don't," she begged hastily. "I - I want you inside."

He did not retire again, nor did he advance.

"You want to know -" he said.

With a stupendous effort she faced and answered him.

"I want to know what made you ask me to marry you."

Tots did not at once reply. He sat on his perch with his back to the light, and contemplated her.

"I should have thought a clever little girl like you might have guessed that," he said at length.

This was intolerable. She felt her courage ebbing fast.

"I'm not clever," she said, a desperate quiver in her voice, "and I - I'm not good at guessing riddles."

In the silence that followed, she wondered wildly if she had made him angry at last. Then he spoke in his usual good-natured drawl, and her heart gave a great throb of relief.

"I think you're chaffin'," he said.

"I'm not," she assured him feverishly. "I'm not indeed. I always mean what I say. That is -"

"Of course," said Tots, with kindly reassurance. "I knew that. Why, my dear child, that's just what made me do it. I took a likin' to you for that very reason."

She stared at him speechlessly. There was absolutely nothing left to say. He really cared for her, it seemed. He really cared! And she? With a gasp of despair she abandoned the unequal strife, and hid her face from him in an agony of tears. Why, why, why, had this knowledge come to her so late?

He was by her side in an instant, stroking, soothing, comforting her, as though she had been a child. When she partially recovered herself her head was against his shoulder, and he was drying her eyes clumsily but tenderly with his own handkerchief.

"There! there!" he said. "Don't cry any more. Some one's been troublin' you. Just let me know who it is, and I'll wring his neck."

She raised herself weakly. The desire to laugh quite left her. She leaned her head in her hands, and forced down her tears.

"You - don't understand," she said at last.

"Don't I?" said Tots. "Why, I thought we were gettin' on so well."

"I know. I know." She was making a supreme effort. It must be now or never. "You have been very good to me. But - but - we never have got on really. It was all a mistake."

"What do you mean?" said Tots.

She fancied his tone had changed a little. It sounded somehow brisker than usual. He was angry, whispered her panting heart, and if she angered him - ah, how should she bear it? But the next instant a big, consoling hand pressed her shoulder, and the misgiving passed.

"Don't tremble like this, little one," he said. "You can't be afraid of me. No one ever was before. There has been a mistake, you say. What was it? Can't you bring yourself to tell me?"

There was something in his voice that moved her strangely, kindling that in her which turned her passionate regret to tragedy. Her head sank a little lower in her hands. How could she tell him? How could she? Yet he must know, even if - even if it transformed his love to hatred. The bare thought hurt her intolerably. He was the only friend she had. And yet - and yet - he must know. She swallowed a desperate sob, and spoke.

"I've been deceiving you. I've trifled with you. When you proposed to me - I didn't know - didn't realise - you were in earnest. No one had ever proposed to me before. I didn't understand. And when I accepted you - I wasn't in earnest either. I - I was just spiteful. Afterwards - when I found out - it was too late. I couldn't tell you then."

The confession went haltingly out into silence. She dared not raise her head. Moreover, she was weeping, and she did not want him to know it.

There was a motionless pause. Then at length the hand on her shoulder began to rub up and down, comfortingly, caressingly.

"Don't cry!" said Tots. "Hadn't you better have some breakfast? That bacon must be gettin' pretty beastly."

He was not angry, then. That was her first thought. And then again came that insane desire to laugh. After all, why was she crying? Tots apparently saw no cause for discomfiture.

With an effort she controlled herself.

"No; I'm not hungry," she said. "Won't you - please - settle this matter now?"

"Only stop cryin'," said Tots. "You have? I say, what a fib! Well, I suppose I must take your word for it. Now, little one, what is it you want me to do?"

She raised her head in sheer astonishment.

No, there was no trace of anger in his face, neither did it betray any disappointment. Complacent, kindly, quizzical, his eyes met hers, and her heart gave a sudden, inexplicable bound.

"I - thought you would understand," she faltered. "We - we can't go on being engaged, can we?"

"No," said Tots with instant decision. "Shouldn't dream of borin' you to that extent. I've had enough of it myself as well." He uttered his pleasant, careless laugh. "I really don't wonder that my courtin' made you feel spiteful," he said. "I'm glad you're in favour of cuttin' it too."

Ruth stared at him blankly. Was he laughing at her? Was this to be her punishment?

He had straightened himself and was smiling down at her, his head within a foot of the bulging ceiling.

"Tell you what!" he suddenly said. "You eat some breakfast like a good girl, and then - I'll show you somethin'. Perhaps you'll let me join you?"

He did not wait for her consent, but sat down at the table. Ruth rose. He was putting her off, she felt, and she could not bear it. It had cost her more than he would ever realise to tell him the truth.

"I'm very sorry," she said unsteadily, "but - I don't think we quite understand each other yet. You know" - her voice failed suddenly, but she struggled to recover it, and succeeded - "I am not clever - like other women. I want plain speaking, not hints, I want to be told - in so many words - that you have set me free."

"Why should I tell you what isn't true?" said Tots. He stretched out his hand to her without rising. "I haven't set you free," he said, "and I'm not goin' to. Is that plain enough?"

He caught her hand with the words and drew her gently towards him. "I'll tell you what I am goin' to do," he said. "Come quite close. I want to whisper. You needn't be anxious. This chair is strong enough for two."

Gentle as he was in speech and action, there was something irresistible about him at that moment - something to which Ruth yielded because there was no alternative. She went to him trembling, and he drew her down beside him, holding her every instant closer to him.

"Still frightened?" he asked her very tenderly. "Still wantin' to run away?"

She hid her face against him dumbly. She could not answer him in words.

He went on speaking, softly, soothingly, as if she had been a child.

"People make a ridiculous fuss about gettin' married," he said. "It's the fashion nowadays to make a sort of Punch and Judy show of it for all the people one ever met, and a few hundreds besides, to come and gape at. But you and I are not goin' to do that. We're goin' to show some sense, and get married on the quiet, in a little village church I know of; and then we're goin' into retirement for a time, and when we come out we shall be old married people, and no one will want to pelt us with shoes and things. Now I've got a weddin'-ring in my pocket, and I hope it'll fit better than the other. And I've got a special license too. It's a nice, fine mornin', isn't it? And that's all we want. Let's have some breakfast, and then go and get married!"

Ruth raised her head with a gasp. Unexpected as was the whole turn of events, she was utterly unprepared for this astounding suggestion.

"But - but -" she faltered.

And then for the first time she saw Tots's eyes, opened wide and looking at her with an expression there was no mistaking. He took her face between his hands.

"Yes, I know all that," he said, speaking below his breath. "But it doesn't count, dear - believe me, it doesn't. The only thing that is really indispensable, we have. So why not - make that do?"

"Oh, I don't know," she gasped. "I don't know."

She was quivering as a harp quivers under the fingers of one who knows, and her whole soul was thrilling to the wild, tumultuous music that he had called into being there. It was almost more than she could bear - this miracle that had been wrought upon her. Tots's eyes still held her own, and it was as if thereby he showed her all that was best in life.

"Why not?" he said again very softly.

And suddenly she realised overwhelmingly how close his lips were to her own. In that moment she also knew that greater thing which is immortal. And so she answered him at last in his own words, with a rush of passionate willingness that swept away all fear:

"Why not?"

As their lips met, it seemed to her that her eyes were opened for the first time in her life; and everywhere - above, around, within her - were living sparks, dazzling, wonderful, unquenchable, of the Eternal Flame.

Choose from Thousands of 1stWorldLibrary Classics By

A. M. Barnard
Ada Leverson
Adolphus William Ward
Aesop
Agatha Christie
Alexander Aaronsohn
Alexander Kielland
Alexandre Dumas
Alfred Gatty
Alfred Ollivant
Alice Duer Miller
Alice Turner Curtis
Alice Dunbar
Allen Chapman
Ambrose Bierce
Amelia E. Barr
Amory H. Bradford
Andrew Lang
Andrew McFarland Davis
Andy Adams
Anna Alice Chapin
Anna Sewell
Annie Besant
Annie Hamilton Donnell
Annie Payson Call
Annie Roe Carr
Annonaymous
Anton Chekhov
Arnold Bennett
Arthur Conan Doyle
Arthur M. Winfield
Arthur Ransome
Arthur Schnitzler
Atticus
B.H. Baden-Powell
B. M. Bower
B. C. Chatterjee
Baroness Emmuska Orczy
Baroness Orczy
Basil King
Bayard Taylor
Ben Macomber
Bertha Muzzy Bower
Bjornstjerne Bjornson
Booth Tarkington
Boyd Cable
Bram Stoker
C. Collodi
C. E. Orr

C. M. Ingleby
Carolyn Wells
Catherine Parr Traill
Charles A. Eastman
Charles Amory Beach
Charles Dickens
Charles Dudley Warner
Charles Farrar Browne
Charles Ives
Charles Kingsley
Charles Klein
Charles Hanson Towne
Charles Lathrop Pack
Charles Romyn Dake
Charles Whibley
Charles Willing Beale
Charlotte M. Braeme
Charlotte M. Yonge
Charlotte Perkins Stetson
Clair W. Hayes
Clarence Day Jr.
Clarence E. Mulford
Clemence Housman
Confucius
Coningsby Dawson
Cornelis DeWitt Wilcox
Cyril Burleigh
D. H. Lawrence
Daniel Defoe
David Garnett
Dinah Craik
Don Carlos Janes
Donald Keyhoe
Dorothy Kilner
Dougan Clark
Douglas Fairbanks
E. Nesbit
E.P.Roe
E. Phillips Oppenheim
Earl Barnes
Edgar Rice Burroughs
Edith Van Dyne
Edith Wharton
Edward Everett Hale
Edward J. O'Biren
Edward S. Ellis
Edwin L. Arnold
Eleanor Atkins
Eliot Gregory

Elizabeth Gaskell
Elizabeth McCracken
Elizabeth Von Arnim
Ellem Key
Emerson Hough
Emilie F. Carlen
Emily Dickinson
Enid Bagnold
Enilor Macartney Lane
Erasmus W. Jones
Ernie Howard Pie
Ethel May Dell
Ethel Turner
Ethel Watts Mumford
Eugenie Foa
Eugene Wood
Eustace Hale Ball
Evelyn Everett-green
Everard Cotes
F. H. Cheley
F. J. Cross
F. Marion Crawford
Federick Austin Ogg
Ferdinand Ossendowski
Francis Bacon
Francis Darwin
Frances Hodgson Burnett
Frances Parkinson Keyes
Frank Gee Patchin
Frank Harris
Frank Jewett Mather
Frank L. Packard
Frank V. Webster
Frederic Stewart Isham
Frederick Trevor Hill
Frederick Winslow Taylor
Friedrich Kerst
Friedrich Nietzsche
Fyodor Dostoyevsky
G.A. Henty
G.K. Chesterton
Gabrielle E. Jackson
Garrett P. Serviss
Gaston Leroux
George A. Warren
George Ade
Geroge Bernard Shaw
George Durston
George Ebers

George Eliot
George Gissing
George MacDonald
George Meredith
George Orwell
George Sylvester Viereck
George Tucker
George W. Cable
George Wharton James
Gertrude Atherton
Gordon Casserly
Grace E. King
Grace Gallatin
Grace Greenwood
Grant Allen
Guillermo A. Sherwell
Gulielma Zollinger
Gustav Flaubert
H. A. Cody
H. B. Irving
H.C. Bailey
H. G. Wells
H. H. Munro
H. Irving Hancock
H. Rider Haggard
H. W. C. Davis
Haldeman Julius
Hall Caine
Hamilton Wright Mabie
Hans Christian Andersen
Harold Avery
Harold McGrath
Harriet Beecher Stowe
Harry Castlemon
Harry Coghill
Harry Houidini
Hayden Carruth
Helent Hunt Jackson
Helen Nicolay
Hendrik Conscience
Hendy David Thoreau
Henri Barbusse
Henrik Ibsen
Henry Adams
Henry Ford
Henry Frost
Henry James
Henry Jones Ford
Henry Seton Merriman
Henry W Longfellow
Herbert A. Giles

Herbert Carter
Herbert N. Casson
Herman Hesse
Hildegard G. Frey
Homer
Honore De Balzac
Horace B. Day
Horace Walpole
Horatio Alger Jr.
Howard Pyle
Howard R. Garis
Hugh Lofting
Hugh Walpole
Humphry Ward
Ian Maclaren
Inez Haynes Gillmore
Irving Bacheller
Isabel Hornibrook
Israel Abrahams
Ivan Turgenev
J.G.Austin
J. Henri Fabre
J. M. Barrie
J. Macdonald Oxley
J. S. Fletcher
J. S. Knowles
J. Storer Clouston
Jack London
Jacob Abbott
James Allen
James Andrews
James Baldwin
James Branch Cabell
James DeMille
James Joyce
James Lane Allen
James Lane Allen
James Oliver Curwood
James Oppenheim
James Otis
James R. Driscoll
Jane Austen
Jane L. Stewart
Janet Aldridge
Jens Peter Jacobsen
Jerome K. Jerome
John Burroughs
John Cournos
John F. Kennedy
John Gay
John Glasworthy

John Habberton
John Joy Bell
John Kendrick Bangs
John Milton
John Philip Sousa
Jonas Lauritz Idemil Lie
Jonathan Swift
Joseph A. Altsheler
Joseph Carey
Joseph Conrad
Joseph E. Badger Jr
Joseph Hergesheimer
Joseph Jacobs
Jules Vernes
Julian Hawthrone
Julie A Lippmann
Justin Huntly McCarthy
Kakuzo Okakura
Kenneth Grahame
Kenneth McGaffey
Kate Langley Bosher
Kate Langley Bosher
Katherine Cecil Thurston
Katherine Stokes
L. A. Abbot
L. T. Meade
L. Frank Baum
Latta Griswold
Laura Dent Crane
Laura Lee Hope
Laurence Housman
Lawrence Beasley
Leo Tolstoy
Leonid Andreyev
Lewis Carroll
Lewis Sperry Chafer
Lilian Bell
Lloyd Osbourne
Louis Hughes
Louis Tracy
Louisa May Alcott
Lucy Fitch Perkins
Lucy Maud Montgomery
Luther Benson
Lydia Miller Middleton
Lyndon Oii
M. Corvus
M. H. Adams
Margaret E. Sangster
Margret Howth
Margaret Vandercook

Margret Penrose
Maria Edgeworth
Maria Thompson Daviess
Mariano Azuela
Marion Polk Angellotti
Mark Overton
Mark Twain
Mary Austin
Mary Catherine Crowley
Mary Cole
Mary Hastings Bradley
Mary Roberts Rinehart
Mary Rowlandson
M. Wollstonecraft Shelley
Maud Lindsay
Max Beerbohm
Myra Kelly
Nathaniel Hawthrone
Nicolo Machiavelli
O. F. Walton
Oscar Wilde
Owen Johnson
P.G. Wodehouse
Paul and Mabel Thorne
Paul G. Tomlinson
Paul Severing
Percy Brebner
Peter B. Kyne
Plato
R. Derby Holmes
R. L. Stevenson
R. S. Ball
Rabindranath Tagore
Rahul Alvares
Ralph Bonehill
Ralph Henry Barbour
Ralph Victor
Ralph Waldo Emmerson
Rene Descartes
Rex Beach

Rex E. Beach
Richard Harding Davis
Richard Jefferies
Richard Le Gallienne
Robert Barr
Robert Frost
Robert Gordon Anderson
Robert L. Drake
Robert Lansing
Robert Lynd
Robert Michael Ballantyne
Robert W. Chambers
Rosa Nouchette Carey
Rudyard Kipling
Samuel B. Allison
Samuel Hopkins Adams
Sarah Bernhardt
Sarah C. Hallowell
Selma Lagerlof
Sherwood Anderson
Sigmund Freud
Standish O'Grady
Stanley Weyman
Stella Benson
Stella M. Francis
Stephen Crane
Stewart Edward White
Stijn Streuvels
Swami Abhedananda
Swami Parmananda
T. S. Ackland
T. S. Arthur
The Princess Der Ling
Thomas A. Janvier
Thomas A Kempis
Thomas Anderton
Thomas Bailey Aldrich
Thomas Bulfinch
Thomas De Quincey
Thomas Dixon

Thomas H. Huxley
Thomas Hardy
Thomas More
Thornton W. Burgess
U. S. Grant
Valentine Williams
Various Authors
Vaughan Kester
Victor Appleton
Victoria Cross
Virginia Woolf
Wadsworth Camp
Walter Camp
Walter Scott
Washington Irving
Wilbur Lawton
Wilkie Collins
Willa Cather
Willard F. Baker
William Dean Howells
William le Queux
W. Makepeace Thackeray
William W. Walter
William Shakespeare
Winston Churchill
Yei Theodora Ozaki
Yogi Ramacharaka
Young E. Allison
Zane Grey

www.ingramcontent.com/pod-product-compliance
Lightning Source LLC
Chambersburg PA
CBHW030359100426
42812CB00028B/2767/J